Life after Gravity

LIFE *after* GRAVITY

ISAAC NEWTON'S LONDON CAREER

PATRICIA FARA

OXFORD
UNIVERSITY PRESS

OXFORD
UNIVERSITY PRESS

Great Clarendon Street, Oxford, OX2 6DP,
United Kingdom

Oxford University Press is a department of the University of Oxford.
It furthers the University's objective of excellence in research, scholarship,
and education by publishing worldwide. Oxford is a registered trade mark of
Oxford University Press in the UK and in certain other countries

© Patricia Fara 2021

The moral rights of the author have been asserted

First Edition published in 2021
Impression: 1

Published in the United States of America by Oxford University Press
198 Madison Avenue, New York, NY 10016, United States of America

British Library Cataloguing in Publication Data
Data available

Library of Congress Control Number: 2020944353

ISBN 978–0–19–884102–9

Printed and bound in Great Britain by
Clays Ltd, Elcograf S.p.A.

For Clarissa

Acknowledgements

This is the second book I have written about Isaac Newton, although I do not regard myself as a specialized expert. Instead, I have leant on the shoulders of many scholars, especially three: Rob Iliffe, Simon Schaffer, and Steven Snobelen. Together they know everything that has ever been discovered about Newton, and individually they have all been very helpful. In addition, I have benefited from the wonderful online Newton Project, currently hosted by Oxford University at http://www.newtonproject.ox.ac.uk/ and freely available to all. Headed by Rob Iliffe and Scott Mandelbrote, around fifty researchers—mostly underpaid and unnamed women—have meticulously transcribed many thousands of documents from different archives.

Other colleagues have also been extremely generous with their time and their expertise. In particular, I should like to thank the anonymous reviewer who made some extremely perceptive comments as well as Will Ashworth, Malcolm Baker, Martin Cherry, Tim Chesters, Sally Dixon-Smith, Sarah Dry, Mark Goldie, James Harriman-Smith, John Leigh, Alex Lindsay, Joanna Marschner, Andrew Odlyzko, Anna Marie Roos, Stuart Sillars, Robert Turner, Simon Werrett, and also Clive Wilmer—alphabetically last in that list but deserving particular gratitude as my sternest critic and strongest supporter.

I am very lucky to have a wonderful agent, Tracy Bohan of the Wylie Agency, and also a delightfully sympathetic team at Oxford University Press, notably Luciana O'Flaherty, Matthew Cotton, Kizzy Taylor-Richelieu, and Kate Shepherd.

Contents

List of Illustrations

The first of all English games is making money. That is an all-absorbing game; and we knock each other down oftener in playing at that, than at football, or any other roughest sport: and it is absolutely without purpose; no one who engages heartily in that game ever knows why. Ask a great money-maker what he wants to do with his money,—he never knows. He doesn't make it to do anything with it. He gets it only that he may get it. 'What will you make of what you have got?' you ask. 'Well, I'll get more,' he says. Just as, at cricket, you get more runs. There's no use in the runs, but to get more of them than other people is the game. And there's no use in the money, but to have more of it than other people is the game.

John Ruskin, *The Crown of Wild Olive*, 1866

Prologue

This book has two subjects: Isaac Newton's three decades in London, and a picture by William Hogarth that is packed with Newtonian references.

Figure 0.1 *The Indian Emperor. Or the Conquest of Mexico. As performed in the year 1731 in Mr Conduitt's, Master of the Mint, before the Duke of Cumberland &c. Act 4, Scene 4*; William Hogarth, 1732

Here are ten facts about Isaac Newton.

Some of them may surprise you.

All of them are discussed in this book.

- He owned two silver chamber pots, twelve bibles, and thirteen copies of the New Testament.
- He lost a small fortune on the stock market by buying high and selling low.
- He lived in London longer than in Cambridge.
- He was twice elected MP for Cambridge University.
- He was paid a bonus for every coin minted from slave-trade gold.
- He had sworn to sexual abstinence, but was plagued by obsessive thoughts.
- He wanted to ban imports of luxury goods from China and India.
- He worked for many years in the Tower of London while it still housed a zoo.
- He hired an experimental assistant who became the Grand Master of English Freemasonry.
- He believed that 666 is the Number of the Name of the Beast.

Precise figures are hard to find, but this table indicates Newton's relative affluence by listing estimates for the wealth at death of twelve other people who appear in this book.[1]

£1000 in 1700 was worth approximately £140,000 in 2018 using measures of price, and £2,500,000 using measures of income.[2]

Hans Sloane	Physician and collector	£100,000
David Garrick	Actor	£100,000
Isaac Newton	Master of the Royal Mint	£32,000
Edward Gibbon	Historian	£26,000
George Handel	Composer	£17,500
Robert Boyle	Chemist	£10,000
Alexander Pope	Poet	£5000–6000
Samuel Johnson	Writer	£2300
John Flamsteed	Astronomer Royal	£2000
Elizabeth Tollet	Poet	£1770+
William Whiston	Former Cambridge professor	£1300+
Daniel Defoe	Author	Nothing
John Desaguliers	Master of Freemasonry	Pauper

To say that all the world's a stage had become a cliché long before William Shakespeare was born.[3] During the eighteenth century, members of England's elite put on their own daily performances. Their elaborate gestures, powdered wigs, tightly drawn-in waists and elliptical phraseology all helped to disguise a personal identity that remained closed off even from husbands and wives. Emotions were to be reined in, not displayed publicly. Born with life-scripts marked up in advance, privileged children were moulded into their adult roles, their futures mapped out in front of them. Posing for family portraits, miniature aristocrats held stiff, formal poses, perhaps clutching a little sword or wearing a dress cut so low that a nipple showed. One major priority for landed families was to preserve their estates intact, and so the oldest son inherited everything; daughters remained the possession of their father until marriage, when they—along with everything they owned—became the property of their husband.

London polite society thrived on financial schemes, sexual intrigues, and political manoeuvres, and it became fashionable for children to perform adult plays that taught them about the survival skills they would need. In 1731, four years after Newton died, the Drury Lane Theatre revived John Dryden's The Indian Emperour, *which had first* been staged in 1665, when Newton was at Cambridge. Soon afterwards, the manager's son—actor and notorious rake Theophilus Cibber—directed a children's performance in the house of John Conduitt, Newton's successor as Master of the Mint. The wealthy audience included the juvenile actors' proud relatives as well as three royal children—Prince William (already the Duke of Cumberland, despite his youth) and his two younger sisters. William must have enjoyed the occasion because, at his request, the play was presented again the following year for their parents—King George II and Queen Caroline—at St James's Palace.[4]

Now largely forgotten, Conduitt was a man of considerable standing, a Member of Parliament and husband of Newton's half-niece. An assiduous social climber, he was proud of the aristocratic entertainment he had provided, and he wanted a permanent record. By the following year, his friends were gossiping that he was 'going to have a conversation piece drawn by Hogarth, of the young people of quality that acted at his house; and if I am not mistaken he hopes to have the honour of the Royal part of the audience in the picture.'[5] He did indeed commission Hogarth to portray this event in an exceptionally large picture, 130 × 145 cm (Figure 0.1). Because it contained so many individual faces, the painting took three years to finish. This domestic scene is still privately owned, and unlike much of Hogarth's work, was not on sale as an engraving until 1791, long after most of its participants had died.

Conduitt made an astute choice of artist. Hogarth is now most famous for his scenes of depravity and corruption, which forced prosperous purchasers to confront the risks of slipping from their comfortable existence to share the misery of London's gin-sodden slum dwellers. But at the time, he was renowned for his conversation pieces. The word 'conversation' carried implicit connotations of sexual as well as verbal encounters, and these carefully constructed group pictures depicted long-term tensions and ambiguities in eighteenth-century culture. Resembling snap-shots in oils of a specific instant in time, they portrayed the wealthy at leisure inside their own homes, displayed on canvas as if participating in a performance.

Conduitt's commission arrived with perfect timing, while Hogarth was beginning to enjoy the success of his Harlot's Progress series.

After celebrating with friends on a trip to Kent, he set to work. Dryden's The Indian Emperour. Or the Conquest of Mexico *was loosely based on the Spanish colonization of the Aztecs in the early sixteenth century. Hogarth had recently painted another play, the theatrical hit* The Beggar's Opera, *when he sat among the Drury Lane audience sketching on blue paper to remain concealed in the dark. Perhaps remembering the five years his father had spent in Fleet Prison, Hogarth depicted a grim scene inside a cell, featuring two women and a man in handcuffs. In five successive versions, he increasingly included the audience as well as the action on stage, so that in retrospect the series seems to have been leading up to a grand finale—his* Indian Emperor.

Again, he showed a prison scene, when two local princesses are vying for the love of Hernán Cortés, a Spanish invader who has been temporarily imprisoned by Montezuma, an Aztec emperor. The adults in the audience would have known that, before the evening was over, Montezuma would die and the Cortés character would emerge as conqueror, but perhaps for the watching children the plot and its savagery came as a surprise.

Hogarth's pictures were rarely unambiguous: he liked stacking them with symbolic references and double meanings. Here shimmering flashes of gold and cream evoke power and aristocracy both on and off the makeshift stage, while the scene ripples with concealed passions. By lacing it with visual references to Newton, Hogarth simultaneously paid tribute to an English icon and emphasized Conduitt's high status in London society.

Physically present as a marble bust surveying the scene from the mantelpiece, Newton also pervades the canvas metaphorically. In the audience, the royal governess is bidding one of her daughters to pick up the fan that has fallen though the force of gravity, while the prompter at the back left is one of Newton's staunchest propagandists. Appropriately enough for an intellectual Titan, only Newton's head is present, glowing like a floodlit reminder of his innovative book on optics. Materially absent from the room as from life, Newton's mind is dominant. Resembling gravitational forces that shoot through empty space, he is both nowhere and everywhere, an all-seeing divine presence looming over these childish human activities.

* * *

When Isaac Newton wanted something, he was willing to pay for the best—and he knew that whatever a person's inner virtues, outward appearances counted. England was renowned as the land of portrait painters and, like other affluent social climbers, Newton commissioned London's top artists to create flattering pictures for winning over his critics and influencing his supporters. This was common practice in England; in contrast, continental Europeans looked down with disdain on such 'Face-Painting', regarding it as inferior to history painting, which showed a specific event such as a famous battle or a mythological scenario. Newton hung many of his portraits in his own home, where his visitors could admire the exclusive good taste that can only be purchased by the wealthy. When he became president of London's Royal Society, one of his first steps was to organize a picture collection of its eminent Fellows. To set a suitable example, Newton donated a large picture of himself, making sure that everyone recognized his elite status by adorning it with gold lettering (in Latin) advertising his role as president.

Among Newton's favourite artists was the German-born Godfrey Kneller, who had studied under Rembrandt van Rijn in Amsterdam before being appointed Principal Painter to the Crown by Charles II. Many years later, when one of Newton's London homes was demolished, Kneller's card was found underneath the floorboards. He painted five different portraits of Newton, although only two of them are well known. Newton's facial characteristics are similar in all of them, and their striking differences are due not to his advancing age but to his desire of repeatedly presenting himself in different roles.

The first time he sat for Kneller, in 1689, Newton was in his mid-forties and had published the *Principia*—his famous book on mechanics and gravity—just two years earlier. (In English, this book's full title is *Mathematical Principles of Natural Philosophy*; because all three editions were published in Latin, it is usually referred to as the *Principia*, short for *Philosophiæ Naturalis Principia Mathematica*). This early portrait shows him as a reclusive academic with unkempt hair and a thin pale face, a dedicated scholar who has temporarily ventured out of solitude before scurrying back to the security of his

Figure 0.2 *Sir Isaac Newton*; Godfrey Kneller, 1702

rooms. It has often been interpreted to confirm what many people want to believe: that Newton was an unsullied scientific genius who disdained all thoughts of material comfort. Although that persona dominates biographies and documentaries, after arriving in London Newton radically refashioned himself, and the sombre picture remained virtually unknown, languishing in the dark corridor of a country mansion until the middle of the nineteenth century.[6]

Kneller's second portrait (Figure 0.2) was very different, and it displays the man-about-town who is the less familiar subject of this book—the metropolitan Newton who thrived in high society for three decades and became extremely rich. When it was painted in 1702, Newton was already Master of the Mint, and within three years he had become President of the Royal Society and been knighted by Queen Anne. More conventional but less intimate than the first, the painting shows a distinguished gentleman wearing a fine white shirt and gazing out arrogantly at the viewer. This Newton appears determined to advertise his elegant worldly status. The glossiness of his wig competes with the sheen of the sumptuous velvet wrap, which is deep crimson, the colour of nobility that remained Newton's favourite. Unlike the previous portrait of 1689, this one was widely circulated. As well as being repeatedly copied in oils, it was engraved in black and white with varying degrees of fidelity. Reproduced in books, prints, and medallions, this version travelled all over Europe and became the standard Enlightenment image of Sir Isaac Newton, Britain's most distinguished natural philosopher.

Perhaps on Kneller's advice, in this second picture Newton's face is surrounded by luxuriant but artificial auburn locks, very similar to the style worn by King George I when he posed for Kneller's coronation portrait. Men's wigs were not mere decoration: they indicated the owner's station in life. Unlike those worn by women, which supplemented their natural hair, men's were a cover-over or even a total replacement: older men might be naturally bald, while younger ones could have their heads shaved. In 1720, an advice manual on hair and teeth made it clear that whereas women chose such adornments to make themselves more beautiful, 'men should dress suitable to their various ranks in life, whether as a magistrate, statesman, warrior, man of pleasure, &c.' Just like theatre actors who change their costume, the author explained, male social performers 'may be dress'd to produce in us different ideas of the qualities of men'.[7] In Kneller's portrait, Newton is acting out the cosmopolitan role that he assumed in 1696, after terminating over three decades of scholarship at Cambridge to live in London for the rest of his life.

This book explores how Newton interacted with elite metropolitan society, a milieu far removed from his previous surroundings of the remote Lincolnshire countryside and the secluded cloisters of Trinity College. He spent the next thirty years running London's Royal Mint, revamping the British economy and moving in fashionable aristocratic circles—a very different character from his previous persona as a reclusive Cambridge academic. Rather than soaring above mundane concerns, this Newton immersed himself in financial negotiations, court intrigues, and international politics. By the time he died, he had revived the ebbing fortunes of the Royal Society, but he had also accumulated a substantial fortune, been knighted by Queen Anne, and launched the international gold standard. As a wealthy Enlightenment gentleman with influential contacts, Newton played a key role in the interlinked growth of science, the state, and British global trade.

Preparing to Leave

This was no overnight metamorphosis. Newton finally abandoned Cambridge in the spring of 1696, but he had been exploring future possibilities for some time, prompted by the publication of the *Principia* in 1687 and the political upheaval of the Glorious Revolution the following year. Each time he tried but failed to get a better position, the metropolis became increasingly attractive. By then, he had already emerged from the sanctuary of his books and experiments to become prominent in university politics. Over the next few years, he often travelled to London, even living there for months at a time. During this transitional period, he established fresh friendships and prepared himself for a fresh future.

Even during his most reclusive years, Newton could never totally isolate himself from Cambridge's intertwined religious and political intrigues: survival demanded tactical secrecy and flexibility. He openly abhorred Catholicism openly, denouncing it as a false religion that posed a dangerous threat to the English nation. In contrast, he kept self-protectively quiet about his aversion to some doctrines of the Anglican Church, subscribing instead to a religious heresy named after Arius, a Christian living in Egypt around the end of the third century. The Arian doctrine maintained that although Jesus Christ was the Son of God, he was born later and was therefore secondary. This conflicted with the Trinitarian creed of the Anglican Church that God comprises three distinct but divine personages: God the Father, God the Son, and God the Holy Spirit.[8]

When Newton was offered a position as Cambridge's second Lucasian Professor of Mathematics, his Arianism presented an awkward obstacle, because Charles II had decreed that in addition to their vow of celibacy, all university fellows should subscribe to the Thirty-Nine Articles, the basic statement of Anglican beliefs. Newton's manuscripts reveal how much he struggled to observe sexual abstinence, but at least it was in line with his own high moral standards. The new requirement presented a greater challenge: even the name of his Cambridge college must have felt alien for a heretic who rejected the validity of the Holy Trinity. Technically, it was possible to obtain a royal dispensation, but several requests had already been rejected. Somehow, although it is still not clear how, Newton managed to wriggle out of the university stipulation for orthodoxy. Mysteriously, after a visit to London, a draft exemption was on its way to the Attorney General. Somebody somewhere— probably his predecessor in the post, Isaac Barrow—had pulled strings. From then on, no Lucasian Professor was obliged to take the oath of Anglicanism. Even so, discretion was essential. While Newton diplomatically kept quiet about his unorthodox beliefs, his successor William Whiston actively advertised his own Arianism, and was soon dismissed from the university in disgrace.

Consumed by his work, and keeping well below the parapet, Newton effectively disappeared from public view. When he was at last nearing the end of the *Principia*, Newton embarked on a new phase in his life, gradually emerging from his self-imposed seclusion. By then, James II had inherited the throne from his brother, Charles II—and James was determined to make England Catholic. Refusing to heed his advisers, he replaced Anglicans in powerful positions by Catholics, despotic behaviour that aroused great resentment across the country. Even his daughters, Anne and Mary, complained that 'the priests have so much power with the King as to make him do things so directly against the Laws of the Land, & indeed contrary to his own promises.'[9]

At Oxford and Cambridge, James began distributing dispensations for Catholics, who were normally banned from the universities. In the spring of 1687, Cambridge University rebelled by making a test case out of a Benedictine monk, Alban Francis, refusing to follow

James's instructions that this ardent Catholic should receive a degree without swearing allegiance to the Thirty-Nine Articles. Angry letters circulated; secret meetings were convened. Hypocrisy does not seem too strong a word for describing Newton's behaviour as he launched himself into the campaign against Francis. The Arian who ten years earlier had refused to take vows himself now defended the Anglican Church, insisting that Francis should not be admitted without signing up to the Thirty-Nine Articles. Newton did have other options: he might have left Cambridge, or he could have kept quiet about his conviction that James had no right to intervene in academic affairs. Instead, he decided that protecting the university against Catholicism and Stuart control was more important.

Agitating when appropriate, but discreetly absenting himself from Cambridge when expedient, Newton became such a key player that he was one of eight representatives chosen to defend the university at an official hearing in London presided over by George Jeffreys, a sycophantic supporter of King James. Already notorious as 'The Hanging Judge', Jeffreys ruthlessly enforced royal policy and was duly rewarded with repeated promotion. For his part, Newton drafted fervent defences of the university's position and rose to prominence. Although details of the negotiations remain murky, the outcome is clear: Newton's side won, sustaining only one casualty, an incompetent vice-chancellor with a drink problem.

By the end of 1688, William of Orange—Protestant husband of James's daughter Mary—had landed in England and seized power. James had fled to France, his Catholic protégés had been forced out of Cambridge, and Jeffreys was confined in the Tower (reportedly, he had been captured in a Wapping pub, despite having shaved off his eyebrows and disguised himself as a sailor). Conspirators tend to be scrupulous about covering their tracks, and it is now impossible to retrieve definite information about Newton's possible involvement in the clandestine discussions that had been taking place all over the country. Even so, stray references make it clear that Newton had powerful patrons who were ready to reward him for past favours—so much took place behind the scenes, so much was hinted at rather than openly stated. Whatever had been happening, Newton rapidly emerged as a powerful figure within the university, commanding enough support to be elected in January 1689 as one of Cambridge University's two Members of Parliament, and subsequently re-elected in 1701.

To fulfil his parliamentary duties, Newton set off for London, where he lived for most of 1689. He was there when the new Parliament made one of its most momentous decisions. Breaking definitively with the past, the house decreed that succession to the throne would no longer be an automatic consequence of birth, but should be decided by statute. In line with Newton's sentiments, the official statement declared that 'it hath been found, by experience, to be inconsistent with the security and welfare of this Protestant Kingdom, to be governed by a Popish Prince.'[10] The former recluse from Cambridge was invited to dinner with King William, and backed him solidly on many occasions. By serving on committees, reporting to the university authorities, and negotiating in unrecorded conversations, Newton helped to ensure that Cambridge fellows would abandon their previous oath of loyalty to James and instead swear allegiance to William and Mary.

When his *Principia* appeared in print, even those who disagreed with Newton's theories—to say nothing of the far larger numbers who failed to grasp what he was talking about—were united in celebrating the middle-aged scholar. Accolades soon started arriving, and Newton began to engage with correspondents and make friends with people who might be useful to him. For example, he went to stay with John Locke at Lady Damaris Masham's house in Essex for a week's intellectual conversation, later inviting him back for a return visit. These two men are now acclaimed as a great scientist and a great philosopher, but they were drawn together by their interest in theology. A devout Christian, Newton dedicated himself to finding God through studying both the Bible and the natural world. Like many of his contemporaries, he regarded science not as an end in itself but as a route towards divine truth. Locke commented that 'Mr. Newton is really a very valuable man, not only for his wonderful skill in mathematics, but in divinity too, and his great knowledge in the Scriptures, wherein I know few his equals.'[11]

Taking advantage of his post-*Principia* fame, Newton started looking for more lucrative positions. Despite King William's support, he was blocked in his attempt to become Provost of King's

College at Cambridge, and London began to seem an increasingly attractive option. By 1690, Locke was trying to engineer him a place at the Mint, where there had been a succession of corruption scandals. The Master was Thomas Neale, an MP and financial opportunist who had contrived to secure a variety of lucrative positions, including acting as royal groom-porter—the man responsible for keeping the king's apartments well supplied with dice, cards, and gaming tables. Nicknamed the 'Lord of Lotteries', Neale was mocked for aiming "To teach the Great ones and the Small / How to get Money and Spend it all".[12]

Newton first came across his future Mint boss in the autumn of 1693, when Neale was dreaming up his Million Adventure, a state lottery designed to raise money for the Exchequer. Calculating the risks was tricky, especially as some central laws of probability had not yet been formulated. Seeking advice, Samuel Pepys—whose name as President of the Royal Society appears on the title page of the *Principia*—set Newton a dice-throwing puzzle to clarify what sort of odds were entailed, although the plan went ahead without Newton's further involvement. Neale had suggested that the government could finance its war against France by offering 100,000 tickets at £10 each, but the project foundered almost immediately. Although the vouchers were marketed as an investment opportunity, purchasers found it difficult to reclaim their money—and naturally, Neale made sure that he received a slice of the profits. This was among the first of many suspect money-making ventures that flourished in England well into the eighteenth century.[13]

To put it bluntly, the national economy was in a mess, partly because King William undertook protracted wars that proved cripplingly expensive. The remedies included founding the Bank of England—which benefited those who were already wealthy—and introducing new taxation systems. Although apparently fair, these fiscal reforms provided plenty of opportunities for bribing corrupt officials and for passing extra costs on to consumers through increased prices. William's supporters—including Newton—knew that if the country went bankrupt, his reign would come to an end. And if that happened, the Glorious Revolution would stand for nothing: James II would regain power, and the Catholic Stuarts would be restored to the throne.

On top of that, the currency was literally shrinking. Unlike now, the standard was set not by gold but by silver, the traditional precious metal. In principle, the weight of silver in a coin represented how much it was worth, but for years criminals had been shaving small slivers from the rims, so that when a coin was melted down, its value was far less than it should have been. Symbolically, Jacobite supporters were whittling away the monarch's head. To make matters worse, many counterfeit coins were circulating. The Chancellor of the Exchequer, Charles Montagu, had run out of ideas—he said 'that when he thought of this matter he was like a monkey thrown into the water which always claps his paws or hands to his eyes and sinks to the bottom'.[14]

Montagu played a uniquely important role in Newton's life. Newton is renowned for his enmities, and only Montagu remained his 'intimate friend' for several decades. It was Montagu who brought him to London, arranged a lucrative position at the Royal Mint, and enabled him to climb ever higher in metropolitan life. Newton first met this valuable ally at Trinity College. Conveniently related to the Master, Montagu arrived in 1679 as a student, and four years later was made a Fellow on the express instructions of Charles II. Although notoriously prickly, he became one of England's most influential Whig politicians, admired by many but also disdained as 'a party-coloured, shallow, maggot-headed statesman'.[15] The relationship between these two men gradually shifted. Initially, Newton was the older, more experienced member of the college, and they joined forces to set up a society for scientific experiments. Yet despite being over twenty years younger, Montagu soon became Newton's wealthy patron, intervening at a crucial stage in the delicate negotiations involved in publishing the *Principia* and also backing him at the Royal Society.

A New Life

By the spring of 1695, while Newton was still in Cambridge but looking for an escape, the national debt had reached crisis level. As the value of golden guineas soared, silver plummeted, making it even more difficult to pay the wages of soldiers fighting overseas. The government decided to consult some of the country's leading financiers and scholars, including John Locke, Christopher Wren, and Isaac Newton. That autumn, Newton submitted his carefully thought-out advice, but after many discussions and half-hearted measures, the government opted for the proposal he had rejected—that all the silver coins in the country should be recalled, melted down, and then reissued. They did, however, adopt his recommendation that this should be carried out in stages, rather than all at once.

Rumours about Newton's intentions began to circulate, but publicly he kept very quiet. In the middle of March 1696, he was still hotly denying any plan of moving to the Mint, although naturally that did little to quell the gossip. After all, he was a prime candidate—politically sound, an ace mathematician, and with the chemical skills essential for assaying metals. A few days later, Montagu sent him some excellent news—he had found Newton a wonderful position as Warden of the Mint. 'I am very glad that at last I can give you a good proof of my friendship, and the esteem the King has of your merits,' Montagu wrote; 'the King has promised Me to make Mr. Newton Warden of the Mint, the office is the most proper for you 'tis the Chief Officer in the Mint, 'tis worth five or six hundred p An. and has not too much bus'ness to require more attendance than you may spare. I desire you will come up as soon as you can, and I will take care of your Warrant in the meantime... Let me see you as soon as you come to Town, that I may carry you to kiss the King's hand.'[16]

The Wardenship was not the most senior position at the Mint, but it came with a fat salary and light responsibilities. Wasting no time, Newton hurried down to London and completed the paperwork so that he could embark immediately on his metropolitan career. He subsequently returned to Cambridge only for brief political visits, and there is no record that he even wrote to anyone he had known there. At first, he continued to collect his income as Lucasian Professor, but after five years he gave that up too.

Newton apparently had no qualms about leaving scholarly Cambridge, his home for thirty-five years. On the contrary, he relished his London life, with its prestigious connections and his appointment into royal service. When the Astronomer Royal, John Flamsteed, asked him for some astronomical data, Newton replied haughtily that he did not want 'to be dunned & teezed by forreigners about Mathematical things or to be thought by our own people to be trifling away my time about them when I should be about ye Kings business'.[17] Flamsteed was one of the enemies Newton most loved to hate, and he must have enjoyed putting him down.

Biographers often glide over those London years as if they were an embarrassment, an unfitting epilogue for the career of an intellectual giant. Even though Newton took his responsibilities at the Mint very seriously, his admirers are determined to maintain his status as a scientific icon. According to standard accounts, Newton sublimated his own intellectual desires for the sake of his country by abandoning the intellectual life he adored and reluctantly devoting his great mind to rescuing the nation's plummeting currency. However unconvincing that argument might sound, it is widely accepted, especially by scientists whose own identity and job satisfaction are tangled up with the unrealistic image of a venerated genius. Perhaps demoting Newton from his pedestal threatens their faith in the purity of scientific research and challenges the value of their own career?[18]

Economists see matters differently. More interested in falling stock markets than in falling apples, they are untrammelled by assumptions that the life scientific is the only one worth living. According to them, once Newton had tasted fame and the possibilities of wealth, he wanted more of both. And that entailed going to London.[19] Despite being educated as a physicist, I side with the economists and their more realistic, if jaundiced, perceptions of human nature. After his scholarly period hiding from public scrutiny, Newton headed south to the capital, where he earned his fortune, won friends, and influenced people. I can only speculate about reasons—professional insecurity, the anguish of an impossible love affair, private worries about intellectual decline as he aged—but Newton engineered his move with great care and deliberation. Determined to make a success of his new life, he broke away from provincial Cambridge with its fussy scholars squabbling over university affairs, and dedicated himself to his new metropolitan existence.

Newton continued to confirm and refine his theories of the natural world, but he was also a member of cosmopolitan society who contributed to Britain's ambitions for global domination. He shared the ambitions of his wealthy friends to make London the world's largest and richest city, the centre of a thriving international economy. Like many of his contemporaries, he invested his own money in merchant shipping companies, hoping to augment his savings by sharing in the profits.

An uncomfortable truth is often glossed over: until 1772, it was legal to buy, own, and sell human beings in Britain. Newton knew that the country's prosperity depended on the triangular trade in enslaved people—and when he was meticulously weighing gold at the Mint, he must have been aware that it had been dug up by Africans whose friends and relatives were being shipped across the Atlantic to cultivate sugar plantations, labour down silver mines, and look after affluent Europeans. This was a collective national culpability, and there is no point in replacing the familiar 'Newton the Superhuman Genius' by the equally unrealistic 'Newton the Incarnation of Evil'. By exploring activities and attitudes that are now deplored, I aim not to condemn Newton, but to provide a more realistic image of this man who was simultaneously unique and a product of his times.

This book presents Isaac Newton as a metropolitan performer, a global actor who played various parts. Theatricality was a favourite Enlightenment metaphor, which related the conduct of daily life to the concealed mechanisms of the natural world being revealed by spectacular experimental performances. Newton and his colleagues hoped to establish a fair and equal society that would mirror God's orderly, law-governed physical universe.[20] Every week, newspaper readers all over the country could absorb the pronouncements of Mr Spectator, an urbane commentator on metropolitan life created by the essayist Joseph Addison. The son of a clergyman, Addison preached secular sermons on appropriate behaviour. Or as he put it,

Mr Spectator 'considers the World as a Theatre, and desires to form a right Judgement of those who are actors on it'.[21]

By using Hogarth's theatrical picture (Figure 0.1) as its framework, this book dispenses with conventional themes for organizing Newton's life—time, place, intellectual preoccupation—to paint an unfamiliar picture of him within his cosmopolitan environment. Confined within its ornate frame, this conversation piece has three major components: the room and its portraits; the aristocratic children, women, and men making up the audience; and the miniature actors on the stage. Similarly, I have divided my narrative into three main parts. The first, called 'The Theatre', explores the physical setting of Hogarth's drawing-room scene, relating it to Newton's residences, acquaintances, and family in his London life. In 'The Audience', I switch the spotlight to the play's fashionable spectators, envisaging this metropolitan Newton moving in aristocratic circles of women as well as of men. Finally, in 'The Play', I discuss Newton's involvement in the capitalist projects—trade, conquest, exploitation—that were inseparable from scientific investigation.

Echoing Dryden's play on Hogarth's painted stage, this prologue summarizing Newton's pre-performance preparations for leaving Cambridge has come to an end. Now the curtain rises—and Newton arrives in London.

ACT I

THE THEATRE

ISAAC NEWTON MOVES TO THE METROPOLIS

Who is talking to whom in this conversation piece? Just as importantly, who is looking at whom? William Hogarth—eighteenth-century mastermind of visual quizzes—specialized in posing questions, but he never provided clear answers. In this portrayal of a play, the members of the painted audience are not the only spectators. A sumptuous London drawing room has temporarily been converted into a performance space, but the entire picture is itself a miniature theatre, with us—viewers three centuries later—peering in at a carefully orchestrated depiction of high-society life in the early eighteenth century. As grand theatrical manager, Hogarth has displayed a spectacle in which everybody is acting out a role.

In the aristocratic but unruly audience, attention is divided. Adult gazes wander between the well-disciplined children on the stage, their acquaintances, and those younger children who are restless and need to be distracted. Such undisciplined behaviour was common in London theatres, where the performance on the stage was forced to compete against the conversations in the pit. In contrast to the shifting spectators, the child actors—all around 10 years old—seem transfixed in stationary poses, symmetrically paired as if Newton himself had disciplined them into mathematical order. Above all, everybody is aware of three small royal visitors on the left, set apart by their own pretend box.

Higher up on the left-hand wall appear three people who are physically absent yet form a crucial part of the stage-set. The most prominent is Newton, his marble eyes staring eternally across the room, separated by the large chimney breast from the living groups on either side below him. To his right, two oval portraits hang directly above the audience. They represent a married couple who are not physically present but who gaze out at us and are very much alive: they own the house, and their daughter Kitty is on the stage. In his rightful place at the top is the husband, John Conduitt, currently Master of the Mint. Just below him is his wife, Catherine Barton, the daughter of Newton's half-sister and the woman who played a major role in his London life.

Newton would never have encountered such a mixed company of smartly dressed families in a Cambridge college, where sombre fellows moved in a resolutely male world. At Trinity, even the room servants were men, although there were probably women behind the scenes carrying out the more menial chores. But in London, Newton became familiar with social events where distinguished men and women mingled in elegant surroundings. The codes of conduct guiding their interactions were just as elaborate and concealed as at any university high table—and Newton learnt how to negotiate his way to the top.

1
Living in Style

Standing centre stage, at the middle of this mini-theatre on a canvas, are two statues—a woman and a mythological creature—who divide the performers on the dais from their friends and families, Hogarth's other actors. They mark a physical and a metaphorical boundary between the dramatic impression of sixteenth-century Mexico being played out to their left, and what purports to be modern metropolitan reality on their other side. Hogarth did not intend his picture to be taken as a completely faithful representation of the day's events; in any case, he had not even been present. Whereas he has depicted the audience sitting comfortably in the Conduitts' drawing room, the stage appears to be set inside a prison cell with stone walls and a barred window, an illusion that is not simply a complicated arrangement of ingenious scenery. As the artist, he has located himself beyond the frame, as though he is observing childhood memories of his father's prison sentence as well as the comfortable surroundings of his affluent patrons.

The two intervening statues may or may not have normally been in the house, but they probably represent the complementary muses of comedy and tragedy. Here, in this painted canvas fiction, they occupy a transitional space between two imagined scenes: a fabricated Mexican prison cell and a carefully posed London audience. They are connected by the garland of flowers on the central pillar, which completes a Hogarthian line of beauty running from right to left across the actors' hands and then through the heads of the audience.

The smaller sculpture depicts a faun or satyr, who is playing the pipes of Pan and glancing upwards towards Newton's bust on the mantelpiece. Pan sometimes signalled comedy and disruption, so his role in this picture may have been to emphasize the contrast between childish play and philosophical seriousness, even though the adult audience is behaving in a less orderly fashion than the small actors on the stage, who are arranged with geometric precision in a neat rectangle. Or perhaps Conduitt suggested to Hogarth that an image of Pan would provide a subtle reference to Newton's cosmology, since the god also represented an elemental force of nature: the whole of creation danced to Pan's music. According to Newton's intricate interpretations, the tunes played on Pan's pipes represented the harmony of the universe, the music of the spheres. When not immersed in the Mint's business, Newton devoted much of his time in London to continuing his Cambridge studies of ancient philosophy. He maintained that during a former era in the remote past scholars had been able to access true, uncorrupted knowledge—and he regarded it as his mission to retrieve that lost wisdom, to act as the privileged initiate who would unpick its symbolic formulations.

The taller stone woman to Pan's right wears a theatrical mask. Since her face is in shadow, it is hard to know whether she represents tragedy or comedy, but she is standing next to the hearth, the traditional Roman location for a home's guardian goddess. She gazes directly at Newton's head, as if to indicate that even after death he continues to preside over family life, just as he had always done. Newton took his position as head of the extended Newton clan very seriously. At times of crisis and illness, he lent emotional as well as financial support to distant relatives, as well as inviting younger ones to stay with him in his comfortable London homes.[1]

* * *

Newton wasted no time in securing the job he had angled so hard to get. As soon as the official letter of invitation arrived, he hurried down to London—a two-day journey by stage-coach—and confirmed his appointment as Warden of the Mint. Less than a month later, on 20 April 1696, the prematurely grey-haired man of 54 left Cambridge and his Trinity rooms for good.

International trade and private enterprise boomed in the early eighteenth century: the metropolis was an ideal location for an ambitious middle-aged man determined to move up in the world. The city was being rebuilt after the devastating fire that had ripped through its wooden buildings thirty years before Newton's arrival.

Now the largest conurbation in Europe, and home to a tenth of the country's population, it was expanding westwards, away from the pollution and slums surrounding the dockland areas. Benefiting from careful planning, London's appearance had already changed dramatically as solid brick and stone houses sprung up, lining the wide streets and elegant squares arranged around central gardens.

Much of the early development was organized by Nicholas Barbon, an unscrupulous speculator whose Puritanical father had given him a middle name that now sounds extraordinary: 'If-Christ-had not died-for-thee-thou-hadst-been-damned' (this is technically described as a hortatory name). Barbon was one of the first economists to stress that money itself has no intrinsic value: whether golden coins or paper notes, currency is worth only what it can be exchanged for. According to him, the government should discourage people from stockpiling their savings and instead urge them to spend so that the national economy would thrive. Rather than buying clothes or plates or chairs for life, he argued, people should follow the dictates of style and replace them regularly. Perhaps remembering his early medical training, Barbon insisted that a good circulation is just as essential for national prosperity as it is for a healthy person. As he put it: 'Fashion or the alteration of Dress, is a great Promoter of Trade, because it occasions the Expense of Cloaths, before the Old ones are worn out: It is the Spirit and Life of Trade: It makes a Circulation, and gives a Value, by Turns, to all sorts of Commodities; keeps the great Body of Trade in Motion.'[2]

One of the great chicken-and-egg questions debated by economic historians of early eighteenth-century England is whether demand stimulated production or whether marketing new goods expanded the number of purchasers. Whichever round it may be theoretically, in actuality what happened is that the nation embarked on a frenzy of consumption, and London began to supplant Amsterdam as the world's commercial centre. Luxury possessions advertised their owner's prosperity, and very gradually the traditional social structure based on inherited status started to break down and be supplemented by a hierarchy based on wealth. Recognizing this burgeoning market for domestic items, traders and skilled artisans flooded in from abroad to supply the expensive products being snapped up by customers eager to create a display of grandeur and flaunt their status.

This increase in visible wealth was promoted by an economic juggling trick: founding the Bank of England, for which Newton's patron, Charles Montagu, was rewarded by being appointed Chancellor of the Exchequer. The directors deliberately enveloped their new venture in an aura of prestige and mystery, so it is perhaps appropriate that the original building lay over the site of the London Mithraeum, ancient centre of a ritualistic cult. After disastrous wars against France, King William needed £1.2 million to rebuild the nation's navy and, in exchange for promising to provide that money (in principle, anyway), in 1694 a small group of men was given the exclusive right to issue bank notes, with a guaranteed return for them of over 13 per cent a year. The first Bank of England notes were hand-written for a specific amount, but fifty years later notes began to be printed in specific denominations. Goldsmiths already circulated notes rather than gold among themselves, but creating the Bank of England meant stepping away from this older practice of personal credit towards a more formalized central organization. The system relied on regarding money as an exchange token of no intrinsic value, so that more notes could be created than the gold or silver available to cover them. The advantage of this new national currency was reliability: if everybody could trust it, then there would be no need to have any personal knowledge of the people involved.[3]

The original Bank of England comprised a consortium of individuals who guaranteed to redeem their notes if asked to, and modern bank notes still bear the legend 'I promise to pay the bearer on demand the sum of...' accompanied by the signature of the Chief Cashier: the system works as long as the Bank does not collapse. Inevitably, without formal accounting, sums of money did mysteriously disappear into hidden coffers, and critics remained apprehensive. The political economist Charles Davenant remarked, among things that 'have Existence only in the Minds of Men, nothing is more fantastical and nice than Credit; 'tis never to be forc'd; it hangs upon Opinion; it depends upon our Passions of Hope and Fear...when once lost, is hardly to be quite recover'd.'[4]

Newton warned government officials about the dangers of relying too heavily on paper money. 'Credit is a present remedy against poverty & like the best remedies in Physick works strongly & has a poisnous quality,' he commented. In his view, 'it inclines the nation to an expensive luxury in forreign commodities.'[5] But under Montagu's supervision, the economy soared, this private company retained its monopoly over English banking, and some very rich people became even richer. Instead of paying their servants more money, wealthy people could convince themselves that it was their civic duty to benefit the nation by spending—by buying ever more goods for themselves in order to stimulate production. There was, of course, no protection for those who were ill or disabled, or the men who could find no work, or the children with no parents, or the single women with no munificent male relatives. Both socially and physically, the country was divided between the haves and the have-nots—and especially so in London, where the poor were trapped in no-go areas towards the east of the city. And then there were the even less visible victims, the many, many thousands of African captives shipped across the Atlantic to work on plantations or down silver mines.

Newton certainly does not have a reputation for extravagance. On the contrary: the mythological shroud that conceals him from view presents him as a parsimonious recluse, an unemotional genius divorced from the trivial pleasures of metropolitan life. Yet judging from the inventory of house contents taken when he died, Newton was as susceptible to the newly created pleasures of retail therapy as his neighbours. Original receipts still survive of the landscapes and Delft plates that he bought to complement the many other fine furnishings of the various London houses in which he lived. Now a wealthy man who lived immersed in fashionable luxury, perhaps his puritanical conscience troubled him from time to time? If so, he could take comfort from the influential Dutch doctor Bernard Mandeville, who persuaded English purchasers that there was no harm in ostentations expenditure. Greed is good, Mandeville argued, because it stimulates the economy—after all, 'clean Linnen weakens a Man no more than Flannel, Tapistry, fine Painting or good Wainscot are no more unwholesome than bare Walls, and a rich Couch, or a gilt Charriot are no more enervating than the cold Floor or a Country Cart.'[6]

In conversations about Newton, the question that crops up again and again is 'What was he really like?' The only honest answer is that nobody knows: even when he was still alive, impressions that conflicted with each other could all claim validity. There are several difficulties. To start with, like most people Newton behaved in different ways at different times, or even at almost the same time. Anecdotes squeeze him into a succinct stereotype—absent-minded genius, ruthless administrator, reclusive alchemist—but he could display several apparently contradictory characteristics simultaneously. For example, after his death several relatives reminisced about the dear old man's love for children and animals, his tears on hearing about cruelty, his vegetarianism. He may well have developed such an armchair sentimentality, but, even so, well into his eighties he remained merciless towards criminals, insisting vindictively that a counterfeiter should be cruelly punished: 'it's better to let him suffer...'[7]

And then there is the problem of finding reliable evidence. Historians are forced to fall back on a fairly random assortment of comments that happen to have survived through the centuries. Lack of information makes some references incomprehensible. Newton once reported that 'Sir Joseph is leaving Mr Toll's house & its probable I may succeed him.'[8] Sir Joseph has been identified as Joseph Tily, vice-chancellor of the Duchy of Lancaster, who had married a wealthy widow and was involved in government-linked banking schemes. But who was Mr Toll, and which position was Newton angling for? The answers to those questions will probably never be found.

No testimonies are neutral and trustworthy, not even (or perhaps that should be especially) those of a person's nearest and dearest. Witnesses tend to provide information confirming expectations. After all, Newtonian stories revealing eccentricity—the neglected dinner, the ill-assorted clothes, the leg stuck out of the carriage window—are just so much more interesting than descriptions of normality. Inevitably, the more often they are repeated, the more difficult it becomes to suggest any alternative, especially in the absence of any personal diary or systematic collection of correspondence. Newton's close relative John Conduitt reported that 'all the time he had to spare from his business & the civilities of life in wch he was scrupulously exact & complaisant was employed the same way [in study] & he was hardly ever alone without a pen in his hand & a book before him.'[9] How easy to interpret that as confirming the conventional view of Newton as an antisocial recluse—but it also reinforces a less familiar version of Newton the wheeler-dealer who punctiliously observed the social responsibilities associated with his prestigious positions.

Moving Around

After his first few months in London, Newton abandoned the live-on-the-job accommodation provided by the Mint, and acquired five different houses in succession, all carefully chosen to reflect his good position in society. Initially, he settled in newly fashionable Westminster, remaining there from 1696 to 1709, when he went to Chelsea for nine months. After that, he stayed in St Martin's Street—near today's National Gallery—for around fifteen years before finally moving to a mansion in the Kensington countryside.

Newton's reclusive existence in Cambridge suggests that he was not a natural party-goer, but he knew that living in London entailed fulfilling social obligations. In his official positions at the head of the Mint as well as the Royal Society, he had to cultivate visitors and potential benefactors. As just one example, Newton arranged for the Royal Society's experimental assistant, a former draper called Francis Hauksbee, to bring a bulky air pump to his Westminster residence so that 'I can get some philosophical persons to see his experiments, who will otherwise be difficultly got together.'[10] In a more private capacity, Newton needed to ingratiate himself with his patrons, and also ensure that he distributed benefits to those who in their turn sought his support. And then on top of all that, there were the demands made on him by his Lincolnshire relatives, who somehow seemed to increase in numbers and affection as he became richer and more distinguished.

The spring of 1715 illustrates how Newton combined home and business. That was when natural philosophers from all over Europe converged on England to witness a total eclipse of the sun. Advertising his Newtonian mathematical skills, the astronomer Edmond Halley had drawn a map demonstrating that a band of darkness would sweep across the south of the country, with a black-out elliptical shape stretching almost from Wales to Kent. Because of some inaccurate moon results, Halley's prediction was twenty miles out, but London sky-watchers did—as promised—enjoy about three and a half minutes of totality. When two visiting Frenchmen and an Italian, Antonio Conti, turned up at Newton's house in St Martin's Street, they found it already crowded with foreigners keen to meet Britain's greatest man of science. After politely welcoming his guests, Newton showed them books and old manuscripts from his collection, and the following day invited them back to admire some of his controversial experiments in optics. Evidently identifying Conti as a valuable international contact, Newton met him several times, inviting him to lunch and encouraging him to attend meetings at the Royal Society. Since their conversations took place through an interpreter, this international diplomacy must have taken up a considerable amount of Newton's time—an investment that paid off when, with Conti's help, the *Opticks* appeared in a handsome French edition.[11]

Newton's first choice of home was just to the south of Piccadilly, in the smarter end of Jermyn Street, a location recommended by his patron Montagu, who had lived there for the past seven years.[12] It formed part of a prestigious new development originally designed for politicians and early-career courtiers who could not yet afford the still more expensive Mayfair homes to the north. Lying conveniently near to the Exchequer in Whitehall, where Newton carried out much of his work, it enabled him to squeeze his physical presence at the Tower into a single day a week. At this stage, there were still open green spaces on the way to Hyde Park Corner, from where

La Route du Roi (the King's Road, later corrupted into Rotten Row) led directly to the royal residence at Kensington Palace; illuminated by 300 oil lamps to ward off highwaymen, it was London's first artificially lit thoroughfare. Piccadilly Circus would not be created for another century, but while Newton still lived there, William Fortnum and Hugh Mason opened up a small grocery shop nearby. Initially they sold half-used candles appropriated from the court of Queen Anne, but before long they had upgraded their enterprise into an up-market store catering for the wealthy.[13]

For the first four years, Newton and his household occupied number 88 Jermyn Street, diagonally opposite St James's Church and now the only one in that stretch whose original bricks have not been concealed by a façade of cream-painted plaster. For some reason, he then moved to the wider building next door. Victorian enthusiasts often complained that little effort was made either to record or to preserve Newton's homes. However, his second house in Jermyn Street—number 87, now a men's clothing store—does boast a commemorative blue plaque, even though the original building was demolished in the early twentieth century. Presumably there were good reasons for not putting it on number 88.

Virtually nothing is known about Newton's third house, except that it was in Chelsea—then a riverside village with no easy transport to London—and that he stayed there for less than a year before moving again. This time he chose another up-and-coming central location—St Martin's Street, which ran along the south side of Leicester Fields. That year, 1710, was a stormy one for Newton at the Royal Society. Eventually, he won a bitter dispute about premises by the strong-arm tactic of exercising his presidential authority, over-riding objectors and buying a house in Crane Court for the Society to move into, near the small alleys behind Fleet Street that were packed with small shops selling scientific books and instruments. For himself, he chose a more prestigious neighbourhood further west, near to one of Dryden's favourite coffee houses, Slaughter's. Plans were already in place for converting the area into Leicester Square (currently home to the only London street sculpture of Newton, an unobtrusive bust with a broken nose). Only a few years after Newton settled there, this part of London had become sufficiently grand for the Prince and Princess of Wales (George and Caroline) to move in nearby, at Leicester House.

Newton's new home at 35 St Martin's Street (Figure 1.1) was substantial and designed to impress his visitors; nearly 70 years old when he arrived, he had his international reputation as President of the Royal Society to maintain. Boasting three main storeys and an eyrie later known as 'Newton's Observatory' up in the roof, during the nineteenth century it was first a hotel and then a refuge for prostitutes. To smarten this home up, Newton splashed out on some new furniture, spending almost £30 (about a third of his annual salary as Lucasian Professor), on wall-hangings, a bed and fire-irons, as well as a sink and other essential equipment.[14]

Newton's study from his St Martin's Street residence has been preserved, although seeing it entails travelling to rural Massachusetts. When the house was demolished in 1913, the London City Council (long since disbanded) had the foresight to put some of its furnishings in storage. Over twenty years later, an American woman called Grace Babson arranged for them to be shipped across the Atlantic and reassembled, rather like an IKEA flat-pack. Her husband was Roger Babson, a self-made businessman from New England, who claimed to have made his fortune on the stock market by applying Newton's third law of motion. For this ambitious entrepreneur, Newton was the guru of determinism whose mathematical laws governed not only gravity but also the profitable ups and downs of international finance.

This room is 300 years old, but it can only be reached by taking an electric lift up to the third floor of an all-purpose academic building, which is part of a business college near the end of Boston's T-line. Entering it is a disconcerting experience: after pushing buttons to operate the lift, any historical tourist must walk across a bland corridor and then through a modern door directly into an early eighteenth-century chamber. As a further disorientation, Newton's original room has been reconstituted so that it resembles a museum or shrine rather than a place of work. Authentic dark wooden panels line the walls, and a freshly polished old brass poker sits ready to stir the unlit logs in the grate, but many of the carefully

Figure 1.1 *Newton's House, 35 St Martin's Street*; C. Lacy after Edward Meredith, 1811

chosen decorations—pictures of London, busts of Newton—date from after his death. Although the heavy velvet curtains are crimson, Newton's favourite colour, they fail to block out the American campus sounds that filter through the modern window panes.

Living centrally was a major advantage for Newton, but he eventually yielded to pressure from his family, who insisted that for the sake of his health, he should move to a less urban environment situated still further west—Kensington, the area picked by asthmatic King William. Even then, Newton continued renting the house in St Martin's Street, installing a maid to care for all the possessions he had left behind in case he should ever return from his rural retreat in Orbell's Buildings, on what is now Kensington Church Street. Built at the end of the seventeenth century, this impressive three-storey mansion was surrounded by trees. The country air did restore Newton to some extent, but by then in his eighties, Newton suffered multiple problems of old age that might now be treatable medically—gout, lung infections, incontinence. His Conduitt relatives managed to prevent him from struggling to work at the Tower, but even going up to town for a Royal Society meeting entailed a round trip of several days to allow him time for recuperation en route.

For each of his house moves, Newton faced a logistical nightmare: how to transport his growing library of books. He ended up with over 2000 volumes in several languages, ranging alphabetically from a pocket-size *Abendana of the Polity of the Jews* (1706) through bibles and other religious books to Xenophon and finally Zozimi's *Procopii &c. Historiæ*, a folio volume of 1610. In between were twenty-three books by Robert Boyle, five copies of Euclid (one of his favourite authors), thirty-four items collected together under H for History, and a *Memoir* on Dutch trade. Compared with other English gentlemen, Newton paid virtually no lip service to the nation's great classics by Geoffrey Chaucer, William Shakespeare, or John Milton. More cumbersome still were the ever-mounting piles of manuscript notes, tracts, and correspondence, which were roughly sorted into topics but lacked any systematic retrieval system. In addition to the boxes stuffed with loose papers, the pamphlets and notebooks weighed in at around fifty kilograms.[15]

Although Newton was clearly declining rapidly during his last couple of years, his colleagues loyally maintained that he preserved all his faculties as well as his teeth and his keen eyesight. Carefully scripted accounts make his death sound painful and protracted— 'the drops of sweat ran down from his face with anguish'—but, naturally, his relatives reported that he endured the ordeal stoically, boasting on his behalf that 'more patience was never shown by any mortal.' His thoughts were sufficiently clear that, in line with his unorthodox religious beliefs, he refused to receive the holy sacrament of the Anglican Church, carefully protecting his reputation by ensuring that only his closest relatives knew.[16]

Entertaining

One stock attribute of a scientific genius is to subsist on a starvation diet, rather like a fasting saint. Many biographers have presented Newton as an abstemious man who cared little for food, appearance, or comfort. Their favourite anecdote depicts a Newton who conforms to this imaginary superhuman status by absent-mindedly ignoring the dinner that had been placed before him. Other unverifiable testimonies confirm this ability to exist on little more than air—he apparently abstained from wine and meat, and washed down his frugal breakfast with tea made from hot water and orange peel.

Whatever his habits may have been in Cambridge, plenty of evidence suggests that in London Newton enjoyed eating and entertaining for many years before he became too old and ill. Contradicting the myths of being an absent-minded, down-at-heel academic, this metropolitan Newton was clearly a big spender. Like his neighbours, he was keen to keep up appearances, and he could certainly afford it. On top of the sizeable estate he had inherited from his mother, his combined income from investments and the Mint grew to several thousand pounds a year, towards the upper end of aristocratic expectations and the equivalent of modern millions.[17]

Newton had apparently come to recognize that puritanical privation was not the only option in life. If you want to eliminate drunkenness, he argued, you should change people's behaviour, not remove the alcohol—there is no point banning 'all the best things because by corruption they become the worst'.[18] Portraits and written comments confirm a new-found pleasure in food: they all depict a man who grew steadily plumper as he aged. Conduitt remarked that Newton 'always lived in a very handsome generous manner thoᵘ without ostentation or vanity, always hospitable & upon proper occasions gave splendid entertainments. He was generous & charitable without bounds...'.[19] After Royal Society meetings, Newton socialized at coffee houses and invited people to dinner. But he was canny with his money: interestingly, he seems to have been particularly munificent when he could charge the bill to his account at the Mint. Drawing up the menu for fourteen eminent guests—including several aristocrats and a bishop—Newton specified 'Fish, Pastry. fricasy of chickens & a dish of puddens. Qᵗʳ Lamb. Wild foul. Peas & Lobsters'.[20]

Reports from his visitors vary, but they are not necessarily trustworthy. A French visitor deemed his dinner to be deplorable, but at that time the French and the English were both equally guilty of slating food from the other side of the Channel. On the other hand, it was in Newton's political interests to be hospitable towards a Dutch ambassador, who commented that Newton spent a long time discussing mathematics with him and then, after showing him round the Mint, 'entertained us most sumptuously'.[21] Some scattered facts do survive, and they indicate that Newton was prepared for offering warm hospitality. His cellar was well stocked with bottles of wine and cider, and in the space of a single week the local butcher delivered one goose, two turkeys, two rabbits, and a chicken. After Newton died, his executors settled suppliers' bills for a range of groceries as well as fifteen barrels of beer totalling around £25—enough money to employ a maid for five years (men were routinely paid double the female rate).[22]

In order to lay on such lavish dinners, Newton needed servants and a well-decorated house. Newton was so wealthy when he died that the hand-written and erratically spelt inventory of the possessions he accumulated in St Martin's Street covered seventeen feet of vellum strips sewn together in a long band. It reveals how well equipped he was to cater for his guests. The kitchen was fitted with three spits, around twenty pans and two fish kettles, to say nothing of pewter dishes, a marble mortar, a cheese toaster, and a chocolate pot. Initially, he took on two maids who slept together in the meagrely furnished garret, and a manservant, who was given a small bed in the corridor. Later, he acquired a housekeeper for supervising the additional staff employed to run the household, including a cook as well as Adam the footman. When Newton began hiring a coach and horses, he also had to pay for a driver and his livery. And as Newton got older, he recruited men to carry his sedan chair—naturally, his house boasted a stable to keep it in.[23]

Among many other possessions, Newton owned well over one hundred drinking glasses, eighty napkins, forty plates of best china with another fifty in the kitchen, and nine glass salvers. Over two hundred prints were stashed away in the drawers of a walnut writing desk, although his wig-stand had been relegated to the stable storage area along with several old tables, curtains, and his silver sword. Then there were the more valuable silver items—cutlery, castors, and candle-snuffers, as well as two urinals (usually referred to as chamber pots by historians). Listed alongside the rest of the silver plate, these were particularly extravagant versions of a home's standard accoutrements provided in the dining room for the benefit of male guests. Modern replicas are available on the Web for discerning customers with a couple of (modern) thousand pounds to spare, and the genuine antiques also on sale show that there were several different styles to choose from. After he was knighted by Queen Anne, did Newton elect to behave like other lords of the realm and have his silver chamber pots engraved with his coat-of-arms? Put together, Newton's silver items weighed over 370 ounces, which would today be worth several thousand pounds (silver is still valued by the ounce on the London market).

That seems a sizeable hoard. By comparison, one of the most obsessive eighteenth-century collectors, the Earl of Warrington, amassed 25,000 ounces of silver, but his was an extreme case: he devoted much of his life to converting his wife's massive dowry into elaborate ornaments, and his estate was worth substantially less than Newton's when he died. However Newton acquired his silverware, much of it—including the chamber pots—had probably been crafted by Huguenot immigrants. Welcomed to England after the French law protecting them was revoked in 1685, Huguenots soon came to dominate many skilled trades. Ingenious metal smiths attracted their spendthrift customers by developing increasingly large, ornate (and often functionless) must-have items of precious metals designed to advertise their owners' opulent lifestyle. At least the chamber pots had a practical function.[24]

Showing Off

As one might expect, Newton's dining room contained eight chairs and an oval table, but in addition it was home to two walnut card tables as well as sundry other pieces of furniture. To complement the silver and crystal sparkling in the candle-light on the dinner table, pictures, mirrors, and landscapes adorned the walls. And to emphasize his wealth still further, Newton commissioned one of the most expensive sculptors in town, David Le Marchand, to carve him twice in ivory, as a picture and as a bust.

Le Marchand, a French Huguenot immigrant, was so prestigious that his clients included Queen Anne and George I, but when his own portrait was painted by the English royal artist Joseph Highmore, he chose to show himself clutching Newton's sculpted head (now owned by the British Museum). Wearing a fine white shirt and elaborate wig, his free hand elegantly outstretched in an elegant classical pose, Le Marchand is advertising his status as an English gentleman of discerning taste (Figure 1.2).[25]

The rest of the house was also comfortably furnished, with plenty of sofas, spare beds, chairs, and pictures. Newton's bedroom was especially well appointed: its contents were worth even more than those of the dining room. Judging from the inventory list, Newton created a crimson boudoir for himself, perhaps emulating the recent refurbishments by William and Mary at Hampton Court. Crimson curtains surrounded his crimson mohair bed with its

Figure 1.2 *David Le Marchand*; Joseph Highmore, 1724

feather bolster, pillows, and quilt. The walls were lined with crimson drapes, and a large mirror in a gilt frame hung over the fireplace. Completing the decorations were a gilt wall sconce (to hold a candle), six walnut chairs, and a commode fitted with an earthenware bowl.

Ostentatious displays of wealth were a new vogue in the early eighteenth century, when the economic boom precipitated the birth of today's highly commercialized society with its throw-away competitive culture. The population was growing rapidly, the country needed money to fund its frequent wars, and the government encouraged trade to stimulate manufacture. Britain grew rich by importing raw materials and converting them into fashionable, desirable objects. Daniel Defoe exclaimed in 1713 that merchants had acquired the purchasing power of aristocrats: 'Here I saw, out of a Shopkeeper's House, Velvet Hangings, Embroidered Chairs,

Damask Curtains...in short, Furniture equal to what, formerly, suffis'd the greatest of our Nobility.'[26] Interior design flourished as aspiring consumers bought and bought and bought again in the hope that expensive purchases would signal their refined taste and rising status.

British merchants were importing manufactured products from Asian countries, notably India and China, which dominated the global market. Consumers ranging along the social scale from Samuel Pepys to Queen Mary were snapping up Indian patterned chintzes and other lightweight fabrics to replace traditional sombre bedspreads and wall-hangings, while China was exporting porcelain ornaments for cupboards and mantelpieces, as well as elaborate coloured silks for curtains, women's dresses, and men's waistcoats. The essayist Joseph Addison rejoiced that London had become 'an emporium for the whole Earth...the single dress of a woman of quality is often a product of a hundred climates...the scarf is sent from the torrid zone...the brocade petticoat rises out of the mines of Peru and the diamond necklace out of the bowels of Indostan.' He neglected to mention the flip-side of globalization—that each item in this imagined outfit also depended on extensive forced labour by men, women, and children working under atrocious conditions.[27]

Many such fashionable items were scattered around Newton's house—silk cushions, a Japan table, a shagreen (probably sharkskin) cutlery box, an Indian screen, a calico quilt (probably also red), muslin curtains. During his first decade in London, Newton benefited personally from sales of these imported luxuries because he invested in the privately owned East India Company, which was reaping huge profits from trading with India, China, and Japan.[28] But as international commerce escalated, fears grew that these foreign imports would undercut British products, and the government stepped in with taxes designed to safeguard local manufacturers and squeeze out foreign competitors. In order to compete in the global market and protect its own enterprises, Britain imposed tariffs that encouraged internal producers to create cheaper imitations of exotic goods and squeeze overseas rivals out of business.[29]

Newton supported that policy, even though it was hard to implement. Writing chummily to a Member of Parliament, he resorted to blaming the womenfolk: 'I perceive our Wives are resolved not to quit...the well dy'd *Callico*, and They (We know) must, and will govern.'[30] The terse labels in Newton's official inventory make it impossible to be sure whether his particular domestic trappings were cheap replicas manufactured at home or had been imported. For example, by the time he was decorating his homes, silk woven in London was readily available, provided by the enterprising Huguenot immigrants who settled in Spitalfields. There is, however, one firm piece of evidence that Newton tried to buy British—the crimson curtains surrounding his bed were made not of silk but of harrateen, a linen-based fabric only recently introduced in England and deliberately intended to supplant expensive equivalents from abroad.

The sources of Newton's domestic decorations may be largely unverifiable, but they mattered—and they mattered to him. Newton encouraged people to buy home-manufactured goods, because he endorsed Britain's mercantilist strategy of stimulating national industrialization at the expense of long-established Asian producers. Concerned to protect the Mint and the currency, he lamented that much of the gold and silver pouring in to the country from Africa and South America was going straight out again to buy goods from Asia, leaving Britain with insufficient funds to pay for its expensive wars. He condemned what he saw as frivolous expenditure that was damaging the national economy. 'For these things serve for nothing but a useless & expensive sort of luxury maintained by the exportation of o[r] gold & silver to the Indies,' he warned.[31] As Master of the Mint, he backed the government's protectionist policy of making foreign goods prohibitively expensive, thus encouraging British opportunists to import raw materials and, with the help of some discreet industrial espionage, reproduce the inventions of their foreign rivals at lower prices.

One raw material preoccupied Newton—African gold, dug out of the ground or panned in rivers by local conscripts who knew that their friends and families were being shipped across the Atlantic to the Americas. Those who survived the voyage might be recruited for sugar plantations or despatched down silver mines to extract the precious metal needed for providing gentlemen like Isaac Newton with silver chamber pots and cutlery. The silver blades of Newton's fashionable knives were embedded in handles of ivory, another material stained with colonial blood. To adorn the cutlery on his dining table and to provide the raw material for the expensive sculptures he commissioned from Le Marchand, many wild elephants must have been killed. Moreover, on the long trek from the hinterland to reach an African port, undernourished porters died, burdened down by their giant loads of sawn-off tusks. Newton probably remained as untroubled as his compatriots by the treatment British merchants and soldiers were meting out to people and animals abroad.

2
The Tower of London

Just below Newton's bust, Hogarth has represented the marble plaque from his tomb in Westminster Abbey. The monument itself—one of the very first to be installed in the Abbey's nave—is a massive, sombre edifice that pays tribute to Newton's intellectual work, and this small bas-relief at its base comes as rather a surprise. It shows eight naked cherubs apparently dancing across the surface as they twist, bend, and lift in the course of their work. Although lacking wings, they are otherwise very similar to the putti that frequently appeared in seventeenth-century illustrations of scientific experiments, where they functioned as God's invisible helpers.

Here they are busily carrying out the type of practical tasks tackled by Newton himself during his lifetime: one peers through the telescope that he built by hand, another slides chemical preparations into a fiery furnace, others are weighed down by the piles of objects they carry. In contrast with the formal sculpted head emanating silent intellect on the mantelpiece, they symbolize a Newtonian avatar who was perpetually in motion—testing samples of gold, persecuting counterfeiters, entertaining distinguished foreign visitors, pronouncing on national taxation policies, devising opportunities for self-advancement.

*   *   *

Under normal circumstances, the only emotions Newton revealed were anger and contempt. In the spring of 1696, when he stepped out of his carriage and into his new home at the Mint, located right inside the Tower of London, even this man of iron self-discipline must have felt excited. Yet after only four months, he had had enough. Moving over three miles away to his first house near Piccadilly, Newton began commuting in on Wednesdays, his only regular day at the Tower.

The problem was not the work, which he continued to carry out with dedication for almost thirty years, but the place. Situated on the bank of the Thames, itself a source of pollution and smell, the Tower lay close to some of London's worst slum areas. Concealed behind its ramparts, the Mint had been haphazardly expanding for four centuries, its assaying chambers and coin workshops crammed into narrow windswept spaces between the Tower's inner and outer fortifications. Around twenty wooden, ramshackle buildings straggled in a line among stables and coach-houses; the residence allocated to Newton did have a small garden, but its view was dominated by high blank walls. Making the castle feel still more cramped, its central area was taken up by a large military administrative block that is no longer there.[1]

And then there was the noise. The Tower was already a busy tourist site, and sightseers swarmed in to marvel at the royal Crown Jewels, hastily reconstructed during the Restoration after having been melted down during Oliver Cromwell's regime. They could also admire the large collection of armour, which emphasized that this was the country's military centre, distributing weapons, soldiers, and provisions all over the world. After the Glorious Revolution of 1688, when the Stuart monarchy was deposed and Parliament's power was strengthened, the display was enhanced by introducing the Line of Kings, fourteen heroic monarchs mounted on life-size wooden horses (James II was *not* included). It was a hundred years since the defeat of the Spanish Armada, and the exhibits of captured torture devices further reinforced the message of English splendour.

What many visitors really wanted to see was the famous menagerie. Elephants, lions, and other spectacular creatures were kept in an enclosure by the river, next to a large pool of water into which the corpses of traitors were thrown. Tower residents such as Newton had to put up with night-time roars, screeches, and bellows, while the nearby yard where the lions were kept 'smelt as frowzily as a dove-house or a dog-kennel'. Only a few years before Newton arrived, Mary Jenkinson had been fatally mauled after stroking a lion's paw. When his acquaintance the Bishop of Carlisle visited in 1704, there were six lions, two leopards (by then, the one that had belonged to Charles I was 'old...lean and Lazy'), several wild cats, sundry birds, and two 'dull and lumpish' Swedish owls.[2] In addition to those wild animals, the Tower accommodated many horses. The Mint itself owned around fifty, which every morning and evening tramped over the cobblestones between their stables and the work-shop, earning their keep by powering the latest French equipment that manufactured coins more efficiently than the traditional man-ual methods. Just carting away the manure (more smells) cost a small fortune, while the nine deafening presses often started up at five in the morning and continued until midnight.

The high levels of security made it difficult to move from one place to another. If Newton arrived by road, he had to brave the menagerie, then travel through two portcullises separated by a drawbridge that passed over the filthy, sewage-laden moat. Negotiating various cannon along the way, he next went past the Stone Kitchen pub towards Mint Street, but then had to confront several cross-walls providing extra protection (no longer in exist-ence). Safety trumped convenience at every point: Tower stairways could not be reached directly from their doorways, and deliberately circuitous routes made offices hard to access. Outside, the nearest bridge was almost a mile (over 1 kilometre) away.

Life in the Tower

Newton endorsed the egalitarian ideals proclaimed during the Glorious Revolution, but, under the new Whig regime that fol-lowed, some people were definitely more equal than others. At the Tower, he was pushed into close proximity with men and women from many different backgrounds, but they shared the desire to improve their own existence. As the gaps between rich and poor, between one nation and another, continued to increase, Newton was determined that he would be moving upwards.

For his first three years at the Mint as Warden, Newton was tech-nically under the command of the Master, Thomas Neale, the lot-tery speculator whom he despised. After Neale died, Newton successfully manoeuvred with the help of his patrons to acquire the top job and a higher salary. Now at the peak of an administrative hierarchy, he was still forced to protect the Mint's interests and his own position by constant negotiations with Whitehall statesmen who held power over him. At the same time, he knew that his staff were playing a similar double-speak game of patronage with him. Nothing was straightforward; the words never meant quite what they said. After dutifully rewarding his clerk Hopton Haynes for translating and copying various documents, Newton learnt that further obligatory gifts were expected. Adopting a suitably grovelling and convoluted tone, Haynes told Newton, 'I am sorry I had not ye good fortune to see You ysday at the Excise, tho' I hope You are so kind, as stil to continue y^r good inclination to favor my pretension, if occasion be. But I have rec^d such demonstrations of y^r friendship, already, for which I never pretend to return, & You, I dare say, never expect any other requital than my gratitude that I cannot but assure myself of Y^r good Offices when a fair occasion presents, by which You'll extremely add to the many obligations You have already layd upon [your humble servant].'[3] To succeed, Newton had to manage both upwards and downwards.

As well as housing the Mint and the menagerie, the Tower was home to many other occupants. When the first Astronomer Royal, John Flamsteed, was waiting impatiently for the new Observatory at Greenwich to be completed, he temporarily took over a medieval turret at the top of the White Tower, struggling up its narrow spiral staircase with his heavy telescopes and instruments. More permanently, the Tower accommodated the Ordnance Office, which was mainly responsible for producing ammunition, storing weapons, and transporting soldiers. And, of course, the castle still functioned as a state prison: only the year after Newton arrived, his one-time patron the Earl of Monmouth was deprived of his political positions and held captive in the Tower for a few months.

The Mint and the Ordnance Office might seem rather strange neighbours, but there were close historical associations between making guns and minting money. Both processes involved heavy machinery that forced (also known as forged or coined) metals into an accurate shape. Guns could themselves be a form of currency, especially in Africa, where they were regularly exchanged for gold as well as people destined to work as slaves. Because England was repeatedly at war, the Ordnance Office kept encroaching on the Mint's domain. By 1703, it employed almost forty clerks on top of storekeepers, craftsmen, and labourers, and its demands for new muskets and pistols continued to escalate. Inside the Tower walls, large warehouses sheltered weapons and explosives, which were made under contract by around 200 self-employed gunsmiths, many of them living nearby. This centralized arrangement doubly benefited the state: it forced the independent gunsmiths to compete against each other and so lower their prices; and it prevented any single external group from gaining power and rebelling. To ensure their income during times of peace, these small gunmakers also dealt with private trading companies, but they increasingly depended on the government for survival.[4]

Newton also needed to ward off members of the garrison, trying to prevent them from taking over buildings and constructing barracks on vacant plots. Tensions ran high in the crowded confines of the Tower, where fights repeatedly erupted, often initiated by a minor incident before escalating into a major confrontation. On one occasion, Newton complained, a Tower warden 'took the Porters son by the throat; whence arose a fray between them which caused such a tumultuous concourse of people as rendred ye money unsafe which was then coming down the street of the Mint in Trays...'. At night, the paved road to the Mint workers' homes was only dimly lit by oil lamps, and it was policed by solitary sentries who—according to Mint employees—stole from the properties they were meant to be guarding. The soldiers told a different version of events, claiming that they had no option but to shoot inhabitants who insulted them.[5]

Many military and naval personnel lived on-site with their wives and children, those subordinated family members who had no choice over their accommodation but experienced many of the same discomforts as Newton. Like him, one of those residents without a voice, a young woman called Elizabeth Tollet, found the constant presence of the army especially disturbing. She commented enviously to her brother, a student at Cambridge, on his good fortune in escaping from the sound of troops marching through the courtyards: 'No noisy Guards disturb your blest Retreat.'[6] In contrast with her, Newton was a single man with a handsome salary, and he could afford to move out, heading westwards across London in the opposite direction to the prevailing winds laden with the stench of the docks and the brown smog of open fires.

Elizabeth Tollet's father, Newton's friend George Tollet, was less fortunate. A widower with nine children, only three of whom survived to become adults, he needed to take advantage of any housing he was offered. After holding various administrative posts, he became an Extra Commissioner of the Navy in 1702, when he moved with his family to the Tower. As a mathematician who was later elected a fellow of the Royal Society, Tollet associated with many eminent London men, including not only Newton but also Samuel Pepys, Edmond Halley, John Evelyn, and the prominent politician Robert Harley, Earl of Oxford. Indeed, he was so well respected that in 1706 he was a pall-bearer at John Evelyn's funeral, and two years later was granted a coat of arms. Despite that eminence, few references survive to George Tollet, who is absent from the standard Newton biographies. Unusually, the main evidence of their friendship stems from the poetic renown of a female dependant, his daughter.[7]

Elizabeth Tollet—an intelligent but small and physically disabled woman—was exceptionally well educated, and she grew up to become a fluent Latin translator who also wrote and published her own poetry. Virtually forgotten until the end of the twentieth century, her emotive verse is now becoming better known because she often focused on female oppression. According to the journal editor John Nichols, Newton 'honoured both [Tollet] and his daughter with his friendship, and was much pleased with some of her first essays [poems]'.[8] Nichols gave no indication of where he obtained that information, but he is acclaimed for bequeathing to posterity anecdotes that once circulated as gossipy general knowledge.

Newton's unexpected praise of Elizabeth Tollet's accomplishments suggests that he had acquired the diplomacy essential for survival in London society. It seems unlikely that he would genuinely appreciate her writing: there were no poetry books in his library, he appears to have had no interest in art apart from commissioning portraits and busts of himself—and although he did once go to an opera, he walked out after the second act. A pedantic stickler for accuracy, Newton wished that words would signify what they claimed to represent and no more. This insistence on plain language was most famously expressed by John Locke in his *Essay concerning Human Understanding* (1690), the book that dominated eighteenth-century philosophy and education. Ambiguous words, Locke objected, inevitably led to uncertainty, and so had no place in natural philosophy. Newton castigated ancient poets for making the work of historians more complicated by not sticking to the straight facts; similarly, determined at the Tower to clean up the nation's currency, he scrutinized witnesses' testimony to eliminate any half-truths that might be conveniently concealing evidence of forgery.[9]

Tollet contributed to Newton's fame because, after his death, some of her poems helped to publicize his ideas. Although Newton liked to promote himself in elite circles, he regarded himself as being one of God's chosen few, and generally disdained the mundane task of communicating his ideas to ordinary people. Because Tollet and other women had no opportunity to study at university, they were hardly in a position to make great discoveries. In contrast, they could and did play significant roles in science communication and education.

Scientific poetry might now seem rather a contradiction in terms, but during the eighteenth century it provided an extremely popular medium for disseminating simplified versions of the latest experiments and theories. When Newton first went to London, his name was little known outside scholarly circles, and natural philosophers were far from being England's great cultural heroes. That accolade was reserved for the nation's literary men—John Milton, John Dryden, Alexander Pope. Rather than being a specialized art form or minority interest, poetry was a favourite genre, whose readers welcomed the metaphorical, allusive power of language. Scientific poems could run to several hundred lines, and often doubled up as theological texts, exhorting readers to admire the beauty of the world designed by a munificent God. These didactic verses were particularly targeted at women and other people unable to attend university—a large category that included not only the poor but also Jews, Catholics, and Dissenters.

Typically, virtually nothing is known about Tollet's mother, but she did benefit from an enlightened father, who enabled her not only to excel at the conventional female skills of music and drawing but also to study topics usually reserved for boys. Before she was born, he had lived for a while in Dublin, where he astounded the local Philosophical Society by showing off the skills of a 10-year-old girl he had been teaching. 'Mr Tollet's Schollar' impressed her audience by her knowledge of mathematics, astronomy, and geography, even surviving an interrogation on Euclid. Nearly twenty years later, perhaps Tollet made his own daughter perform similar mathematical feats for the entertainment of visitors. If so, then his friend Isaac Newton would be an obvious guest to invite.

Apart from a recently discovered portrait, Tollet left little material trace of her existence beyond her books of poems, but through them she bequeathed impressions of living in the Tower, Newton's place of work for three decades. In one stanza, she portrayed herself strolling 'round the Walls and antique Turrets' to admire a scene that Newton must also have contemplated—in one direction the churches and green fields of London, and in the other the sailing ships that travelled up and down the neighbouring Thames, plying the international trade that made the metropolis one of the richest cities in the world (Figure 2.1). Like her contemporaries, Tollet

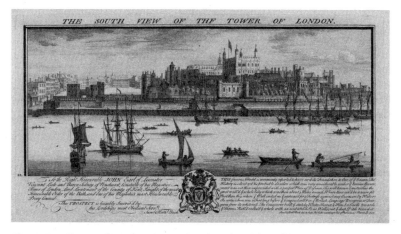

Figure 2.1 *Tower of London*; Samuel and Nathaniel Buck, 1737

celebrated London as the reincarnation of Augustan Rome, the centre of a glorious global empire importing luxury goods:

> See! here Augusta's massive Temples rise,
> There Meads extend, and Hills support the Skies;
> See! there the Ships, an anchor'd Forest ride,
> And either India's Wealth enrich the Tide.[10]

Newton and Tollet were both familiar with the hardships of solitary study, and she fretted at the long lonely days with only her books for companions. Her sense of isolation was intensified by knowing that her two younger brothers were drinking and gambling their way through Oxford and Cambridge, an opportunity that was denied to her. Instead, she devised empathetic translations of Latin aphorisms scratched by Jane Grey into the wall of her cell in the Tower, and composed imaginary verses by another former prisoner, Anne Boleyn:

> Think how I pass the melancholy Hours,
> Alone, immur'd in these relentless Tow'rs,
> My languid Head upon my Hand declin'd,
> Supported only by the conscious Mind.[11]

As well as enduring the Tower's physical confinement, Tollet also felt psychologically compressed within the walls of a female existence. How cruel it was, she protested, that the laws of nature had condemned women to servitude. Only too aware of Francis Bacon's maxim that knowledge means power, Tollet accused men of terrorizing women by denying them access to education:

> That haughty Man, unrival'd and alone,
> May boast the World of Science all his own:
> As barb'rous Tyrants, to secure their Sway,
> Conclude that Ignorance will best obey.[12]

There were many other mathematical daughters scattered around the country. In 1709, the male editor of the annual *Ladies' Diary* announced that, by popular request, recipes would be replaced by 'enigmas, and arithmetical questions, [which] give the greatest satisfaction and delight to the obliging fair'.[13] Every year, answers flooded in from women who could never get a degree but preferred the challenge of mathematics to conventional activities such as flower-arranging or embroidery. Tollet's scientific poetry demonstrates that she had learnt the basic principles of Newtonian physics, either from her family or by private study. Whereas many (male) Newtonian poets made vague references to 'circling spheres' and 'whirling orbs', she provided a more informed summary of the gravitational laws governing planetary motion:

> What Force their destin'd Line obliquely bends,
> And what in vacuous Space their Weight suspends.[14]

As soon as she heard of Newton's death, Tollet composed an eloquent elegy in which she imagined the tomb that would be built for him in the future:

> Soon shall the marble Monument arise,
> And *Newton's* honour'd Name attract our Eyes:
> The finish'd Bust, in curious Sculpture wrought;
> Shall seem to breath, alone absorpt in Thought.[15]

Tollet knew that no such grand memorial awaited her: she was buried in Westham (now West Ham), which is in every sense a long way from Westminster. Unlike Newton, she was trapped within the Tower, dependent on her father's whims or money-earning capacity in order to escape. Even the vagaries of the weather affected her more than they did Newton. During her second year in residence, in November 1703, a devastating hurricane roared over the country and ruined many of the Tower buildings. This was no ordinary storm: a bishop and his wife died in their bed, fifteen warships sank, and Queen Anne pronounced it to be God's punishment for 'the crying Sins of this Nation'.[16] Newton grumbled from a distance about the difficulty of finding money for repairs at the Mint, but only four days later, while the streets were still piled high with rubbish, he was elected President of the Royal

Society. In the meantime, as her father's live-in housekeeper, Tollet would have been responsible for making sure the damage to their home was cleaned up. Similarly, when the coldest winter for 500 years froze the Tower's old elm pipes and water had to be carried in by buckets, Newton was comfortably ensconced in Chelsea with his servants.[17]

Political Promotion

This young female poet shared some of Newton's experiences at the Mint, but scarcely impinged on his awareness. In contrast, another woman was a major presence in his life for many years: Queen Anne, who ascended to the throne in 1702, the same year that the Tollet family moved to the Tower. As a royal princess, she was of course far more privileged than Tollet, yet she was still subordinated to the men in her family. Her uncle—Charles II—had insisted that Anne and her sister Mary be brought up in the Church of England, although their father—Charles's brother, James II—converted to Catholicism. But when it came to choosing a husband for Anne, Charles and James were in accord, handing over their sister to George, the brother of the Danish king.

In 1688, Anne had found herself torn between obedience to her father, James II, and loyalty to her husband, George, who supported William of Orange in his bid to seize the throne. Opting to follow her husband, she slipped down the back stairs of her London residence and climbed into a waiting carriage that swept her away to join the Revolutionary forces in the north of England. That sounds rather cloak-and-dagger, but—like many of her eminent contemporaries—Anne operated by enveloping herself in a miasma of secrecy. All over Europe, rulers relied on intrigue and espionage to overturn plots against them as well as to achieve their own aims. For example, in order to woo a potential prestigious bride whom he had never met, a Hanoverian prince disguised himself as a nobleman, leaving his palace at midnight and travelling incognito through the darkness. Although gossip soon began circulating, the mutually beneficial marriage contract was signed before any objectors could prevent it—and this secret suitor subsequently became George II of Great Britain.[18]

When it came to spying, women at court were perfectly placed, especially those who enjoyed some degree of independence because they were either unmarried or widowed. Go-betweens carried lovers' clandestine letters inside their hats or gloves, or stitched them into curtain linings to prevent discovery. Ironically, women's supposed lack of intelligence put them beyond suspicion, enabling them to move freely between different social and political circles, quietly absorbing essential information before passing it on. When captured, they were assumed to be lying and generally escaped the interrogation under torture inflicted on male spies. Referred to as 'she-intelligencers', they are, of course, extremely hard to identify: a successful spy is one who leaves no trace.[19]

Anne adopted the motto *semper eadem* (always the same) of Queen Elizabeth, who had died a hundred years earlier. No other woman had reigned on her own since then, and Anne knew that she would have to keep control of her ministers and demonstrate that she was capable of tough decisions, especially military ones. One of her greatest coups was to secure a monopoly for England to trade enslaved people in the Americas, and a female poet congratulated Anne for proving that women could be strong rulers:

> Too long her Sex under Reproach has lain,
> And felt a general (oft a just) Disdain:
> But she redeems their Fame; in her we find
> What Excellence there is in Womankind:
> And to her Sex this lasting Honour brings,
> That they are capable of highest things.[20]

Acutely aware that royal patronage mattered, Newton gained sufficient influence to secure a place for his Oxford friend David Gregory as mathematics tutor to the queen's small son, the Duke of Gloucester.[21] Born in 1689, the boy had been named William after the recently crowned king and immediately hailed as a Protestant champion. His favourite occupation was disciplining his miniature army of ninety children, but he died when he was only 11 years old, and the question of the succession hovered over the country throughout Anne's reign. Neither Charles nor William had any surviving children, so there was constant pressure on her to produce another heir.

A Victorian biographer described Anne as 'ugly, corpulent, gouty, sluggish, a glutton and a tippler'. If he had suffered through seventeen pregnancies (plus some phantom ones) and the seventeen young deaths that followed, he might well have gone that way himself. Despite being perpetually ill and/or pregnant, she was an intelligent and knowledgeable patron of the arts, which all flourished during her time in power. In contrast with the rather ascetic approach of her cousin William, Anne was influenced by the more baroque tastes of her father, James II—although definitely without the Catholicism. She sponsored the architect John Vanbrugh to build Blenheim Palace, rewarded George Handel with a royal pension, and commissioned portraits from Kneller and other society artists (in which she naturally does not appear ugly, corpulent, or gouty). It was during her reign that literary stars such as Alexander Pope, Jonathan Swift, and Daniel Defoe appeared on the scene, and she also gave unprecedented encouragement to female playwrights and poets.[22]

Newton was eager to gain Anne's support at the Mint, and throughout her reign he manoeuvred to promote her interests while maintaining the approval of influential politicians and patrons, notably Charles Montagu. Reams of surviving manuscripts covered with spidery columns of numbers show that he deployed the same mathematical skills and obsessive attention to detail when administering royal finances as when calculating cometary orbits. As just one example, mixed in with a host of theological papers is a document analysing Queen Anne's contract with Cornish miners, in which Newton painstakingly lays out all the figures needed to prove that she was paying far above market value for their tin.[23]

In another tactic for ingratiating himself with Anne, Newton made the Tower of London a production centre for royal propaganda by spotting the potential publicity value of commemorative medals. Whereas Newton routinely left the design of images on ordinary coins to the Mint staff, he ensured that these special pieces were under his control. Designed and produced at the Mint, they won him a double goal: gaining favour at court, and spreading covert political messages. Collaborating with engravers, ministers, and other experts, he sought to strengthen Anne's position while also reinforcing the policies of the dominant Whig party, which supported rule by Parliament. Newton effectively became a ministerial agent operating from within his Tower citadel, combining his participation in party politics with his scholarly knowledge of ancient history and mythology.[24]

Most monarchs were experts at self-promotion, but Anne showed an unusual interest in medals. During the twelve years of her rule, Newton oversaw the production of twenty-nine, a far higher number than for her successor, George I. They were expensive luxury items, bought to be displayed in glass-fronted cabinets, or worn around the owner's neck as a visible badge of allegiance, or as diplomatic gifts for foreign visitors. Newton personally controlled every stage of their manufacture, recommending that 'no medals be made in ye mint without order from her Matie to ye Master & Worker of ye mint.'[25] As an additional safeguard, before going into production any design had to be approved right at the very top—by the Lord High Chancellor, Robert Harley, member of the same social circle as George Tollet.

Unravelling Newton's involvement is complicated because he reserved no special notebook for sketching designs. Instead, while he was working on something apparently unrelated—revising his *Principia*, or recalculating the timetables of Persian history—he sketched possibilities in the margins. When planning a promotional medal, Newton realized that its message needed to be clear, just like any advertising slogan. The images were intended to be deciphered, their allusions disentangled as if they were complex texts, and so they relied on mythological figures and symbols that would then have been familiar but have now been largely forgotten. The chief expert was John Evelyn, who is now more famous for his deliciously gossipy diaries than for his distinguished tome on numismatics, but Newton's own copy of this learned work survives at Cambridge, and its dog-eared pages reveal how he scoured it for hints. He learnt from Evelyn that medals were 'Vocal Monuments': like Elizabeth Tollet's scientific poetry, they had to be read and interpreted. For promoting Anne, Newton adopted the language of mythology, now the domain of classical experts but then as much a part of everyday vocabulary as Santa Claus or Robin Hood today.

Newton's first opportunity came with Anne's coronation in 1702. Since her father was a Catholic, Newton and his colleagues were keen to downplay any inherited right to the throne. Instead, they emphasized that she had become queen by statute, not by common law: according to the Whig point of view, it was Parliament that had decided Anne should follow William and Mary, and Parliament that decreed the crown would go to the Hanoverian branch of the family in the absence of a living heir. Newton wanted to portray Anne as William's constitutional successor, not as a Stuart descendant, and to stress her aggressive foreign policy.

Thanks to his extensive historical research, Newton possessed huge reservoirs of mythological knowledge: years of meticulous scholarship now yielded practical political dividends. On Anne's coronation medal (Figure 2.2), he portrayed Anne as Pallas Athene, Greek goddess of wisdom and war, and the favourite daughter of Zeus (Roman Jupiter or Jove), ruler of the gods and traditionally shown carrying the thunderbolt of a warrior. In William's coronation medal, Jupiter had symbolized the king, but now Newton gave the thunderbolt to Pallas—that is, to Anne, William's successor— who towers above a four-armed giant on the ground. In a note probably intended for Anne's approval, and scattered with biblical

Figure 2.2 *Queen Anne's coronation medal*; Isaac Newton and John Croker, 1702

references, Newton spelt out the symbolism, 'She succeeds y^e Thunderer...& y^e Thunderer is here the late King William who in his coronation medal was represented by Iupiter with a thunderbolt in his hand.... The Giant with many heads and hands signifies not a single person but a body politic & may represent any kingdom principality nation people or body of men wth whom her Maj^{ty} hath or may have war.'[26] Engraved by the Mint's top craftsman, John Croker, Newton's medal proclaimed that, despite being a female invalid, Anne was leading England to victory.

Newton's endeavours paid off. From his personal perspective, Anne's backing later came in particularly useful during his protracted, bitter dispute with the Astronomer Royal, John Flamsteed. Moreover, he had negotiated himself into a protected place for supporting the Whigs against the Tories and for preventing the return of the Catholic Stuarts. As he had probably intended, his coronation medal proved valuable for Whig propagandists. With elections being held every three years, they needed campaign material for defeating the Tories, their opponents in the two-party system. Whig pamphlets and poems picked up on Newton's coded imagery by emphasizing that Anne was continuing to enforce William's revolutionary principles. For example, this is the opening couplet of a long but anonymous verse reference:

> If Mighty *Jove*'s Auspicious Reign be o'er,
> To thunder is alone in *Anna*'s Pow'r...[27]

Soon after Anne's coronation, it seemed that her troops were faring badly abroad, but, by taking advantage of a potential disaster, Newton contrived a fresh opportunity to demonstrate his loyalty. Spain also confronted the problem of a childless monarch, and after the king's death the War of Spanish Succession erupted all over Europe in an attempt to prevent the Austrians or the French from building up a massive power bloc. England had been faring badly, but just as all seemed lost, news arrived that a Spanish fleet was due to arrive in Vigo Bay (north-west Spain), loaded down with gold and silver from South America. In a stunning victory, the English stripped the galleons of their precious cargo and shipped it back to

London, where Newton personally superintended its landing. The inside story, which he knew perfectly well, was that the Spanish had secretly unloaded most of their bullion in advance, so that only a paltry £14,000 worth of silver came to London—but Newton kept diplomatically quiet about that. Instead, the Mint contributed to the government's celebrations of this naval triumph by issuing commemorative gold coins, including a massive five-guinea piece showing Anne's bust with VIGO inscribed directly beneath it.[28]

Eager to symbolize Britain's increasing global domination, in 1711 Anne donated the marble for a large baroque sculpture to be placed right in front of the new St Paul's Cathedral. This early tribute to British imperialism is still there (albeit as a nineteenth-century replica), showing the queen with her gilded orb and sceptre standing on a pedestal surrounded by four stone women. Of these, three traditional sculptures draped in classical robes represent Britain, Ireland, and France (Anne was initially crowned as queen of England, Scotland, and Ireland, but after the Act of Union between England and Scotland in 1707, she ruled over Great Britain and Ireland; France was included because, on paper, the country still counted as part of the monarch's inheritance and featured on the guineas Newton produced at the Mint).

By contrast, the fourth statue depicting America confirms how little British people knew about people overseas. Modelled on Brazilians captured by Portuguese invaders in the sixteenth century, she rests her foot on the severed head of a European. Half-naked, she wears a generic feather skirt and headdress to indicate 'Indian', an ambiguous word that could refer to the Mexicans in Dryden's play, to the inhabitants of India, or (as here) to the non-Europeans living in North America. In 1710, four Iroquois ambassadors had visited London to solicit support for invading Canada. Erroneously described as 'kings', they were formally presented to Queen Anne in English-designed costumes, wearing turbans and slippers more appropriate for Muslim Turks. Despite their courteous behaviour, these unfamiliar Indians were also portrayed as untamed savages:

> Chiefs who full Bowls of hostile Blood had quaff'd,
> Fam'd for the Javelin, and invenom'd Shaft.[29]

The diplomats from America prudently kept their thoughts to themselves, but a clever satirist was probably spot on when he imagined their contemptuous description of their hosts in a letter back home: 'Instead of those beautiful feathers with which we adorn our heads, they often buy up a monstrous bush of hair, which covers their heads, and falls down in a large fleece below the middle of their backs.'[30] Warmly welcomed, and accompanied back across the Atlantic by an armed fleet, the Iroquois believed their mission had been successful. They were wrong. In a private letter, Anne made it clear that her ulterior motive was to expel French settlers so that 'the several Indian Nations will be under Our Subjection and Our Subjects will enjoy the whole Trade of Furr and Peltry, which they purchase with the Woollen Manufacture of this Kingdom, and with Guns, Powder, Shott, Knives, Scissars, Beads & Toys.'[31]

There is probably no way of ever being sure that Newton heard about this visit, but it was well publicized and he was fully aware of British policy overseas—indeed, so much so that, in 1713, he actively supported Robert Harley's Whig campaign to exit the War of Spanish Succession under terms giving Britain a greater share of the lucrative slave trade. Although the state normally funded only coronation medals, for this special occasion Newton designed a medal portraying Anne as Britannia, olive branch in her hand, rising up from a bucolic scene of bountiful land and sea. His records show that for 562 golden pieces of this imperial publicity, the Treasury spent over £2500.[32]

The government continued to spend lavishly on regal display. When she died, Britain's last Stuart monarch was given a funeral that cost more than £10,000. But despite the ostentatious splendour, Anne was treated with less than royal courtesy. Some of the chief mourners were people she disliked, and the ceremonial crown she wore to the grave was made of tin covered with gold paint.[33] Her final public event was delayed for two days until the new king—George I—arrived from Hanover, but Newton soon realized that the next monarch would be paying far less attention to matters of the Mint.

3
Family Trees

Hogarth's drawing room was owned by a man—John Conduitt—who owned a wife—Catherine Barton—to care for him, his houses, and his child. Here she has a virtual presence, suspended below her husband, who had inherited Newton's position as Master of the Mint. Looking out from her oval frame towards the viewer, her gaze is directed away from the stage and away from Newton. Perhaps by then she had tired of being an adjunct to her ambitious husband and her demanding uncle. Hogarth has colour-coordinated her with the room's furnishings—the pale blue window curtains to her right, the draped swags on the far side of the mantelpiece—as if she were merely a decorative item in Conduitt's inventory of treasured possessions. Perhaps the original picture is hanging in the dim corridor of a remote country house, unidentified and forgotten. Or perhaps it never existed—Hogarth may have conjured this portrait out of his imagination, placing it on the wall as a symbolic reminder that women as well as men were important in Newton's life.

*   *   *

It was a truth universally acknowledged, that a single man in possession of a good fortune, must be in want of…somebody to look after both him and his house (as Jane Austen did not put it). This was a common male problem, but the solution was not necessarily an Austen-style marriage. Since women were legally the possession of their menfolk, those who remained unmarried became a collective family responsibility, an obligation often fulfilled by installing them as unpaid housekeepers for the bachelors and widowers among the relatives. Sisters, daughters, and nieces could easily become consigned to perpetual servitude, effectively forced into unwelcome spinsterhood.[1] Elizabeth Tollet was only 8 years old when her mother died and her father brought her to the Tower with her two younger brothers. She probably realized from childhood that she had no choice but to assume the wifely roles of house-keeper, childcarer, and hostess without ever acquiring her own husband. Lonely women all over the country could empathize with her protest:

> What cruel laws depress the female Kind,
> To humble Cares and servile tasks confin'd?[2]

The young woman that Newton recruited to organize his life was very different from Tollet. Soon after he moved out of the Tower and into Jermyn Street, he was joined by Catherine Barton, the daughter of his younger half-sister, Hannah. The exact date is uncertain, but Barton was probably around 17 years old when she arrived in the metropolis and—in contrast with Tollet—was all set to enjoy herself. Whereas Tollet endured long periods of secluded isolation, drifting around the Tower with only her Latin books for company, Barton became a gossip-column party-goer, publicly referred to as 'the famous, witty Miss Barton' in the *Gentleman's Magazine*.[3] She was definitely no home-loving innocent from Lincolnshire who had decided to sacrifice her youth by caring for elderly Uncle Isaac.

Although Barton's exact status in the Newton household is not clear, she apparently managed to maintain her independence while also ensuring that Newton would continue to value her presence and support her financially. Surviving references suggest that although she remained close to Newton throughout his life, she also engineered a separate existence, even before she married in 1717. In particular, she regularly entertained intimate friends such as Jonathan Swift, who was a close confidant long before he wrote *Gulliver's Travels*.[4] When Newton died around thirty years later, she and her husband were by his bedside in Kensington, although she had not been a permanent resident for all of that time. Perhaps she was responsible for persuading Newton to smarten up his homes by buying new furniture, decorations, and tableware? In the St Martin's Street house they shared, her private apartment ran to at least a couple of rooms, and the list of their contents is twice as long as those in Newton's bedroom—but they were worth only half as much. Among other pieces, there were four tables, six chairs and a settee, several sets of curtains, a silk and feather bed, tapestries, mirrors, chests, and a commode.[5]

Barton is usually referred to as Newton's niece, but during the seventeenth and eighteenth centuries that word conveniently covered a range of associations between men and younger women, and could be used even when they were not tied together by blood. Complementing that ambiguity, more intimate so-called avunculate relationships were openly acknowledged, even though they were not positively endorsed. Whatever Barton's position in her uncle's household, other attractive nieces became sexually involved with their protectors. One particularly relevant example is Grace Hooke, niece of Newton's arch-enemy Robert Hooke. She first arrived from her home on the Isle of Wight at the age of 12, when her father—Hooke's brother—began paying for her to go to school in London. Newton had much in common with his slightly older rival at the Royal Society: both obsessive workers who seized every opportunity for an argument with each other, they both became extremely rich (although, unlike Newton, Hooke lived like a pauper and hid his fortune in a chest under his bed, where it was discovered after his death). In addition, they were both cared for by charming live-in nieces who had their own similarities: they each enjoyed at least one aristocratic affair, and they each survived a severe case of smallpox.

There is, however, a major contrast between these two examples: unlike Hooke, it is improbable that Newton engaged in full sexual activity with his niece. Hooke kept an extraordinary diary, in which he recorded every orgasm with the symbol of Pisces, and it reveals that the first time Grace and Robert Hooke slept together, she was 16 and he was 40. He had apparently been besotted with her even before that, and they lived together more or less continuously until she died. Grace Hooke did, however, spend a mysterious ten-month interlude on the Isle of Wight, when it seems extremely likely that she had a baby. It might have been her uncle's: his sexual diary shows that the dates would match. On the other hand, it might have

been fathered by another older man with whom she spent time—
Sir Robert Holmes, the island's 55-year-old governor with an illustrious reputation as the swashbuckling naval officer who had ousted
the Dutch to secure King Charles's privileges in the lucrative West
African slave trade. He certainly believed that a small girl born during that period was his illegitimate daughter and rightful heir, Mary.[6]

Shocking now, but far less so in the late seventeenth century,
when large age differences between husbands, wives, and other
sexual partners were quite common. At the time, incest was not a
criminal offence, and it remained legal (although banned by Church
law) right through until the early twentieth century. Even then,
nieces were not specified in the list of taboos and a long line of distinguished incestuous uncles includes sundry aristocrats as well as
Voltaire.[7] Of course, these examples yield no information about
Newton's friendship with his niece. On the other hand, they do
indicate how differently close family relationships were viewed in
the past.

After Newton's niece moved in to his London home, did his
contemporaries assume that he was sleeping with her? Possibly, but
if so, all traces of any insinuations have vanished. In any case,
substantial evidence suggests his emotional preference for men.
When homosexuality was illegal or still widely frowned upon,
many biographers were reticent about exploring this topic. 'Was
Newton gay?' is the wrong question to ask, because—like nieces
and uncles—male and female friendships of all types were conducted differently from now, and the category 'homosexual' had
not yet been created. Sodomy was technically an ecclesiastical
offence carrying the death penalty, but during the seventeenth century same-sex couples could and did enjoy pleasurable relationships
together, sometimes feeling themselves intimately bound by their
mutual seraphic love, a divine friendship in which souls soared
pure and high above bodily concerns.[8]

Despite—or perhaps because—he professed sexual abstinence,
Newton wrote a fair amount about lust. From a young age, he
repeatedly castigated himself for even the slightest deviation from
his self-imposed restraint. As an adult in London, when he wrote a
female servant's reference, he scrupulously crossed out the words

'lived with me two or three years' and substituted 'served me as a cook'.[9] Even on his deathbed, he insisted on his celibacy, an assertion that many historians have unquestioningly accepted as incontrovertible proof, apparently assuming that he was too saintly to lie. Newton reportedly told his doctor that he was still a virgin, which might seem an odd status to insist upon at that late stage. The word occurs in one of his favourite biblical texts, the Book of Revelation, where he found confirmation that he was destined for spiritual leadership provided he practised abstinence. Those who were chosen 'were they which were not defiled with women; for they are virgins,' he read; 'they are without fault before the throne of God.'[10]

Newton was plagued with thoughts of sexual sin. In his diatribes against Roman Catholicism, he railed against monks' self-denial, maintaining that their practices served only to inflame desire. 'The cell, the solitude, the habit, hunger, thirst, vigils, every ascetic practice will constantly bring to mind the reason for these things, and the more effort he puts into them, the more often and powerfully it will do so.' Newton was writing from personal experience: as a Cambridge fellow, he had led a similar life of self-discipline, closeted apart from society. Too much privation, he warned, 'at length brings men to a sort of distraction & madnesse so as to make them think they have visions of women conversing with 'em & sitting upon their knees.'[11]

Unsurprisingly, there are few concrete facts, especially after Newton moved permanently to London. At Trinity, he was a close colleague of another fellow, John Wickins, for twenty years, but it is now impossible to know exactly what their relationship was, why it ended, or even whether any aspect was deliberately concealed. Around the end of 1689, Newton became deeply involved with Nicolas Fatio de Duillier, a Swiss mathematician living in London who was over twenty years younger than him. It was in Fatio's interests to flatter Newton and secure his patronage in the competitive world of natural philosophy—and reciprocally, Fatio was trying to secure a position for Newton in London. Snippets of surviving correspondence suggest that Fatio and Locke belonged to a small circle centred on Charles Mordaunt (First Earl of Monmouth): Newton was very keen to ingratiate himself with this influential politician, a powerful Whig close to the monarch.[12]

Whatever its nature, Newton's relationship with Fatio seems to have been immensely important for him, because its demise corresponded with a period of psychological collapse followed by a renewed determination to start life afresh. Only a few months after their first introduction, Newton invited himself to visit Fatio from Cambridge. 'I intend to be in London ye next week & should be very glad to be in ye same lodgings wth you,' he wrote. 'Pray let me know by a line or two whether you can have lodgings for us both in ye same house at present or whether you would have me take some other lodgings for a time till...'[13] Till what? Oddly (and annoyingly), this is the third place in this letter where words have been cut out of the paper. The records kept by Trinity College reveal Newton's numerous absences, but not where he went while he was away. After Newton moved to the Mint, Fatio got in touch from time to time (especially when he needed some money), and later composed a poetic eulogy hymning him as a Christ-like figure destined to make great discoveries.[14] No solid information has yet been dug up confirming that Newton conducted any clandestine London romances. But there were plenty of rumours about his niece.

Scandalmongers circulated various spiced-up versions of two basic questions. Did Catherine Barton have an affair with Newton's wealthy friend and patron, the distinguished politician Charles Montagu? And had Montagu persuaded Newton to keep quiet by offering him a cushy position at the Mint? Those claims ran the gossip rounds at the time, and have preoccupied biographers ever since. For three centuries, historians have devised convoluted arguments designed to protect the reputations of one, two, or even all three protagonists. Victorians vehemently refuted both assertions. More recently, the first—the affair—but not the second—the bribe—has become generally accepted.[15] My answer is yes to both accusations, even though some crucial evidence about dates is missing.

That can only, of course, be surmise. Everybody was desperately covering up for each other, and three centuries later there are large holes in the timetable of Newton's life. Basically, it boils down to a choice. You can—as I do—accept allegations voiced at the time; or, you can be so confident of Newton's unimpeachable moral integrity that you deny them.

Catherine Barton

Newton acquired his first house in Jermyn Street in 1696, and Barton probably left her family home in Northamptonshire and moved to London fairly soon afterwards. There is no way of being absolutely sure that they had already met each other, but it does seem extremely likely. To the end of his life, Newton remained in close touch with his extended family, supporting numerous relatives and attending their weddings. He spent time with Catherine's mother Hannah (his half-sister) in Cambridge as well as in Woolsthorpe, and they presumably also saw each other several times in 1689—the year Catherine was born—while Newton was caring for their sick mother in Stamford, fairly near to the Bartons' home. When Catherine's father was dying in 1693, Hannah sent a tearful plea for comfort to her 'Dear Brother'.[16] Had she perhaps already tried to cement the bond with her increasingly wealthy half-brother by bringing the family to London during the year he lived there as MP for Cambridge University? Or perhaps he visited them during one of his mysterious absences from Cambridge—or they might have met at Woolsthorpe, where Newton returned every few years to visit other relatives and keep a close eye on his Lincolnshire property. Possible, even likely—but impossible to verify.

Unfortunately for historians, when people meet regularly they have no need to correspond with each other. Only one letter survives from Isaac Newton to Catherine Barton, sent in the summer of 1700, when she had already been away from his London house for some time, staying with friends near Oxford to recover from her smallpox infection. Ever economical with paper, Newton recycled a hand-written sheet of information about the coinage systems in different countries by writing on the back of it. He promised to send up some wine for her host, and his affectionate tone suggests close familiarity with a warm concern for her appearance, every sufferer's nightmare. 'I had your two letters & am glad ye air agrees wth you & th[ough y^e] fever is loath to leave you yet I hope it abates, & y^t y^e [re]mains of ye small pox are dropping off apace...Pray let me know by your next how your f[ace is] & if your fevour be going. Perhaps warm milk from ye Cow may [help] to abate it. I am Your very loving Unkle, Is. Newton.'[17]

That recommendation to bathe in fresh milk is less strange than it might sound. Milkmaids were rumoured to have wonderful complexions, and modern medical knowledge suggests that they were often effectively immunized against smallpox by catching a less dangerous form, cowpox. More generally, Newton quite fancied himself as a dispenser of medical advice. A few years earlier he had achieved great success with his pregnant sister-in-law (Barton's aunt by marriage), whose chest infection had cleared up after she applied the poultice he had prescribed. He even tried to cure the chronic headaches of his lifelong rival the Astronomer Royal John Flamsteed, recommending (vindictively?) that he should bind his head tightly until his skull went numb.[18]

In the same letter, Newton also offered his niece a gentle reprimand: 'My La[dy] Norris thinks you forget your promis of writing to her, & wants [a] letter from you.' This casual reference indicates that Newton had already introduced his niece into London's fashionable political circles. At the time, Elizabeth Norris's husband was representing the East India Company on a diplomatic mission to India, where he was faced with the near-impossible task of persuading Mughal officials that he could obtain special trading privileges for them. Like Newton, as a fellow of Trinity College he had resisted the attempts of James II to introduce Catholics into Cambridge, and was a keen Whig supporter, so presumably they had known each other for some considerable time. A couple of years later, Norris died of dysentery on the way home, but his wealthy widow felt sufficiently at ease with Newton to solicit his advice about marrying for a fifth time. Perhaps she was angling for an approach from him—but if so, he ignored the hint.[19]

Whether or not the cow's milk did the trick, Barton's face was preserved unblemished. As well as being beautiful, she was very intelligent, and much admired by Newton's friends, as well as her own. Her circle included the poet John Dryden, author of *The Indian Emperour*, who wrote a flowery tribute before he died in 1700. She habitually dined with celebrated socialites—Lady Betty Germain, Anne Long, Lady Frances Worsley—and for many years, she remained a close confidante of Jonathan Swift, often entertaining him alone, especially after he moved into the same street. 'I love her better than anybody here, and see her seldomer,' he wrote to Stella, who had been his elusive passion since she was 8 years old and seems to have been rather concerned about this relationship. Only half-jokingly, Swift reprimanded Stella for making catty jokes about Barton.[20]

Barton delighted in telling Swift risqué stories, such as the one about a woman reputedly destined to remain unburied until the Resurrection because, before her death, she had insisted that the parson and the pall-bearers should be virgins (not very funny, perhaps, but Swift appreciated it). While he lived in London, they remained close, worrying together one year when Whig supporters planned to burn effigies of the Pope and the devil during celebrations commemorating the birth of Elizabeth I.[21] Barton also supplied Swift with biographical titbits and political gossip that came in useful for his satires. 'Mrs Bart[on] is still in my good Graces,' he told a friend in 1709; 'the best Intelligence I get of Publick Affairs is from Ladies, for the Ministers never tell me any thing.'[22] After Swift switched political sides to support the Tories, he used Barton as his mouthpiece to transmit messages from his political leaders. For example, through Swift and Barton, the powerful Henry Bolingbroke warned Newton not to be too confident of retaining his place at the Mint, telling him that he 'thought it a sin his thoughts should be diverted by his place at the Mint & that the Queen would settle upon him a pension.'[23]

While Swift remained in London, he refrained from attacking Newton directly, but many others found his satires offensive, including Queen Anne, who effectively exiled him to Ireland. No longer in contact with Barton, no longer dining at her uncle's house, Swift felt free of any obligations. During a bitter dispute about the Irish currency, he accused Newton of falsifying evidence and tyrannically imposing English power; after a prolonged conflict, Newton backed down. This very public controversy took place while Swift was writing *Gulliver's Travels* (1726), for which he concocted the Academy of Lagado to satirize the Royal Society and ambitious scientific innovators. He must have thought back to those private dining sessions with gossip-mongering Barton, when she may well have entertained him by dressing up an anecdote that she later told her husband, who in turn used it to depict Newton as hopelessly absent-minded. According to Barton, Newton often became so engrossed in his thoughts that he would forget to eat his dinner and instead consume it for breakfast the following morning, not even realizing his error. Perhaps this insider titbit became transformed into Swift's parable of the flappers, whose function was to strike their dysfunctional masters gently and recall their constantly wandering attention.

Presumably Swift became a sensitive topic of conversation in the St Martin Street household, although there is no record of rows between Newton and Barton on the topic—but since there are so few traces of any conversations between them, that is hardly surprising. No letters between Barton and Swift survive from this period, although several years after Newton died, the two friends renewed their correspondence with great familiarity and affection.[24]

Charles Montagu

Negotiating eighteenth-century families is complicated. Like most aristocrats, Charles Montagu was referred to by several different names and titles. By 1695, when confronted with England's monetary emergency, he had already become the first Baron Halifax; nearly twenty years later, he was created Earl of Halifax with the courtesy title Viscount Sunbury (not to be confused with the Marquess of Halifax, who was not a Montagu and was born George Savile). In addition, Montagu was at various times known as President of the Royal Society, Chancellor of the Exchequer, First Lord of the Treasury, and High Steward of Cambridge University. Making it even more difficult to pin him down, the Montagu family was so large and well connected that, after the 1695 election, seven

Montagus—including Charles—were sitting as MPs. Many of the other Montagus also bore additional names, such as the Earl of Manchester, who was Charles Montagu's cousin.[25]

Soon after she arrived in London, Barton became a favourite at the Kit-Kat club, which was renowned not only for its drunken revelries but also for actively supporting Whig policies. This privileged political group included Newton's preferred artist Godfrey Kneller, whose forty-eight portraits of his friends now provide the nearest thing to a membership list. Painted over a period of twenty years, and all mounted in identical frames, they show wealthy aristocrats as well as the philosopher John Locke, the architect John Vanbrugh, and the playwright William Congreve—and also Newton's patron, Charles Montagu. Traditionally, the Kit-Kat drinking companions honoured a woman of particular distinction by toasting her health with a custom-composed verse and engraving her name on a fine glass goblet. In 1703, when it was Catherine Barton's turn, Montagu probably wrote the tribute. As Samuel Johnson remarked, his couplets were not great poetry, but by then it seems to have been a general assumption that they were lovers.

> Beauty and Wit strove each, in vain,
> To vanquish Bacchus and his Train;
> But Barton with successful Charms
> From both their Quivers drew her Arms;
> The roving God his Sway resigns,
> And awfully submits his Vines.[26]

Now wealthy and influential, Montagu had been so desperate for money when he was 27 years old that he married the rich widow of his cousin the Earl of Manchester; then in her sixties, she died in 1698. Whether or not he had met Barton before that, he later openly pulled strings for her, such as recommending her brother to the Duke of Marlborough for a captain's commission, even though he was said to be an incompetent soldier. By 1706, they clearly knew each other extremely well, because just before leaving for several months in Europe, he revised his will by adding an intriguing codicil. Whereas he had originally bequeathed £1000 to each of his brothers, Montagu now stipulated that £3000 and all his jewels should go to Barton. Six years later, he increased that to £5000 plus two country estates and an annuity. This was, he emphasized unconvincingly, solely in recognition of 'the great Esteem he had for her Wit and most exquisite Understanding'. Claiming that she was merely his housekeeper, he defended her against critics who 'pass'd a judgement upon her which she no Ways merited, since she was a Woman of strict Honour and Virtue'.[27] Did he seriously expect anybody to believe him? Far from being dismissive of this future windfall for his niece, Newton positively connived at it, since Montagu's will stipulated that he would be involved in the administration.

When Montagu died unexpectedly in 1715 from a lung infection, Barton sent a plaintive note to Newton wondering what she should do. 'I desire to know whether you would have me wait here...or come home,' she asked, presumably writing from Montagu's house to her uncle in St Martin's Street. Aware that women were legally the possession of their nearest male relative, she signed her letter 'Your Obedient Neece and Humble serv^t, C. Barton'.[28] Newton—then aged 72—promptly cancelled all his social engagements. 'The concern I am in for the loss of my Lord Halifax [Montagu] & the circumstances in wch I stand related to his family,' he wrote to a relative, 'will not suffer me to go abroad till his funeral is over'.[29] Newton owned a golden mourning ring that is now at the British Museum, and for the rest of his life he kept a portrait of Montagu in his room.

As Newton may well have realized, the allegations did not stop at a mere affair. With its oblique reference to the Mint, the last line of this anonymous Kit-Kat verse hints at a patronage relationship between Barton, Montagu, and Newton:

> Stampt with her Reigning Charms, the Standard Glass,
> Shall current thro' the Realms of *Bacchus* pass;
> Full fraught with Beauty shall new Flames impart,
> And Mint her shining Image on the Heart.[30]

Further insinuations were levelled by the notorious playwright Delarivier Manley. In *Memoirs of Europe*, one of her scurrilous satires about London life, she lent the couple only wafer-thin disguises. For enlivening the humour of this extraordinary tale, purportedly set in the eighth century, she assumed that her readers would immediately identify Barton with the 'charming *Bartica*', and Montagu with Julius Sergius, the maudlin drunkard at a gambling party who had recently been deserted.[31] More scandalously, Manley made an additional accusation—that Montagu had bought Newton's silence about their illicit affair. In her fictionalized account, Sergius (aka Montagu) sobbed that la Bartica was 'a Traitress, an inconsistent proud Baggage, yet I love her dearly, and have lavish'd Myriads upon her, besides getting her worthy ancient Parent a good Post for Connivance'.[32]

For admirers of Barton's 'worthy ancient Parent', it is unthinkable that Newton should have engaged in such a bargain. They stress the lack of hard evidence that Montagu met Barton before 1696, when he offered Newton his first lucrative position in London. But absence of evidence is not evidence of absence: that aphorism may be well worn, but there are indeed many empty gaps in the relevant historical records. Montagu could easily have met Barton earlier—in Cambridge, for example—or heard the rumours that a beautiful young niece was about to arrive.

On their own, such suppositions might easily be dismissed, but their likelihood is strengthened by knowing that Voltaire—who met Barton—made a similar claim. His testimony is particularly convincing because he was a great fan of Newton, admiring him to the point of obsession. His accusation did not appear in print until long after Barton, Montagu, and Newton had all died, but presumably it reiterated suspicions that had been prevalent at the time. 'I thought in my youth that Newton made his fortune by his merit,' Voltaire reported. 'I supposed that the Court and the City of London named him Master of the Mint by acclamation. No such thing. Newton had a very charming niece, Madame Conduitt, who made a conquest of the minister Halifax. Fluxions and gravitation would have been of no use without a pretty niece.'[33]

Despite the gossip, Newton remained close to Barton, setting her up with a substantial dowry, and endowing her daughter Kitty with a Kensington estate worth £4000. He was also well disposed towards other members of their extended family, staying in close contact until the end of his life. After Barton's brother (the incompetent soldier) was killed in a shipwreck near Quebec, she fulfilled only the minimum of mourning obligations, whereas Newton ensured that his widow and children were adequately cared for. At one stage, Barton's cousin, Benjamin Smith, arrived to live with them in London, although that was not a successful experiment—Smith's behaviour was so appalling that Newton threw him out. Frustratingly, his letters were destroyed by a well-meaning clergyman who was scandalized by their language, but they might have revealed a fascinatingly non-sanitized aspect of Newton's character.

Newton's origins lay in Lincolnshire, and he never relinquished his connections with Woolsthorpe, the hamlet where he grew up. He owned property there until the end of his life, and he donated money to restore the nearby church. Judging from his spelling of some key words, Newton retained his childhood accent at a time when English was spoken and spelt far less uniformly than nowadays. His speech may well have resembled that of Alfred, Lord Tennyson, also brought up in a small Lincolnshire village, whose voice can be heard on a crackly recording made in 1890.[34] As Newton became rich and famous, relatives and friends constantly tapped him for funds. He often responded generously—making regular payments for the children of his half-sisters, donating wedding gifts of money and wine, and setting up a pension for the widow of Barton's brother and a loan for his uncle's grandson.[35]

Letters also flooded in from people claiming any sort of vague connection, including one from an unrelated Newton detained in Marshalsea prison. Scores of these appeals survive because Newton economically re-used the paper they were written on for drafting his own documents, but in this period, long before any state welfare system, there must have been many more that have vanished. Even the village rector tried to cash in, informing Conduitt after Newton's death that he 'used to talk pretty much ab't founding & endowing a school in Woolsthorpe for ye use of ye Parish'.[36] However liberal Newton might himself have been, Conduitt had different priorities. He committed over £700 on Newton's spectacular monument in Westminster Abbey, but pledged only £20 to alleviate the plight of the Woolsthorpe poor.

Rewriting the Past

In 1696, Newton had abandoned Cambridge, disillusioned by his failure to secure a better position in the university. Although no 'Dear Diary' entry records his feelings, one might imagine his gloating exultation when nine years later, on 16 April 1705, he returned briefly to participate in a grand ceremony celebrated throughout the city. Now a wealthy metropolitan administrator, he knelt before Queen Anne, who tapped him on both shoulders with a sword and dubbed him a knight. When Flamsteed congratulated him a few days later, he wrote to a friend that Newton 'was more than usually gay and cheerful.'[37] Luckily for Newton's self-esteem, he died before Swift lampooned him as an 'Instrument Maker [who] it seems, was knighted for making Sun-Dyals better than others of his Trade.'[38]

There were, of course, several tedious speeches during the ceremony, but Cambridge University did put on a splendid reception. 'The Ways were all along strowed with Flowers,' wrote one reporter; 'the Bells rung, and the Conduits run with Wine'. Welcoming scholars lined the main road up to Trinity College, which hosted a magnificent dinner for 200 distinguished guests. Perched above them on a makeshift throne five feet high, Anne knighted Newton and two other friends of Charles Montagu, whom she honoured by admitting him as a Doctor in Law. The tables were scattered with poems, reportedly written by students, which sycophantically elevated her above Henry VIII and Edward III, the founders of Trinity.[39]

This was a political event through and through. Newton had earned his accolade not because he was a famous mathematician, but as a reward for loyalty: he had let Montagu persuade him to stand as a Whig candidate in the forthcoming parliamentary election. He had been an MP before settling in London, but this time Newton made the time-consuming journey up to Cambridge three times—six days of travelling in a single month. Determined to gratify Montagu, he campaigned hard, liberally donating money to the right pockets, but he complained constantly of being squeezed out. He was right: after humiliating public protests against 'Occasional Conformers' who signed up to orthodox Anglicanism when it suited them, he came a bad last of four. That was the end of Newton's parliamentary career—but he still had his knighthood, which interested him far more. During that summer, he dedicated himself to consolidating this honour by assiduously tracing his ancestry. Relying mainly on church records, which probably explains why he included so little information about the women of the family, he diligently researched back over several generations to his sixteenth-century great-great-grandfather, drawing up a pedigree that he filed at the College of Arms in November (Figure 3.1).

Newton was already an expert on family trees. While he lived in London, he became increasingly obsessed with calculating the timetables and genealogies of ancient dynasties, a project that he had begun years earlier at Cambridge. When he died, by far the largest bundle of his manuscripts was labelled 'relating to the Chronology'—that is, to rewriting the dates of ancient history. At a quick glance, Newton's sprawling messy trees of his own family look very similar to those he compiled for the Egyptians and Hittites who had thrived many thousands of years before the Newtons

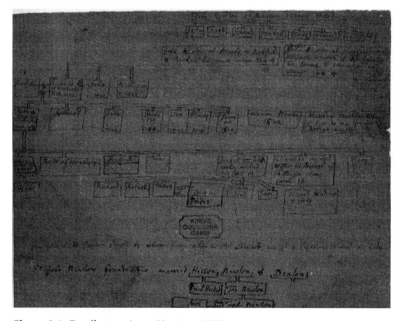

Figure 3.1 Family tree; Isaac Newton, 1705

arrived in Woolsthorpe. This expertise must have come in handy when he wanted to create a noble ancestry for himself and design a suitable coat of arms.

Newton thought creatively during this search to establish past facts. Ingeniously, he managed to suggest a link with Sir John Newton of Thorpe, who may or may not have been distantly related but was in any case willing to let a connection be established. Isaac Newton appropriated Sir John's family crest, which featured crossed shin bones (although during the nineteenth century some Cambridge sculptors inadvertently transformed them into pirate-like thigh bones). Later on, Newton changed his mind about his origins, this time deciding that his ancestors hailed from Scotland and came south with James I in the early seventeenth century.[40]

Several different versions of Newton's tree have survived, but the one that somehow ended up in the University of Texas includes dates.[41] Resembling the way he found it necessary to reconcile timetables between different civilizations, Newton was obliged to operate under one dating system in England but to use another in Europe: then, as now, the offshore island was out of step with the mainland. Towards the end of the sixteenth century, Pope Gregory had revised the older Julian calendar (named after Julius Caesar), most significantly by altering the leap years pattern. But Protestant England had refused to adopt this Catholic innovation, and by the time of Newton's birth lagged ten days behind the rest of Europe; by his death, the divergence had increased to eleven days. For English people, Newton might seem to have been specially chosen by God because he was born on Christmas Day 1642, whereas in France his birth was recorded as 4 January 1643. As an added complication, the English new year started on 25 March rather than January 1—and that explains why, in the Texas manuscript, Newton has recorded being born on 25 December 1642 yet baptized a week later on (confusingly) 1 January 1642.

Changing the calendar made astronomical sense, but, for Whig patriots such as Newton, it also implied kowtowing to pressure from Rome and aligning England with Europe at the expense of Scotland and the colonies. When several Protestant countries adopted a compromise system in 1699, they put pressure on

England to follow their example, and Newton was asked to supply some relevant figures. He complied reluctantly, even though he shared the Royal Society's lack of enthusiasm for accommodating foreign Catholics. 'The King has of his own subjects Chronologers and Mathematicians as good as any that Europe can boast off [sic],' the Fellows protested patriotically; 'If we reform let us go to ye root of ye matter and not be led by any example hitherto extant. Our King is as fit to arbitrate this business as any Monarch in Europe...' Newton promptly set about going to 'ye root of ye matter', after several attempts coming up with a mathematically elegant yet hopelessly nationalistic solution that would have put England ten days ahead of the Continent. Britain remained out of step until 1752.[42]

In the *Principia*, Newton had laid bare the fundamental laws of nature that govern the universe. Ten years later, in London, he became convinced that he could bring similar harmony to the apparently disorderly development of human civilization. In page after ink-splodged page, his tiny spidery scrawl calculates the reigns of Israeli kings, the dates of ancient Greek poets, the genealogy of Egyptian deities, the duration of the Trojan War, the invasion of Judea...each sheet must have taken hours to write out, let alone to research. Deciding that the key to ancient pagan chronologies lay in the Masoretic Bible, the authoritative Hebrew text of the Jewish Old Testament, he worked out the time needed for repopulating the world after Noah's flood—then a hotly debated topic among chronological cognoscenti. Relying heavily on numbers in the Masoretic Bible, Newton drastically revised previous timetables, redating key episodes such as the voyage of the Argonauts and the reigns of the Egyptian pharaohs.

Unfortunately for historians trying to track his thought processes, Newton adopted a very simple storage system: arrange everything in large piles. He rarely dated his documents, and a single page might include undergraduate inspirations alongside meandering musings of old age on a completely different topic. Whether genealogical tables or mathematical treatises or alchemical recipes or shopping lists, his manuscripts are no longer piled up in loose heaps: sheet by sheet, they have been systematically numbered and the originals are now carefully preserved inside air-conditioned archives scattered around the world. As an added resource, experts have already embarked on the mammoth project of transcribing all those documents—including the deletions, repetitions, and false starts—and making them available digitally. But of course, however easily this material can be accessed, making sense of it remains far more difficult. Like Newton himself, scholars can only begin to decipher his immense legacy after undertaking an arduous self-tuition course in ancient history and biblical hermeneutics.

4
The Rise and Rise of John Conduitt

John Conduitt married into the family of England's most famous scholar, inherited his position at the Mint, and ensured that he would himself be buried in Westminster Abbey close to the eminent relative he had acquired. As a record for posterity, Conduitt commissioned Hogarth to create this conversation piece, which includes—at the top left—the only known painting of Conduitt himself.

A picture may be worth a thousand words, but it does not necessarily tell the literal truth. The four children on the stage include John Conduitt's daughter, Kitty, but according to the script, she should not have been there at that point: her father had requested that she be included in the painting. On the chimney-breast, Hogarth has reproduced the marble plaque from the base of Newton's monument in Westminster Abbey, although this plaster replica may or may not have been installed in the real-life drawing room; similarly, Newton's bust above it on the mantelpiece seems to be an imagined amalgam of actual versions. Newton's double presence above the hearth—symbolic centre of the home—emphasizes that this is a dynastic portrait advertising Conduitt's prestige and noble ancestry.

The only two other surviving images of Conduitt appear on a medal that was struck at the Mint after he died (Figure 4.1). While he features on one side as a well-fed Roman emperor, on the reverse he is being ceremonially presented to two residents of the Elysian Fields—Isaac Newton and John Hampden, the Civil War hero who symbolized the rights of Parliament. Accompanying them is a voluptuous, scantily clad Goddess of Truth, but somebody has slipped up: Newton is clutching a diagram that shows the planets orbiting in circles instead of ellipses, a blunder that the former Master of the Mint would never have permitted.

*   *   *

Figure 4.1 Medal of John Conduitt; designed by Gravelot, engraved by John Sigismund Tanner, 1737

After Charles Darwin returned from his voyage on the *Beagle*, he debated with himself whether or not to get married. To clarify his thoughts, he drew up a list of pros and cons. It would, he noted, be rather nice to have a docile companion who would take care of the house and give him some children; on the other hand, his freedom would be restricted, and he would have less money available to buy books. But, he concluded, a wife was probably better value than a dog, and he decided to take the risk.

In the summer of 1717, Newton and his niece were faced with a similar quandary. Barton's lover Charles Montagu had died two years earlier, which left her in an awkward position. Born in 1679, she was already old for a first marriage, and anyone who counted in London was aware of her ambiguous reputation as a Kit-Kat toast. John Conduitt was eleven years younger than her, and although handsome he came from an undistinguished family and had left Cambridge without a degree. As two major points in his favour, he had been abroad almost continuously for the past ten years, so was less likely to be familiar with London scandal, and had probably accumulated quite a bit of money while he was serving with the army in Gibraltar. The exact details of his occupation overseas remain obscure, but, like many military men, he somehow contrived to return wealthier than when he left. Bribery and corruption were the norm for landing lucrative contracts that benefited privileged individuals but pushed up prices for ordinary consumers.[1]

The couple presumably met around the end of June 1717, when Conduitt presented a paper at the Royal Society. Newton was in the chair, learning about Conduitt's one and only claim to academic distinction: identifying Carteia, a hill-top Roman trading city on the southern tip of Spain. Fortuitously, this fitted in with Newton's investigations into ancient migrations through the Mediterranean basin.[2] Only a couple of months later, Barton and Conduitt were granted a licence to marry, although the surviving document reveals that she sliced six years off her age. Did he realize? For some reason they were in a great rush, and the wedding was held only three days later. The motive for the hurry remains mysterious: if Barton was pregnant, she presumably suffered a miscarriage, because their only recorded child, their daughter Kitty, was born two years later.

One great advantage for Conduitt was that he acquired a rich and eminent relative: Newton effectively became his father-in-law and an extremely valuable patron. After three years, he (or Newton on his behalf?) bought a large sixteenth-century estate near Winchester, and embarked on a new career as a Whig MP. When not in Hampshire, the Conduitts lived in London, and as Newton aged, they spent an increasing amount of their time caring for him. For the year or so before Newton died in 1727, Conduitt was more or less running the Mint on his behalf and seems to have been a fairly constant companion. As well as listening to Newton's reminiscences and taking over his responsibilities, Conduitt tried to protect him. For example, when a French scholar published a vitriolic attack on Newton's ideas about chronology, Conduitt commissioned a censored summary that excluded the most vitriolic remarks. To his gratification, Newton did not embark on a campaign of vindictive revenge, but tranquilly concluded that the author was ignorant.[3]

Newton realized that he was dying, and he planned for the future by dispensing gifts to relatives and struggling to condense a publishable book from his millions of words on ancient chronology. Frustratingly, as part of these preparations, he burnt some papers whose contents will remain for ever unknown. Surprisingly, what he did not do was make a will. During the following ten years, until his own death, Conduitt dedicated himself to sorting out Newton's estate as well as preserving and enhancing the fame of his relative by marriage.

Creative Writing

As Newton aged, Conduitt made himself increasingly indispensable. That blunt summary might sound cynical, but taking advantage of a family relationship does not preclude feeling genuine affection and admiration. While Conduitt pursued his own parliamentary career, he undoubtedly gained wealth and status by inheriting Newton's position at the Mint and boosting his reputation. Yet he also showed deep commitment, immersing himself in the tedious administrative responsibilities of dealing with Newton's estate as well as commissioning written, sculpted, and painted tributes to honour his memory.

Considering he prided himself on being such a methodical and logical thinker, Newton did not have a very effective filing system for his papers. When he died, he left behind him a huge assortment of disorganized manuscripts, between them carrying around eleven million words. Unsurprisingly, the members of Newton's extended clan were more interested in land and money (I wonder what did happen to those silver chamber pots...) than in the teetering stacks of scarcely decipherable documents. Conduitt struck a deal with the other relatives. Because Newton had died in office as Master of the Mint (even though Conduitt was already doing all the work), he was in principle liable for the entire cost of producing Britain's new coins until (and if) they passed a compulsory quality test. Conduitt agreed to take on this potential debt and to pay for any imperfections that were discovered. He also set aside some money to ensure that Newton's family could share in any profits from future publications. In exchange, he took charge of all Newton's manuscripts.

As a versatile material, paper was put to many different uses. By the time of Newton's death, manufacturers had successfully persuaded their customers to adopt a lifestyle based on lavish expenditure and conspicuous consumption. But he had been brought up to deem such behaviour immoral, and the prevailing attitude more closely resembled the 'Waste Not–Want Not' approach of wartime Britain. The word 'recycling' had not yet been invented, although the concept was certainly there—not because people were worried about global warming, but in the interests of optimizing God's gifts to the human race. As just one example of Newton's own minor economies, he squeezed some notes on ancient history into the spaces between the lines of a letter from Marcus Tollet (presumably some relative of the Tower Tollets) soliciting a favour for a friend.[4]

Other scholars repeatedly complained about women and servants who had purloined their latest masterpiece to slip under a pie or cut into hair-curling papers. Many learned manuscripts ended up wrapped round fish, placed over food while it cooled, or twisted into implements for loading powder into guns. It can be tempting to mock Conduitt's over-egged adulation—'his virtues proved him a Saint & his discoveries might well pass for miracles'[5]—but on the other hand, it is owing to his devotion that the bulk of Newton's papers were preserved. Without his intervention, many others would have been destroyed in addition to those that Newton himself ordered to be burnt, perhaps eventually finding their way into outhouses ('bumf' was abbreviated from 'bum fodder' during the First World War). Determined to protect Newton's papers from such a fate, Conduitt conserved everything he could find.[6]

Although paper was not exorbitantly expensive—as a rough guide, a labourer could earn enough in a day to buy seventy-five large sheets—Newton rationed his out. The standard way of sending a letter was to fold a large piece of paper in half, and then write on only one side so that it could be folded over again for the address. In preference to consuming several pages, correspondents would thriftily continue in the margins, or even write transversely across the original script (a challenge for historical transcribers). For his personal notes, Newton folded his sheets in four, but although he left one side blank for further thoughts, he rarely dated anything. His habit of re-using old documents and notebooks from years earlier makes it very difficult for historians to work out the timing of his ideas. Sometimes he scribbled his profoundest thoughts on the nearest available scrap—such as a laundry list—or superimposed fresh inspirations on hastily crossed-out texts or tables.[7]

Newton's mathematical approach to different topics that he juxtaposed on the same page can be disconcerting. A single sheet of an undated paper in the Royal Mint archives carries trigonometrical arguments on one side, while the other has apparently consecutive calculations on customs duty and on Herod's Temple. The original is peppered with illegible words and deletions, but if copied out neatly, the result would look something like this:

Question

To find the net duty upon East-India goods by 12 Ann

Answer

Let D be the duty per cent upon 100^{li} by former Acts of Parliament & say, As the value, 100^{li} + D to the net duty D so is 1 to N. And the number N being once found the Question will be thus answered. From the value by the candle subduct the allowances for prompt payment & warehouse room & the remainder multiplied by N will be the net duty desired

Proof

For let the Remainder by R & NR will be the duty per cent upon R − NR, the remainder of that duty. For as the value 100^{li} + D is to the net duty D, so is 1 to N, & so is the value R to the net duty NR the remainder R is the value upon which the net duty is to be paid & this value is to the net duty upon it in a given proportion & this proportion is that of 100^{li} + D to D or 1 to N.

The Iews who first published the measures of Herods Temple, omitted some measures on either side of the altar & the summ of the cubits & the following Iewish writers dividing the summ of the cubits omitted into two equal parts placed the altar nearer to the south side of the court then to the north side: whereas they should have divided that summ unequally so that the altar might have stood in the center of the court.[8]

As well as trying to instil some sort of order on Newton's collection, Conduitt also created more material of his own. After obtaining professional advice on Newton's unfinished works, he arranged for two books to be published posthumously, one on ancient chronology and the other on biblical prophecy. And although he never did get round to producing a final version, Conduitt also made copious notes for writing Newton's biography, soliciting information from colleagues and recording his own memories of conversations. Conduitt does hint delicately from time to time that elderly raconteurs can be tedious, but he was clearly a good listener and his surviving hand-written drafts provide the basic source of many familiar anecdotes about Newton. Some of them he heard directly, others he learnt from his wife, who seems to have retained her youthful predilection for racy stories—she gleefully told him an off-colour joke about a nun that Newton had found deeply offensive.

Conduitt exerted an enormous influence on how Newton was remembered after his death. Rather than presenting Newton as a wealthy metropolitan, he emphasized the frugality, purity, and intellectual brilliance of the man who had already been in his mid-seventies when they first met. Multiple drafts have been preserved of letters that he sent soliciting information, as well as their answers. Together, they demonstrate how Conduitt gradually refined Newton's legacy by withholding discreditable items, yet simultaneously releasing more flattering snippets of information that later became incorporated in other memoirs. Reading his various accounts feels like eavesdropping on countless conversations he must have had during the twenty years between his first encounter with Newton and his own death, only ten years after Newton's. By then, Conduitt had consolidated Newton's reputation as a lone genius who was also a model of patient perseverance.[9]

Conduitt was not embarrassed to portray a man who was notoriously forthright as a quasi-saint. According to him, 'An innate modesty & simplicity shewed it self in all his actions & expressions, his whole life was one continued series of labour patience charity generosity temperance piety goodness & all other virtues without a mixture of any vice whatsoever.'[10] Any rival who had been subjected to Newton's vindictive accusations of plagiarism would have been surprised to learn that 'he was so little vain & desirous of glory' that if only colleagues had not talked him into objecting, he would have 'lett others run away with the glory of those inventions which have done so much honour to humane nature'.[11]

Most famously, Conduitt bequeathed one of the four accounts of Newton's reminiscences about sitting beneath an apple tree at Woolsthorpe and (supposedly) conceiving the theory of gravity in a flash of inspiration. He also listened patiently to Newton boasting about buying his first prism at a fair just outside Cambridge so that he could carry out optical experiments in his student room. Apparently, after realizing he needed a second prism to confirm his ideas, Newton had to wait until the fair returned the following Saturday. A nice story, and one that is now solidly embedded in the Newtonian mythology—but the dates prove that it could not have happened exactly like that.[12]

Like all good anecdotes, Conduitt's grew in splendour as he repeatedly retold them. His first attempt at reporting Newton's birth is probably closest to the one he actually heard from Newton—that the infant was so weak and tiny that he was not expected to live. Soon that frailty had become a positive strength: like other superior mortals, the lack of physical vigour indicated that all available energy had been poured into intellectual splendour. Before long, Conduitt was bracketing the Lincolnshire super-baby with Caesar and Homer. He also placed increasing emphasis on the royal family's appreciation, adding in superlatives and eventually claiming that the monarchs often spent hours on end with Newton.[13]

As Conduitt tried to control Newton's reputation, he began to recognize the enormity of potential problems lying ahead. At the same time as keeping French biographers onside, he had to worry about damaging revelations from disillusioned British colleagues, such as the Arian William Whiston, Newton's former protégé and successor as Cambridge's Lucasian Professor. Looking through his stacks of inherited manuscripts, Conduitt realized that glorifying Newton was more complicated than he had thought. Unsanctioned previews of his work on ancient chronology were already arousing controversy both at home and abroad—and how was the family going to gloss over Newton's Cambridge obsession with alchemy? And what if word spread of his unorthodox religious sentiments? Barton wanted to publish Newton's theological writings, but was that necessarily a good idea? Keeping quiet seemed the best policy, and Conduitt only published two edited selections from the mass of Newton's papers, the first on ancient history, the second five years later on biblical prophecy.

After the Conduitt couple died, Newton's papers passed to their daughter, who had married upwards into the nobility. Most of the bundles got sent to the Hampshire country house of her descendants, who stashed them away in obscure cupboards and guarded the manuscripts closely. Favoured Victorian scientists were given permission to retrieve documents on optics, gravity, and mathematics, but anything else was protectively deemed to be worthless and retained in storage. That censorship finally ended in the 1930s, when the family fell on hard times and auctioned off the entire collection that remained in its possession. While the religious material mostly went to Jerusalem, where it is still preserved in the National Library archives, Newton's copious alchemical writings were snapped up by the Cambridge economist John Maynard Keynes.

Because of the Second World War, the 1942 festivities for the 300th anniversary of Newton's birth were somewhat muted, but Maynard Keynes eventually revealed what many others had desperately tried to conceal over the centuries—Newton had been a closet alchemist while he was at Cambridge, a fascination that he retained throughout his life and that affected his cosmological ideas. Shock waves of disbelief reverberated through the international scientific community, promptly followed by denial. Many physicists still find it hard to accept that their greatest hero was not indulging in alchemy as a mere pastime, but was so deeply committed to this collection of ancient practices that its precepts pervaded his cosmological theories. By the twentieth century, Newton's reputation was so well established that his splendour was only slightly tarnished by this controversial news, but he might never have achieved his status of international scientific genius if Conduitt and other propagandists had not decided to conceal his alchemical pursuits.

Enlightenment Display

Conduitt never did publish his biography of Newton, but it would probably not have been a best-seller. Controversies sell books, and he was aiming at bland panegyric. Even so, he ensured that many millions of people learnt about his version of Newton's prowess because he also commissioned visual commemorations. As well as Hogarth's conversation piece and pictures by other artists, Conduitt masterminded and paid for a magnificent monument in one of London's most important buildings, Westminster Abbey, which was fast becoming a major tourist attraction. Conduitt's sycophancy, adulation, and perseverance paid off: he, his wife, and his daughter were all honoured by being buried in the Abbey nave close to Newton. Conduitt and Barton may have embarked on a marriage of mutual convenience, but they both reaped eternal dividends.

For this impressive memorial to Newton, Conduitt picked a prominent position at the head of the nave, where it would have had a far greater immediate impact than it does now—during the nineteenth century, an ornate decorative screen was installed, and its coloured tracery clashes with the monument's marble austerity. The need to corral modern tourists has also detracted from the view. Whereas worshippers used to enter through the great west door, from where they could see the monument straight ahead of them in the aisle, modern ticket purchasers are guided along a winding route that obscures the grandiosity of the building's original design.

Newton's large, expensive tomb was not the tribute of a grateful nation to its greatest scientific hero. In the land of liberty, private enterprise reigned over state benefaction, and Conduitt's marble edifice was a personal celebration of Newton paid for by the man who had contrived to inherit his lucrative position at the Mint. Conduitt scored quite a coup. For hundreds of years, the Abbey had been essentially reserved for monarchs and saints, whose Gothic stone tombs still lie to the eastern end of the Abbey behind the altar. From the early eighteenth century, the nave in the western part of the building became home to a new Enlightenment glorification of intellectual and military achievement. Conduitt installed Newton as an early member of this secular male pantheon, whose diverse assembly of privately commissioned marble monuments differed from the uniform style imposed in France. Together, these new-style heroes displayed a strong political statement endorsing the maxims of the Whig party that dominated British politics for much of the eighteenth century—constitutional monarchy, anti-Catholicism, and individual freedom.

Newton was, of course, being lauded for his individual achievements; nevertheless, in death as he had in life, he fulfilled political and symbolic functions. Renowned for his scholarly work and his Mastership of the Mint, he was also on display as a national icon embodying Whig ideals. Newton's monument is one of a pair, complemented on the other side of the aisle by Lord Stanhope, whose reclining posture is a mirror-image version of Newton's. Like Newton, this Whig military hero rests on one elbow dressed as a Roman, but he is attended by winged cherubs to indicate an exemplary Christian who has passed into the afterlife with his works. While Newton personifies contemplative virtue on the left, Stanhope provides the traditional contrast of active virtue on the right.

The country's oldest religious centre was being converted into a national shrine for genius, and Newton was later joined by other Enlightenment luminaries such as George Handel, David Garrick, and Samuel Johnson (who successfully ousted a female actor temporarily buried next to Shakespeare's commemorative statue). Even Newton's physics meshed with ideals of political liberty. In his gravitational model of the universe, independent particles resemble citizens who interact to varying degrees with those moving around them, each enjoying freedom of choice yet simultaneously constrained by a stronger central power. Britain—at least, so ran the ideology—was a hierarchical country harmoniously bound together by the gravity of love: just as wives and children respected the man of the family, so, too, courtiers bowed to the will of the monarch, who in turn was obedient to God.

Conduitt commissioned the prestigious artist and landscape designer William Kent, also employed by the royal family, to draw up the preliminary sketches. The carving was executed by Michael

Rysbrack, the fashionable Dutch sculptor who had made the bust of Newton sitting on Conduitt's mantelpiece. In addition to the plaque Hogarth showed in Conduitt's drawing room, Rysbrack carved a grand marble chimney-piece for the new headquarters of the East India Company.[14]

Since Conduitt was paying, he could specify which aspects of Newton's life should be featured most prominently. He had come to know Newton only during the last decade of his life, when he was devoting himself mainly to the historical and biblical studies that have since been largely forgotten. Although Conduitt did choose to depict the scientific innovations for which Newton is now far more famous, he was himself more closely involved in other aspects of Newton's achievements. Neither Newton nor Conduitt had any way of knowing that Newton would become celebrated as a secular saint in a world dominated by science and technology. For them, the physical world was inseparable from the divine cosmos, and the second half of his career was not divorced from the first.

The Abbey monument is dominated by a large globe with a Greek goddess draped across its top. She is Urania, muse of astronomy, fulfilling the stereotypical female function of symbolizing a science without being allowed to practise it. Like other celestial spheres, this one displays a curved map of the stars as they would be seen by an observer positioned at the centre of the earth. In an oblique reference to Newton's *Principia*, it shows the path of the 1680 comet that had proved crucial for his ideas about gravity. More surprisingly for modern viewers, the constellations on Urania's globe indicate how Newton set out to calculate a more accurate date for the voyage of the Argonauts. By using astronomical data, Newton concluded that the expedition had taken place three centuries later than usually thought—an adjustment that conveniently gave priority to the ancient Israelites, his favoured civilization. In the years leading up to his death, Newton spent more time refining the details of that analysis than in fine-tuning the niceties of universal gravity.

Newton's elbow rests on four marble books, whose carved spine labels imply that Theology and Chronology formed as crucial a component of his intellectual legacy as Gravity and Optics. This parity reflected Newton's own conviction that correcting the timelines of ancient history and interpreting the Bible were no mere hobbies to pass the time but formed a central component of his intellectual endeavours. As part of his investigations into God's world, Newton obsessively researched the history of ancient dynasties from the Persians up to Alexander the Great, collating a wide range of textual and physical evidence. At the time, such topics seemed far from arcane and he was internationally regarded as a great expert. Edward Gibbon—famous chronicler of the Roman Empire—thought that quantifying ancient history was a valuable initiative, declaring: 'The name of Newton raises the image of a profound Genius, luminous and original. His System of Chronology would alone be sufficient to assure him immortality.' As another example, Newton's meticulous comparisons of textual variants were incorporated into a massive critical edition of the Greek New Testament that appeared in 1707.[15]

For Newton, the timetables of ancient history were intertwined with biblical accounts and divine cosmology. Unlike earlier biblical exegetes such as Archbishop James Ussher, he refrained from assigning particular dates to the Creation or the Flood, but hoped to establish a new timeline without explicitly contradicting the old one.[16] On his eighty-third birthday—25 December 1725 on the British calendar—Newton was visited by his admirer William Stukeley, an expert on Stonehenge, the ancient monument that fascinated them both. Newton maintained that long ago, before original knowledge had been lost and when one single religion was followed all over the world, Stonehenge had functioned as a temple where worshippers could cluster around a central fire, like the planets revolving around the sun. That day, he chose to regale Stukeley with his similar ideas about King Solomon's Temple, revered by Jews and Christians alike as ancient Jerusalem's holiest of holies. The Temple was, he thought, the physical manifestation on earth of a divine abode.

The original Temple's exact history is still uncertain, although Newton maintained it was established in 1015 BC. Whatever the precise date of its origin, well over two thousand years ago the building was ransacked and burnt down by Babylonian invaders.

Chatting companionably over Newton's drawings, the two theologians agreed that his sketches were unlike any others (presumably a compliment from Stukeley to the uniqueness of Newton's insights rather than to any regrettable deviation from standard thinking on the topic). They decided that the unknown architects had influenced first their Egyptian and then their Greek successors, a historical sequence that was compatible with the reconstruction work required after the biblical flood, which they also discussed.

Newton believed he had a lifelong mission to establish the Temple's structure, which had been ordained by God as a blueprint of heaven—so the Altar represented the sun, but also God's presence. As he put it, 'Temples were anciently contrived to represent the frame of the Universe as the true Temple of the great God.' From his historical and mathematical research, he concluded that the Temple's Altar of Burnt Offerings lay at the centre of a square with sides of 500 cubits (according to him, the dimensions of the Egyptian pyramids suggested that a cubit was 22 inches, or 55.8 centimetres). For Newton, the Temple was important not only as a template for the cosmos, but also as a key to understanding the Apocalypse and the millennial kingdom of God that would follow.[17]

After Newton died, Conduitt confronted the tricky task of converting Newton's enormous archive of private research into public knowledge. Eventually, after arduous processes of amalgamation and condensation, he produced two related books posthumously attributed to Newton: *The Chronology of Ancient Kingdoms Amended* (1728) and *Observations on the Prophecies of Daniel* (1733). His first step was to sort through the millions of relevant words scattered among Newton's piled-up boxes of papers. The Master of the Mint may have basked in a virtuous glow of economy when he scribbled his latest intellectual insight on the back of an old letter, but presumably Conduitt found this lifelong habit frustrating. When Newton jotted down a note about the Apocalypse on a Mint document, was he sitting alone in his office or zoning out of a tedious committee meeting? Or might it have been years later, after he had economized by taking spare paper back home? People's convictions often change as they get older—and Newton's certainly did—but without dates, such shifts are hard to track. What does seem clear is that during the last ten years or so of his life, Newton picked up a key phase of his earlier intellectual life at Cambridge by resuming his passions for biblical studies and ancient history. As he aged, he continually supplemented and also revised previous work, although he never arrived at definitive versions.

Newton's astronomical fame rested on calculating when an eclipse or other celestial events might occur in the future. Conversely, looking back into the past, he could give accurate dates to events that had been described in ancient documents. For him, numbers were what counted: words were slippery, as suspect as the stories dreamt up by the counterfeiters he persecuted at the Mint. As he ploughed on through historical records, he repeatedly encountered puzzling complexities. Frustratingly, he discovered not only that metaphorical terms were of limited reliability, but also that mythological characters had often been confused and that constellation maps were inconsistent.

This natural philosopher who famously scorned hypotheses adopted a surprisingly cavalier approach towards his information. 'I shall not stand to recite other men's opinions, but propose as shortly as I can what I take to be ye truth,' he declared.[18] To arrive at his unique version of the truth, Newton invented a method of mathematical averaging that was designed to overcome the shortcomings of inconsistent records inherited from the past. In a reiterative process of refinement, he checked conflicting facts one against the other to adjust them in sequence and hence produce new ones of supposedly higher reliability. Even his one-time acolyte and fellow Arian William Whiston was contemptuous, remarking that Newton 'seems to have digged long in the deepest Mines of Scripture and Antiquity for his precious Ore himself; and very rarely to have condescended to make use of the Thoughts or Discoveries of others on these Occasions'.[19] Eventually but controversially, Newton sliced five centuries or more from traditional chronologies, generating a version of humanity's history that was internally consistent but differed from those of his contemporaries.

Newton regarded biblical prophecy as being conceptually very different from astronomical prediction. He condemned as false prophets those arithmetical exegetes who deciphered the scriptures in order to provide an accurate forecast for the Day of Judgement or the end of the world. Instead, he insisted, God foretold events not so that human beings might know about them in advance, but so that afterwards, interpreted in retrospect, they could be seen to have fulfilled God's intentions. Proclaiming his own superior insight, Newton described how these divine plans had previously been concealed, encoded in enigmatic pronouncements, and obscured by textual corruptions. He discerned no firm boundaries between the physical world and theological belief; similarly, there was for him no disjunction between God's prophecies as recorded in scriptural texts, the successive civilizations of humanity, and the unknown futures lying ahead—the new heavens and the new earth promised in the Bible.

In his later years, Newton increasingly focused on the Book of Daniel: the dog-eared corners and well-thumbed pages of his own bible, now preserved in the University Library at Cambridge, show how thoroughly he perused its chapters in his attempts to recover their uncorrupted meanings. In particular, he searched for divine testimony exposing Catholicism as a false religion, although he gradually became less rabid in his denunciations. Newton regarded himself as a divinely appointed interpreter, a member of the intellectual elite who had been chosen by God to unravel the obscure messages of the Bible and explain to lesser mortals how the unfolding of human events confirms the predictions of the scriptures.

As Conduitt sifted through reams of notes, he had to select for publication sections that were neither too controversial nor too arcane. For instance, he omitted Newton's attempt to quash scare-mongering rumours about the immediate end of the world by post-poning until 2060 the apocalyptic fall of the corrupt Trinitarian Church.[20] In contrast, this sentence did pass Conduitt's tests: 'The whole scene of sacred prophecy is composed of three principal parts: the regions beyond Euphrates, represented by the two beasts of Daniel, the empire of the Greeks on this side of Euphrates, represented by the Leopard and the He-Goat; and the empire of the Latins on this side of Greece, represented by the beast with ten horns.'[21] It was then standard practice to identify the four beasts of Daniel with four ancient empires.

Sometimes Newton opted for numerical or cabbalistic calculations, substituting numbers for letters to decode hidden references. Most notoriously, this style of analysis meant that the number 666 could be equated with the name of the Beast with seven heads and ten horns that emerges from the sea. The mystic significance of 666 is described in the last book of the Bible, Revelation: 'Here is wisdom. Let him that hath understanding, count the number of the beast: for it is the number of a man; and his number *is* Six hundred threescore *and* six.'[22]

Newton's personal fascination with the number 666 might well have been sparked during the lead-up to 1666, when he was an undergraduate at Cambridge. As the fateful date grew nearer, dire prognostications circulated about the doom to be visited on the world. Confirmation of these pessimistic predictions duly arrived. First came the Plague, which cut short the first run of John Dryden's *Indian Emperour*. And then in the year itself, the Great Fire of London was accompanied by some disastrous defeats in naval battles against the Dutch. Dryden emerged as the spin doctor who converted this gloomy despondency into a positive message. Towards the end of 1666, the English fleet at last won a glorious victory that enabled Dryden to reconfigure the year in a long and enormously popular poem, the Year of Wonders or *Annus Mirabilis*. This phrase is now often used to describe Newton's apparently miraculous period at Woolsthorpe, but Dryden knew nothing of that. Patriotically, he insisted in what now seems a somewhat tortured argument that the nation should be grateful to God for protecting England from even worse devastation, and for giving Londoners the opportunity to rebuild their city and make it the richest in the world. Here the third line refers to Mexico, imagined location of *The Indian Emperour*:

> Me-thinks already, from this Chymick flame,
> I see a city of more precious mold:
> Rich as the town which gives the *Indies* name,
> With Silver pav'd, and all divine with Gold.[23]

Whether or not he was indeed God's messenger on earth as he thought, Newton certainly knew how to win enemies. He protected his chronological theories as closely and as malevolently as his version of calculus. During the last two years of his life, he became involved in a vindictive row with the Venetian aristocrat Antonio Conti. A decade earlier, during the Italian's visit to London for the solar eclipse, they had seemed to be the best of friends, but after a leaked version of Newton's chronological views was illicitly published in Paris, he rounded on Conti, choosing to savage him in the Royal Society's journal, the *Philosophical Transactions*, which was widely distributed and summarized overseas. Aggrieved, and anticipating further accusations, Conti asked (the italics are his): '*is he not obliged*, according to his own principle, to prove them, *at the risk of becoming* guilty of calumny? Now how will he demonstrate, as he would a geometric curve…my masquerade of friendship, my clandestine intervention, and other chimeras with which it has suited him to embellish the opinion he has formed of me?' By challenging Newton to justify his sudden transition from close colleague to bitter enemy, Conti had put his finger on a fundamental paradox in Newton's behaviour: although he prided himself on being a meticulous scholar who relied on logical argument, he apparently had no qualms about resorting to unsubstantiated invective when it suited him, almost as if he already lived in a post-truth era.[24]

This dispute preoccupied Newton during the last few years of his life and continued raging for a century after his death, as gossipy philosophers distributed pirated accounts of his *Chronology* across Europe. Although Newton had previously pursued his research in secrecy, it seems that he could not resist boasting about it to Caroline, Princess of Wales (wife of the future George II). Unable to refuse her royal request for a summary, he drew up a short abstract of around twenty pages. Before long, several versions—whose origins are unclear—were circulating around London, and further details had also leaked out from other Newtonian confidants. Conduitt was so terrified of Newton's reaction that he concealed the most vicious critiques, but it was Conti who formed the prime target of Newton's fury.

At first, chronological experts were delighted that such a distinguished mathematician as Newton had turned his attention to an antiquarian subject, but disappointment soon set in. The accepted timetable had been provided by Archbishop Ussher, the same clergyman who decreed so influentially that the world was created in 4004 BC. Placing great emphasis on the voyage of the Argonauts, Newton shaved several centuries from traditional outlines of Greek history, and telescoped earlier kingdoms even more dramatically. While critics competed to compile objections, their central accusation was that although Newton had achieved mathematical accuracy by using astronomical calculations about the relative positions of the sun and the earth (or to put it more technically, the retrogression of the equinoctial points across the constellation of Aries), he had also been forced to use documentary and mythological evidence, seen as far less reliable. Of what use were his sophisticated techniques if he could only make informed guesses about the length of a ruler's reign?

Trying to calm Newton down, the Bishop of Rochester diplomatically suggested that the best way of vanquishing his mistaken critics was to publish his own account. Shortly before Newton died, the Bishop spotted a visitor leaving his bedroom—a bookseller who later claimed that Newton had promised him the commission of printing his *Chronology*. Stepping inside, the Bishop found Newton contentedly revising, once again, the manuscript that Conduitt published only a year later. By then, Caroline had become queen. Never one to pass up a patronage opportunity, Conduitt obsequiously dedicated Newton's posthumous book to the new monarch, whose 'hours of leisure are employed in cultivating in Your Self That Learning, which You so warmly patronize in Others'.[25]

ACT II

THE AUDIENCE

ISAAC NEWTON IN LONDON SOCIETY

The true stars of Conduitt's show are not the actors on the stage but the three royal children near the fireplace. Dressed as miniature adults, all three had already had regal responsibilities thrust upon them. To set a good example for the nation, their mother Queen Caroline risked their lives by insisting that they become test cases for inoculation against smallpox. At that stage, the treatment was uncertain and unpleasant, inducing a mild form of the illness that could last for several weeks and might result in death or permanent scarring. Caroline's gamble paid off: following her initiative, thousands of other small children were subjected to the same procedure, and she gained credit for her maternal solicitude.

Hogarth's title makes the hierarchy clear: this play may be being performed in Mr Conduitt's house, but the most important person present is the Duke of Cumberland, the boy in the white wig and the red jacket standing behind the makeshift box accommodating his two small sisters. Based on the private sitting, Hogarth also produced a virtually identical separate portrait of the young prince. Although William Augustus never inherited the throne, he was his parents' favourite, the darling they preferred to his older brother Frederick. Born soon after three failed pregnancies—a miscarriage, a still birth, and an early death—he was indulged throughout his childhood. Here only 10 years old, William Augustus already possessed a string of titles and an annual income of £6000. He owned his own laboratory as well as a printing press down in the palace basement, while his astronomy tutor was Newton's friend Edmond Halley. When Newton died in

1727, the 6-year-old Prince had insisted on attending his funeral, but as an adult he acquired multiple lovers and pursued a successful military career until he was wounded in the knee and grew so fat that he died in his forties.[1]

In front of him are his two younger sisters, the princesses Mary and little Louisa, who were brought up far less indulgently. Close by, the woman wearing white is their governess Mary, Countess of Deloraine. Recently appointed, she was kind but not very bright; prone to over-drinking, she later became the king's mistress, apparently on one occasion pulling away his chair so that he fell on the floor. Here she is accompanied by her own two daughters, Georgia and Elizabeth.[2] Although one of them is captivated by the scene on the stage, the other is retrieving a fallen fan that has succumbed to the power of Newtonian gravity.

The elegant aristocrats in the audience come from the highest echelons of London society: Conduitt was an ambitious social climber. In the foreground, the man with a diagonal blue sash across his back is the Duke of Richmond, keen cricketer and grandson of Charles II (through the king's extramarital relationship with Louise de Kérouaille). He is leaning on the chair of his wife Sarah, one of the queen's favourites, and their eyes are fondly fixed on the stage actor dressed in white satin, who is their oldest daughter Caroline. Their marriage was a great success, even though it had been arranged when Sarah was only 13 but endowed with a large dowry to pay off the debts he had already incurred.

Beneath the Conduitt portraits are three men who show little interest in the rest of the proceedings and are probably talking shop. Standing with his back to the wall is the second Duke of Montagu, who had inherited his father's position at court as Master of the Great Wardrobe. Belonging to the same extended Montagu clan as Newton's patron Charles, he, too, was a Whig politician. The other two are the Queen's Master of the Horse, the Earl of Pomfret—a new title created personally for him by George I—and Thomas Hill, Secretary to the Board of Trade, which King William had commissioned to promote lucrative relationships with the American colonies. While Conduitt was living in his Hampshire house, Hill visited Hogarth's London studio and reported on this picture's progress.

The person paying closest attention to the performance is the least flashily dressed. Swathed in black, the clergyman John Theophilus Desaguliers stands behind the stage, his back turned but his script open at the right place for prompting the children if they fluff their lines. As Newton's henchman and a distinguished Fellow of the Royal Society, he is here to ensure that Newtonian order prevails among the play's youthful cast.

5

Fortune Hunters

Skulking in the back corner of Hogarth's picture, Desaguliers may appear an insignificant figure, but he is the lynchpin of these apparently disparate groups. He worked closely with two of the adult aristocrats in the audience—the Dukes of Richmond and Montagu—as well as being employed in the royal household. Moreover, he was Newton's chief propagandist both before and after his patron's death, a key performer who executed the Newtonian experimental programme at the Royal Society, converted critics to the cause, and consolidated Newton's international glory.

Caricaturists emphasized his short-sightedness, and here his nose is buried close to his prompt book—yet ironically it was Desaguliers who did most to promote Newtonian optics in Europe. Constantly short of money, he was an expert in oily diplomacy, taking full advantage of his wealthy acquaintances to consolidate his position and to secure lucrative engineering contracts. An Enlightenment entrepreneur par excellence, Desaguliers showed the commercial world that Newtonian physics was not merely the preserve of reclusive academics but could earn money for ambitious investors and make Britain a great industrial nation.

* * *

At the beginning of the eighteenth century, an intelligent young man who wanted to earn his living without going into the army had three professions from which to choose: the law, medicine, and the Church. Desaguliers opted for the third, but he was not very effective as a clergyman. Although he once took legal proceedings against his parishioners for refusing to pay their tithes, his aristocratic backer, the Duke of Chandos, pointed out how unreasonably he was behaving: 'A corpse has lain three days in the church waiting Christian burial and neither you nor your curate thought fit to attend till today.'[1] In one engraving, Hogarth portrayed Desaguliers preaching from a pulpit, peering myopically at his sermon through a magnifying-glass and holding forth long after the sand in the hour-glass beside him has run through to the bottom. The title says it all: *The sleeping congregation*. Even a fat priest appears to be dozing, although he is probably leering down the low-cut dress of the buxom but somnolent young woman reclining nearby.

Rather than carrying out his clerical duties, Desaguliers preferred to spend his time performing experiments or designing roads and fountains. Even so, religion was extremely important in his life. For one thing, it was the reason why he was brought up in England and not France. His parents were Huguenots, Reformed Protestants who were subjected to increasing persecution by hostile Catholics. Desaguliers was a toddler when his family fled across the Channel in the early 1680s, settling initially in French-speaking Guernsey. As a child he grew up speaking French, but his life changed abruptly when he was 9, and the family—now officially Anglican—moved to London, where they survived on a combination of charity and his father's low-paid teaching job. After learning to speak English like a native, Desaguliers studied at Oxford and then settled in London, where he lived for the rest of his life.[2]

A new word was coined to describe men like Desaguliers: 'refugee'. Towards the end of the seventeenth century, Huguenots migrated all over Europe after a shift in French law that removed their official protection (the Revocation of the Edict of Nantes, 1685). Many of the wealthier families came to England, where Charles II had already welcomed these affluent immigrants. Under government encouragement, initial instinctive hostility to the incomers faded. Even so, they were welcomed not from compassion, but because the expertise of these skilled workers would enable more goods to be produced locally, and so reduce the need for expensive imports. A Whig writer explained that by undercutting competition from abroad, they could help to boost the British economy: 'We are now supplied from *foreign parts* with divers Commodities, which, if the kingdom were replenished with Artisans, they would furnish us with here at home.' As well as dominating the luxury end of the silver market, Huguenots transformed the silk, paper, and linen industries into efficient profit-making ventures, thus contributing to the emergence of Great Britain as an industrial leader. By 1713, French commentators were envying their upstart national rival, reporting that 'the refugees have carried the manufactories to such a degree of perfection that even we begin now to import some of their output.'[3]

A refugee with no family wealth behind him, Desaguliers rose in Hanoverian society through intelligence, diplomacy, and sycophancy. Although honourable ancestry was still a great advantage, in this competitive profit-hungry age enterprise brought rewards. In parallel with Conduitt, Desaguliers played a key part in Newton's London life and was crucial for establishing his international reputation. Within only a couple of years, Newton had singled Desaguliers out for special treatment, and he rapidly became one of the Royal Society's most active Fellows. Taking advantage of his language skills, Desaguliers developed influential contacts across Europe, especially in France and the Netherlands, while at home he ingratiated himself into aristocratic circles. By cultivating wealthy patrons, he demonstrated the practical value of Newtonian physics. While some of his Huguenot compatriots were engraving fine silverware or manufacturing silk, he was using his engineering expertise to transform London by modernizing water systems, advising on Westminster Bridge, and renovating the antiquated ventilation system in the House of Commons. And although this short round man suffered from limited eyesight, he had the vision to place himself at the forefront of a new and powerful English organization—the Freemasons.

In Pursuit of Profit

The key to success during the Enlightenment was networking, and masonic lodges provided the ideal environment for would-be entrepreneurs to meet influential aristocrats and wealthy businessmen. One ambitious young fortune seeker who had recently arrived in London condescendingly explained in a letter to his father that 'Masonry here is upon another footing to what it is in the country;

it is not a dozen pots of beer, nor a dozen gallons of Wine'; instead, membership gave access to those all-important court circles and 'no small advantage to a man who would rise in the world and one of the principal reasons why I would be a Mason'.[4] Desaguliers had the same idea. Probably initiated in 1713, the year after coming to London from Oxford, he became a leading figure in London's new Grand Lodge.

Hogarth was himself a Mason, and so were most of the men in his conversation piece. (Or perhaps they all were: there are insufficient records to confirm the Earl of Pomfret, aka Thomas Fermor aka 2nd Baron of Leominster aka Master of the Queen's Horse.) Montagu and his two friends, Hill and the Duke of Richmond (aka Charles Lennox or the Duke of Aubigny) were all Freemasons, and although the Duke of Cumberland (Prince William) was still too young, in time he and his elder brother Frederick would both be initiated. In 1719, Desaguliers became one of the earliest Grand Masters, and his successor was the Duke of Montagu, the man in the white wig and blue jacket standing just below Barton's portrait.

Newton's assistant Desaguliers played an important part in drawing up the first official constitution of English Masonry, published in 1723, or 5723 in the Masonic calendar (Figure 5.1). Its frontispiece shows Desaguliers on the far right wearing his black clerical robes; like the other men, he may be holding his hands in symbolic gestures. Dressed in his ceremonial costume as a Knight of the Garter, the Duke of Montagu is presenting a scroll of the constitution and symbolic pair of compasses to his successor as Grand Master, the Duke of Wharton, witnessed by various high-ranking personnel. On the tiled floor between them is a diagram of Pythagoras's theorem to illustrate Masonry's foundation in geometry, accompanied by a Greek inscription reading 'Eureka' (Figure 5.2).[5]

Freemasonry may or may not go back to the Rosicrucians, but some basic facts are well established. England's Grand Lodge, the first in Europe, was founded in 1717, when four smaller London lodges joined together. During the eighteenth century, Freemasonry rapidly expanded throughout the country and also spread abroad. Despite many satirical poems and caricatures, membership rose rapidly. Initially, meetings took place in inns or taverns, but as the

THE

CONSTITUTIONS

OF THE

FREE-MASONS.

CONTAINING THE

History, Charges, Regulations, &c.
of that most Ancient and Right
Worshipful *FRATERNITY.*

For the Use of the LODGES.

L O N D O N:
Printed by WILLIAM HUNTER, for JOHN SENEX at the *Globe,*
and JOHN HOOKE at the *Flower-de-luce* over-against *St. Dunstan's
Church,* in *Fleet-street.*

In the Year of Masonry —— 5723
Anno Domini —— —— 1723

Figure 5.1 Title page *The Constitution of the Free-Masons*; James Anderson, 1723

Figure 5.2 Frontispiece, *The Constitution of the Free-Masons*, 1723; engraving by John Pine

movement swelled, lodges were able to build their own halls, and soon enterprising Huguenots and other skilled artisans were creating a lucrative masonic market for engraved drinking vessels and ceremonial regalia. The Whig-oriented Grand Lodge maintained particularly close contact with the Netherlands, where the Duke of Richmond and Desaguliers—who acted as Deputy Grand Master several times—established a lodge in 1734. Recollecting his own impoverished childhood, Desaguliers steered the Grand Lodge towards charitable activities, which included raising money for distressed brethren to settle in the new American colony of Georgia.

Apart from engaging in plenty of eating and drinking, the precise activities of Enlightenment Freemasons are notoriously difficult to pin down. They based their structure and activities on those of traditional guilds, many of which had been in existence for centuries. Masonic brothers dressed elaborately, performed esoteric rituals, constructed lavish halls, enjoyed an annual Grand Feast and were led by a Grand Master. In those respects, they closely resembled the liveried guilds, many of which still retain elaborate ceremonial occasions. The written rules specifically encouraged religious toleration and promoted learning, but outlawed political discussions. The lodges varied in character, and many of them provided ideal opportunities for quiet business discussions. Unconstrained by the restrictions of a routine nine-to-five job, eighteenth-century gentlemen frequented clubs and coffee houses to discuss the latest news, boast about their recent expensive purchases, and engage in some lucrative deals.

At one time—and possibly under Desaguliers's influence—around a quarter of the Fellows of the Royal Society were Freemasons, including Martin Folkes, appointed by Newton as his vice-president. But that substantial overlap does not necessarily indicate any strong ideological alignment between the two groups. Unlike now, Fellows were often elected for their prestige rather than their scientific expertise, and wealthy London gentlemen routinely belonged to several different societies and clubs. Drinks and dinners provided ample time for quiet chats in corners, irrespective of whether the main event of the evening was an elaborate initiation rite in a lodge or a dramatic demonstration at the Royal Society. There is no evidence that Newton was a Freemason, nor that masonic ideas permeated scientific theories. On the other hand, it was definitely advantageous for Newton to have a strong advocate with contacts all over Britain as well as in France and the Netherlands. Desaguliers often travelled on masonic business, when he could also arrange meetings, lectures, and experimental displays vindicating Newtonian theories.

Freemasonry was dominated by wealthy Whigs, including the most powerful man in the government, Sir Robert Walpole. Like his masonic colleagues, he turned the meetings to his own advantage, infiltrating the membership with spies whose information contributed to his exceptionally long ministerial regime—twenty years without interruption.[6] Whigs claimed allegiance to the 1688 Revolution that had toppled the Stuart monarchy, although in practice many of them endorsed rather than opposed traditional hierarchies. In a metaphor that prevailed throughout eighteenth-century Britain, Desaguliers compared the British constitution with the orderly structure of a smooth-running clockwork universe. He judged 'that Form of it to be most perfect, which did most nearly resemble the Natural Government of our System, according to the Laws settled by the *All-wise* and *Almighty Architect* of the Universe'.[7] He thus neatly introduced a masonic image of an architectural God into a Newtonian vision of a monarch who ruled courtiers just like the sun controls the planets and fathers direct their families. Protected by this stable patriarchal system, individuals could seek to improve their own position.

The Whig ideologues of the early eighteenth century—including Newton—promoted trade and commerce, profit and competition, liberty and self-advancement. Ambitious social climbers bought into the idea that, by making and spending money, their status would improve; since wealth implied prestige, financial gain became an over-riding aim. Fortunes seemed to be there for the making, but in the absence of stock market experience and legal protection, they could also be lost. The most notorious example is the South Sea Bubble, British investors' first experience of a major crash. Newton was used to keeping secrets, and he may well have concealed the awkward fact that he lost over £20,000.

The initial success of the South Sea Company (referring mainly to the South Pacific area) depended on a long-standing European fantasy that the Americas would yield wealth far exceeding the financial investment required to get there. An expensive map commissioned from Herman Moll, one of Europe's most distinguished cartographers, was of little practical use for navigators, but it did advertise the Company's sole right to trade up to 300 leagues out to

Figure 5.3 *A New & Exact Map of the Coast, Countries and Islands within ye Limits of ye South Sea Company*; Hermann Moll, 1711

sea (Figure 5.3). British entrepreneurs felt they had a God-given mandate to take advantage of natural riches, but the Company also specialized in buying and selling people. Claiming that profits of up to 4000 per cent might be realized, Moll stressed the value of slavery, emphasizing that 'the greatest Trade, and the most beneficial the *English* ever had with the *Spaniards* on the Continent, was for

Negroes.'[8] Customers poured money into shares in the new Company, never envisaging what would actually happen—their price soared, but then abruptly collapsed, resulting in many bank-ruptcies and suicides.

Insider trading, political bribery, false advertising: in retrospect, the Bubble seems to have been a harbinger of the corruption and sharp talk that still pervade international finance. Viewed with the luxury of hindsight, Newton and his fellow investors appear to have behaved stupidly, but decisions were hard to make during a crisis that was unprecedented and evolved rapidly. Amongst eminent Freemasons, the artist James Thornhill contrived to sell at the peak, while the Duke of Montagu was so hopeful of still further profit that he lost everything he had gained, although unlike many of his fellow gamblers, he was sufficiently well connected to continue accumulating honours and well-paid positions. A contemporary ballad summed up the mixture of pity and contempt felt by those lucky enough to escape unscathed:

> Jews, Turks and Christians, hear my song
> I'll make you rich before it's long...
> Farewell your Houses, Lands and Flocks
> For all you have is now in Stocks.[9]

Finding out exactly what went wrong for Newton and so many other investors is difficult, because the gossipy conversations that induced first enthusiasm and then panic mostly took place secretly in coffee houses, inns, and club corridors. Daniel Defoe contributed to the rumour mill that precipitated the disaster, but a few years later—and mindful of his own losses—he blamed greed: 'Avarice is the ruin of many people besides tradesmen; and I might give the late South-sea calamity for an example, in which the longest heads were most over-reached, not so much by the wit or cunning of those they had to deal with, as by the secret promptings of their own avarice.'[10]

For the first few years after it was set up in 1711, the South Sea Company represented a successful financial experiment that tied together the interests of individual investors, the government, and wealthy merchants. The dream-child of Tory politicians, it was designed to raise the vast sums of money needed to pay off the ever-escalating national debt incurred by repeated wars. Britain was engaged in military action for much of the eighteenth century, and even when officially at peace, the nation was either recovering from the previous conflict or preparing itself for the next one. A similar system was launched in Paris, dreamt up by a Scottish opportunist and escaped murderer, John Law, in an attempt to rescue the French economy, which was also failing. His Mississippi Scheme, dedicated to exploiting the French colony of Louisiana, made so much money that in the autumn of 1719 a new word was invented to describe him: millionaire. For 500 days, Law was the most powerful man in France, but he lost his fortune when confidence collapsed and share prices crashed.[11]

Whereas Law focused on French possessions in northern America and eastern Asia, the South Sea Company was granted a monopoly to trade in the South American region and transport enslaved Africans when needed for working the silver mines or tending plantations. According to Defoe, it was 'a real beauty' compared with the 'painted Whore' of the Mississippi Scheme.[12] Private investors were lending money that would (in principle) be repaid with interest, but other perks were also available. One of the navy's chief contractors, Abraham Crowley, had stopped supplying nails to the Royal Navy because his bills were not being paid. After being given enough South Sea stock to become a director, he resumed deliveries that were essential for the nation's ships.[13] As an incentive to preserve their human cargoes intact, for every 104 captives delivered alive, the ships' captains were offered a bonus of four to own as slaves, valued at £20 each.[14]

Many British investors regarded this venture as a wonderful opportunity to increase their own wealth. Even the poet Alexander Pope, who condemned slavery, boasted about his investments and the amount of money he might have made (if only...) by selling at the right time.[15] Initially, Newton had begun buying shares as a stable, long-term investment to provide him with a steady income, but he gradually changed his mind and became profit-hungry. Acting on his own initiative, not on professional advice, he built up his holdings until, by 1720, 40 per cent of his wealth was in South Sea stock.

By then, it was already becoming clear to those in the know that the sums were not adding up. Recognizing too late that the scheme was running into serious trouble, the Company and the government attempted to forestall disaster by circulating hollow predictions of the vast profits to be made. As sweeteners, influential officials and royalty were offered special deals enabling them to buy shares on credit at a particularly low price. With no need to hand over money until later, they had a strong incentive to keep quiet and help push prices up. Benefiting from insider knowledge, George I quintupled his money, but as more and more speculators decided to risk their funds, the share price rocketed: between January and May 1720, it rose from £128 to £550. When the value rapidly deflated in the summer—when the Bubble burst—any available cash had already been spent in bribes, and the greatest losses were suffered by private individuals.

Not everybody got burnt. Thanks to a fortuitous delay in the post, Robert Walpole was prevented from buying more shares at their peak price. Although shrewd Sir Thomas Guy owned around five times as much stock as Newton, he began liquidating early on, well before prices had rocketed, which yielded enough profit for him to build the London hospital bearing his name. Newton initially hung on for slightly longer than Guy before selling, and so reaped a still greater profit—but astonishingly, just as Guy was completing his sales, Newton bought in again at a higher price. He had once flippantly remarked that he could calculate the movements of the planets although not the madness of investors, yet at this late stage, he mistakenly placed so much confidence in the scheme that he also invested money on behalf of an estate for which he was an executor. He even continued purchasing stock after the graph had begun to plummet. At the end of September, shares that had touched £1000 in July were worth only £200. Even sitting tight and doing nothing throughout the Bubble period would have been more profitable than buying, selling, and then buying again as Newton had done.

The government worked hard to suppress the facts, which were just too embarrassing for public circulation. By screening everyone responsible from proper scrutiny, Walpole—mocked as the

'Skreen-Master General'—managed to restore confidence, and the Company continued to thrive. The following May, Walpole effectively became Britain's first prime minister, retaining power by filling important posts with his friends and relatives, and by pushing through savage laws that made any form of public protest pretty much impossible. This was the Whig government, the champions of liberty, which Newton had helped to put in power.

Engineering the Future

Like other talented young women, the poet Elizabeth Tollet may well have enjoyed challenging herself with the mathematical puzzles that featured regularly in the *Ladies' Diary*. Perhaps she pondered a *Prize Ænigma* that appeared in 1725. If so, although she would have been intrigued, she would probably have deplored the anonymous author's literary skills. These were the first two lines:

> I Sprung, like Pallas, from a fruitful Brain,
> About the Time of CHARLES the Second's Reign.[16]

Eager readers had to wait an entire year before learning the answer: a steam engine (then called a fire engine) originally designed to pump water out of Cornish mines. At the time, Britain's greatest engineering expert was Desaguliers, who was a close friend of the *Diary*'s editor and also a not very talented poet. Whether or not he composed the poem's nine heroic couplets, he definitely did write the authoritative account that later introduced James Watt to the power of steam.

The Huguenot refugees who settled in London followed many different trades. As well as silk manufacturers and silversmiths, they included apothecaries, distillers, brewers, inventors, and instrument makers. Like many immigrants, they were ambitious and hard-working people who stimulated the economy by introducing new skills and spotting profitable gaps in the market. Many of the men were well educated: for example, the community of weavers based in Spitalfields set up an influential Mathematical Society that flourished well into the nineteenth century.[17] Desaguliers was unusual in being a scientific lecturer with an Oxford degree, but he shared his compatriots' adaptability, initiative, and commitment to practical money-earning projects.

Only a year after he arrived in London, Desaguliers managed to attract the attention of Newton, who promptly employed him to devise and demonstrate experiments at the Royal Society. This position of Curator had originally been held by Robert Hooke, and both men succeeded because they were mechanically as well as intellectually gifted. But as they both discovered, the Royal Society salary would not fund the life they envisaged, and Desaguliers sought out other means of support. By piecing together a variety of different occupations, he contrived to earn a fair amount of money, although he always spent more than came in and was constantly short of cash. Patronage was crucial: Newton was helped by Charles Montagu, John Conduitt benefited by acquiring Newton as a relative, and Desaguliers was supported not only by Newton but also by profiteers who hoped to gain from his technical expertise. Desaguliers found his first patron while he was still at Oxford, and spent much of his subsequent career persuading wealthy contacts to recommend him among their friends and to invest in schemes that promised much, and sometimes delivered.

Desaguliers's major industrial patron was the Duke of Chandos (aka James Brydges or the Earl of Carnarvon). Although not portrayed in Hogarth's picture, Chandos moved in the same circles as its aristocratic audience—and he, too, lost a fortune in the South Sea Bubble. Like many other Fellows of the Royal Society, he spent his days looking after his investments, gossiping in coffee houses, renovating his various estates, learning about the latest engineering inventions, attending and throwing parties—basically, multiplying his money and having a good time. A favourite of Queen Anne's, Chandos occupied several prestigious government positions, and—as with many other opportunists of this period—question marks hover over the sources of his great wealth. Apart from his titles, he had inherited little from his father except responsibilities, although he did adopt Conduitt's tactic of marrying a wife who was older than him and endowed with rich relatives.

Wives have left few traces in history books. After a series of negotiations, it was through Mary Lake that Chandos acquired Cannons, a large estate near Edgware. Now the site of North London Collegiate School, its development became the central project of his entire life, preoccupying him long after her death and soaking up her fortune. Lake was, of course, a unique person, but her experiences were not untypical for the daughter of a rich aristocrat. Of their nine children, only two survived, and her husband failed to attend any of the funerals. The first baby was born in London, but that night he was busy entertaining several other women in Hereford 'and after dinner wee danc't till 3 in the morning'.[18] Chandos professed himself inconsolable when Lake died, but only a couple of months later his lawyer was drafting documents for his next marriage. Wives resembled landed estates in being possessions, and the marble monument in the local church shows Chandos standing in the costume of a noble Roman, a dead wife kneeling in tribute at either side. The third wife was still alive, but no record survives of her thoughts about the design.

Chandos's first gift to clergyman Desaguliers was the chaplaincy of that church (before the monument was erected), but both men were more interested in the palatial mansion that Chandos was building on his wife's estate. Patronage brings power, and Chandos had no qualms about ordering Desaguliers to sort out the smoking chimneys, escort his two surviving sons around the country, and take over the awkward task of firing a distinguished gardener suspected of theft. At special dinners, Desaguliers was relegated to the Chaplains' table, kept apart from Chandos's aristocratic friends and their ladies. When it came to providing advice, Desaguliers was expected to be omniscient. Chandos requisitioned him as consultant on various schemes, which included supporting the African slave trade as well as persuading an alcoholic Dutch baron to divulge his secret recipe for refining gold.

But there were compensations. In particular, Desaguliers was being paid to put Newtonian principles into action for the engineering work that he loved. With Desaguliers as his technical adviser, Chandos developed the property of his wife's family to create a hyper-extravagant edifice that was lavishly decorated by the finest artists from across Europe. In 1722, Daniel Defoe pronounced the mansion at Cannons to be the most magnificent in England: 'I venture to say that not Italy itself can show such a building rais'd from the common surface, by one private hand, and in so little time as this. The inside of this house is as glorious as the outside is fine; the lodgings are indeed most exquisitely finish'd, and if I may call it so, royally furnish'd.'[19]

A spectacular gilt statue of a gladiator stood in the gardens next to the canal: if gold chamber pots were ever made, this house would have had some (it seems that, unlike silver ones, they existed only as a satirical whim in the imagined world of Thomas More's *Utopia*). Purchases included 150 oaks for the avenue, an organ and two harpsichords, ostriches and flamingos, numerous blocks of Italian marble, 200 geese, and water closets worth around £400. The inventory of Newton's bedroom was valued at about £80, while the best bed chamber at Cannons ran to almost £2500. Yet, symbolically, Chandos's massive mansion was as ephemeral as the South Sea Bubble, vandalized after thirty-five years in a grand demolition sale to pay off family debts. Various architectural features were recycled, and its Palladian pillars still adorn the portico of the National Gallery in Trafalgar Square. Little else survives from its overblown splendour apart from the sales catalogues, the Chandos monument in the church, and the *Chandos Anthems* composed by George Handel while he was resident organist.

If Desaguliers read Defoe's account (which seems likely), he would have been especially gratified by the writer's praise of 'a large basin or fountain of water, and the coaches drive round it on either side'. Creating spectacular hydro-effects was one of Desaguliers's specialities. Admittedly, things did not always go to plan. He once unintentionally sabotaged a Thames barge full of elegant ladies and gentlemen when his underwater rockets unexpectedly leapt up right beneath them. More successful projects included designing the ornamental fountains at Cannons, and fixing a problem with pipes in Edinburgh when he was attending a Masonic event.

Even so, Desaguliers discovered that being a Newtonian entrepreneur was time-consuming and not necessarily profitable. For example, although he produced wonderfully ingenious designs for constructing large London reservoirs, many of the schemes fell through, the victims of conflicting interests, technical problems, and insufficient private funding. Chandos and other rich investors who were determined to make a business out of selling water were trying to undermine each other and needed more efficient pumping engines to reduce their expenditure on coal. Desperate to win a contract, Desaguliers even resorted to publishing an anonymous satire on one scheme, although only two months later, he switched sides to extol his former rival.[20] Unsurprisingly, proposals to divert water were contested by local residents who would lose their own source of power, while Desaguliers suffered from fines for leaking pipes and late completion (naturally, he blamed the workmen). And, of course, nobody wanted their part of town to be defiled by the large and noisy steam engines needed to lift water from one level to another.

Desaguliers was more successful with other Newtonian ventures. Anybody who has ever lived in a house heated solely by coal fires will appreciate the marketing appeal of his promise to remedy 'the usual Inconveniences of being obliged to creep near, or to sit at such a Distance from the Fire that we are either starv'd before or roasted behind'. After his improved fireplaces became popular, he was commissioned to produce one device for circulating warm air in the House of Lords, and another to freshen up the atmosphere in the crowded House of Commons. He went on to invent equipment for forcing air down mine shafts, improving the below-deck ventilation on ships, and reducing fire risks by using steam for drying inflammable materials such as gunpowder.[21]

Advertising his inventions presented a dilemma. Naturally, Desaguliers wanted to make his machines sound the most desirable, efficient, and cheapest available, but it was hard for ambitious speculators to distinguish between Desaguliers's untested yet potentially profitable schemes and others that were intrinsically unfeasible because they were based on unsound principles. He reminded potential clients of his close links with Newton, griping that 'I know five or six persons who have been taken in…even after I had told them that the Persons applying to them were ignorant Pretenders. What they lost by them, and reading this, will make them remember it.' He was particularly angry about the ignorance that led to disastrous investments in perpetual motion machines: 'These bold Undertakers, who are generally Perpetual-Motion Men, are so ignorant as not to understand the Language whereby they should be shown their Error.'[22]

Desaguliers also needed to avoid being confused with over-opportunistic opportunists and their unrealizable promises. He must have known that in *Gulliver's Travels*, Barton's friend Jonathan Swift mocked Newtonian projectors who vainly tried to extract sunbeams from cucumbers so that greenhouses could be kept warm during inclement summers. That inspiration sounds uncomfortably close to Desaguliers's 'new invented Chimneys' as recommended by Lord Chandos's gardener in his popular instruction manual: 'nothing can be contriv'd more for our Purpose of preserving Plants in the Winter from Frosts and Damps, than one of them plac'd artificially in some Part of a Green-House.'[23] Satire is at its most effective when painfully close to reality.

Liaising between investors and inventors, Desaguliers argued that Newtonian physics would improve efficiency and protect speculators from backing schemes that were bound to fail because they defied the laws of nature. Following the massive losses sustained during the South Sea Bubble, he warned wealthy opportunists against over-enthusiasm, against risking their money 'to supply boasting Engineers with it in the hopes of great Returns'.[24] Familiar with the details of Chandos's expenditures and economies, Desaguliers knew that his Edgware patron had managed to recover from his disastrous venture. Was he aware that Newton had gambled and won, but then gambled and lost?

6

The Royal Society

Beneath their former president's bust, Hogarth has included pictures of four living Royal Society Fellows.

The Duke of Richmond (the man leaning on his wife's chair) was elected not merely for his aristocratic status but also for his learning. Interested in medicine, he collected data about the success rate of the new smallpox inoculations and reported to the Society on the latest biological experiments.

Nominated by President Newton, John Conduitt was elected a Fellow about eighteen months after his marriage to Catherine Barton, although there is no record of his being a keen participant in Society business.

In contrast, Newton's patron Charles Montagu had previously been President of the Royal Society, but he does not appear in Hogarth's picture because he died about fifteen years before the children performed their play. Otherwise, he might well have been included, although in his absence his extended clan has been represented by John, the second Duke of Montagu, the blue-jacketed man furthest to the left. Like Charles, John had strong connections with both Newton and Barton, because he, too, was a Fellow of the Royal Society and a member of the Kit-Kat club. His London residence, Montagu House, became the first home of the British Museum, established by the Royal Society to care for the legacy of Sir Hans Sloane, Newton's successor as president.

Compared with those three Fellows, the fourth one shown here—Newton's experimental assistant Desaguliers—played a crucial part in the Royal Society's activities. Although half-concealed at the back of the stage, he is superintending the play—and he fulfilled an equally important behind-the-scenes role in real life. Frequently overlooked, this deceptively insignificant, liminal figure performed on several Newtonian stages.

*   *   *

Newton would never have dreamt of expressing his gratitude to Joanna Pudsey, but, like other scarcely visible women, she helped to enhance his status both before and after his death. Her uncle was a knight, but in 1712 she moved socially downwards by marrying an impoverished French Huguenot, John Theophilus Desaguliers. Her parents may well have disapproved: at that stage, they had no way of knowing that the bridegroom would later become a leading Freemason, hand-picked by Newton for Fellowship of the Royal Society. As a woman, Pudsey was excluded from those aspects of her husband's life. She did, however, have first-hand experience of helping him to earn his living.

Three years into their marriage, Desaguliers took Pudsey and their first child to live in Channel Row, a run-down area described by Jonathan Swift as 'a dirty street near the Parliament-House, Westminster'; Newton's patron Charles Montagu had once lived there, but moved out after marrying a widow with a fortune.[1] The Desaguliers couple stayed in that house for twenty-five years, until it was demolished to make way for Westminster Bridge, which— ironically or self-punitively?—Desaguliers had helped to design. By then, five of their seven children had died, and Pudsey had had enough of married life. Unusually for this period, instead of con- tinuing to suffer, she went to live on her own while he retreated to the Bedford Coffee House. Chronically short of money, he died in extreme poverty.

For a quarter-century, Pudsey's domestic duties included run- ning a residential school as well as a family. Any spare cash went on buying expensive pieces of equipment for Desaguliers's lectures and experiments on Newtonian mechanics. Knowing that audiences were impressed by dramatic displays, he tended to build large: his space-consuming bellows was eight feet wide, designed for clearing fetid air from mines and ships. When he was on one of his frequent trips away from London, either on business for Chandos or attend- ing Freemasonry meetings, she was presumably left in charge of the lodgers—and his frequent attacks of gout must inevitably have cast greater day-to-day responsibilities on to her.

One unusual visitor was disconcerted by this Newtonian house- hold—the celebrated bluestocking Elizabeth Carter, the woman who boosted Newton's reputation by translating a small popular Italian book she called *Newtonianism for the Ladies*. 'I have two or 3 times been at his House which is the strangest looking place I ever beheld & appears very much like the Abode of a Wizard,' she wrote to a friend; 'The Company that frequents it is equally singular consisting chiefly of a set of queer looking people called Philosophers... Tis well if amongst all these conjurors I do not turn Witch...'[2] She made no mention of Joanna Pudsey, the non-witch who made it possible for her husband to become Newton's leading international propagandist, and for her son Thomas to expand his father's spectacular ambitions into Russia.

Experimental Demonstrations

Arrogantly assuming a privileged status as one of God's chosen few, Newton had little interest in communicating his theories beyond a restricted academic sphere. For those outside the Royal Society, scientific knowledge became a commodity to be bought. As part of a larger shift towards commercialization, scientific experimenters and writers developed new opportunities for turning a profit, so that access to the latest discoveries depended on paying a fee to attend a public lecture or buying one of the new Science Made Easy educational books.

That Newton did become famous well beyond university walls and scholarly societies was due less to his own efforts than to the collective initiative of many disciples who energetically disseminated his ideas. The greatest enthusiasts were those who saw scientific education as a money-making opportunity, but by taking advantage of the growing market in popular science, they also helped to create it. Their tactics varied—performing experiments, devising parlour tricks, writing books for women (sub-text: if a woman can understand science, then anyone can), and designing machines. Together, they made it essential for any fashionable person to be familiar with at least a smattering of Newtonian knowledge.

In 1703, when Newton became President of the Royal Society, that process of packaging Newtonianism into commercial products had scarcely begun. So far, he had published only one major book, the *Principia*, which was written in Latin and stuffed with mathematics so complex that even academics failed to make much headway. Most Fellows of the Royal Society were even less capable of understanding it than their more learned university contemporaries. This fee-paying Society was primarily a metropolitan club for wealthy gentlemen with intellectual pretensions who appreciated some weekly entertainment. Half a century previously, Robert Hooke had been appointed as the Society's first Curator of Experiments, but by the time Newton took over, the position was held by a former draper, Francis Hauksbee. In retrospect, Hauksbee's greatest innovation was his electrical machine—an evacuated glass globe that, apparently miraculously, glowed in the dark when it was rotated between an experimenter's hands. Preoccupied at that stage with the properties of glass, Newton failed to spot one of the eighteenth century's key inventions, the device that stimulated intensive research into the powers and properties of static electricity.

Newton did, however, identify an excellent experimenter to take over the position permanently: Desaguliers. Although more highly educated than his immediate predecessors, Desaguliers was chronically short of money, which meant that Newton could rely on him to work hard and obey orders. As an added advantage, his position as Grand Master of England's Freemasons ensured valuable contacts all over Europe. Newton was so appreciative that—conforming to his role as patron—he agreed to become godfather to Desaguliers's third son, John Isaac (one of the five who died in infancy). Presumably, Newton turned up for the baptism at Desaguliers's local church, duly admired the baby and his mother, and handed over a suitable silver gift, such as an engraved mug. He could be confident that on his side of the unspoken bargain, Desaguliers would assiduously promote Newton's interests.

Justifying Newton's choice, at the Royal Society Desaguliers worked hard to make himself indispensable and to maximize his remuneration. Since he was paid for published articles, he made sure that the *Philosophical Transactions* was kept regularly supplied with his experimental reports. On top of performing demonstrations to entertain the Fellows, he sold them one of his fireplaces to remedy a smoking chimney, translated foreign documents, and installed a ventilation system to protect the dried animal and vegetable specimens in the Society's museum.

Desaguliers was not unusual in lecturing and writing about Newton, but he was uniquely placed as Newton's experimental assistant, and became the most influential of his early propagandists, both in England and abroad. Earning money was a major priority. His endeavours as an engineer, Fellow of the Royal Society, and lecturer were all oriented towards one personal goal: financial survival. From the perspective of the future, Desaguliers helped to ensure that Newtonian ideology would prevail. Fluent in English, Latin, and French, Desaguliers translated important text books, built instruments to demonstrate the principles of physics, insinuated himself into the royal court, insisted on sound scientific principles for engineering projects, and taught a high proportion of the foreign lecturers who went on to spread Newtonianism around Europe.

National politics mattered in science: although natural philosophers boasted about a European intellectual community transcending boundaries, in practice chauvinism was rife. Newton was initially slated by French critics, but by rejigging some of his key optics experiments, Desaguliers convinced them that Newton was right, and that their own hero—René Descartes—was wrong. Like many immigrants, Desaguliers was determined to prove his patriotism, and he loyally proclaimed that 'It is to Sir Isaac Newton's Application of Geometry to Philosophy, that we owe the routing of this Army of Goths and Vandals in the Philosophical World.'[3]

Presidential Power

The Royal Society was not in good shape when Newton became president in 1703. The previous two presidents—one of them Newton's patron Charles Montagu—had been elected not for their scientific prowess but because they were influential politicians. Neither of them, however, had done much beyond murmur words of encouragement, and it was the secretary, Hans Sloane, who carried out all the work. Whatever the Society's professed aspirations, by the time Newton was elected president, it was an elite institution whose membership was determined as much by social status as by intellectual ability. Newton intended to keep it that way: the Royal Society should, he insisted to Queen Anne, be housed near the government at Westminster so that it would be 'more convenient for persons of Quality'. Only applicants who passed a concealed entrance examination were allowed to join.[4]

Sloane was probably responsible for getting Newton elected as president, although Montagu may have intervened behind the scenes. There was little enthusiasm among the Fellows for this candidate who had so far shown scant interest in the Society during his seven years in London. According to a foreign visitor, he did very little during the next seven years either: 'The president, Newton, is an old man, and too much occupied as master of the mint, with his own affairs, to trouble himself much about the society.'[5] That judgement was over-harsh, but the level of intellectual discussion was not always high. Perhaps strategically, in 1705 Newton inducted the Bishop of Carlisle, who noted that the highlight of the occasion was hearing 'an Account of an extraordinary involution of the Gutts; which occasioned such an invincible Stoppage, that the patient had not a Stool in seven months before his Death.'[6] Even Newton joined in such visceral discussions, reminiscing about worms he had unearthed inside dogs' noses and kidneys.

As soon as he became president, Newton judged the Society's weak financial position to be a top priority. He and Sloane were both strong-willed, stubborn men who repeatedly antagonized one another, but they did join forces to remedy this situation. At the Mint, Newton already excelled at chasing forgers, and now he began clamping down on Royal Society defaulters. He launched legal actions to recover rents that were due on property owned by the Society, and demanded that members sign bonds to cover their annual subscription. Although this strategy succeeded financially— there was even enough spare cash for the Society to invest in South Sea bonds—it meant that membership was determined by wealth and influence as much as by scientific skills. Did Newton ever think back to 1675, when his savings had run out and his position at

Trinity seemed increasingly untenable? He had become so desperate that he begged for a subscription waiver, writing, 'For ye time draws near y^t I am to part wth my Fellowship, & as my incomes contract, I find it will be convenient that I contract my expenses.'[7] Presumably he read and dismissed similar pleas.

A second major administrative problem Newton faced was finding new premises. While Hooke was alive, the Society had been able to meet at Gresham College, where he was a professor, but the Fellows were now facing eviction. Newton approached Montagu for help, but there were limits even to his power. Christopher Wren drew up ambitious plans for a government property that the Society presumptuously assumed would be theirs free of charge, but a parliamentary committee turned down their request. Eventually, spending £110 of his own money but making himself unpopular by abruptly quashing opposition, Newton arranged for the Royal Society to buy a house in Crane Court.

Regularly presiding over meetings, Newton gradually yet systematically consolidated his hold over a Society that was wracked by internal divisions. One ally wrote obsequiously that he would like to make Newton 'Perpetual Dictator of the Society'—and that is effectively what happened.[8] Unlike his predecessors, he chaired most of the meetings himself, and also employed some dubious tactics. By marking a list of council members with an X against the names of those he wanted to replace, he successfully squeezed Sloane out of office and substituted his own ally, Edmond Halley. One of his acrimonious enemies, the Astronomer Royal John Flamsteed, reported that 'There were high and furious debates...Sr I. Newton sees now that he is understood.'[9] He was right: President Newton had made the fellows understand that he was in charge, even changing the day of the weekly meetings to suit his own diary. As council members resigned or died, he wheeled in his supporters as well as allotting greater power to himself and making the meetings more formal.

In 1714, when King George I of Hanover succeeded Queen Anne, Newton promptly enlisted the new monarch as a Fellow (Anne had been ineligible as a woman). Newton was now firmly in control and beginning to behave with quasi-regal grandiosity himself. '[T]here were no whispering, talking, nor loud laughters,' reported the Stonehenge expert William Stukeley; 'every thing was transacted with great attention, & solemnity, & decency...indeed his presence created a natural awe in the assembly.'[10] The Royal Society was a political as well as an intellectual organization, and Newton made sure that eminent statesmen and distinguished visitors from Europe were invited to join, even though—like the king—they had no obligation to attend meetings. One particular proposed candidate was refused election: Francis Williams of Jamaica. His British education was said to have been paid for by a courtier in Hogarth's painting, John Montagu, but he happened to be black, and hence—like women—lay low down the social hierarchy.[11]

Attacking Enemies

Newton was a serial slanderer: as soon as he had vanquished one opponent, he moved on to the next. Considering that he became embroiled in so many disputes, it is rather surprising that he professed to hate them. After a long gripe to Edmond Halley about Hooke's perfidious behaviour, Newton reported that he would be suppressing part of the *Principia* in the hope of avoiding controversy. 'Philosophy is such a litigious Lady,' he commented, 'that a man had as good be engaged in Law suits as have to do with her.'[12] Even so, he created many philosophical enemies over the years, although the three that he particularly loathed and yet also feared were Robert Hooke, John Flamsteed, and Gottfried Leibniz. While he lived in Cambridge, his major foe had been Hooke, who died in 1703, only a few months before Newton became President of the Royal Society. One of Newton's earliest initiatives was to donate and display his own portrait with a golden inscription proclaiming him as president. Since other Fellows were invited to join him on the walls—where they form the heart of the Society's current collection—can it just be coincidence that no picture of Hooke survives?

Whatever Newton's culpability may have been in excluding Hooke from London's painted pantheon of fame, he shamelessly took advantage of his powerful position to sabotage the next two rivals. At one stage he had enjoyed playing backgammon with Flamsteed, the first Astronomer Royal, but in 1704 long-standing coldness escalated into open confrontation. Their quarrel revolved around ownership of astronomical observations that Flamsteed had made at Greenwich Observatory, although it is difficult to work out exactly what happened because all the accounts are biased towards one side or the other. According to one interpretation, Flamsteed was a lazy, secretive, bad-tempered man who persistently refused to supply Newton with the data he needed. In contrast, Flamsteed and his supporters accused Newton of illicitly publishing the catalogue that Flamsteed had compiled at his own expense, even altering its contents.

With his long-term reputation in mind, Flamsteed was determined to produce an ambitious historical review of astronomical records. For that, he needed money to hire assistants who could complete all the calculations. Through Charles Montagu, Newton learnt that Prince George—Queen Anne's Danish husband—might be interested in financing the publication of Flamsteed's catalogue. Because he desperately wanted to get hold of Flamsteed's data, Newton welcomed that suggestion, which he felt would serve his own interests: he was preparing a second edition of the *Principia* and needed to sort out some problems with his calculations about the moon. So he took a boat down to Greenwich, and—solicitously but hypocritically—encouraged Flamsteed to contact Prince George.

Flamsteed may well have been a difficult man to deal with, but Newton does not emerge creditably from this prolonged and savage quarrel, whose complicated twists and turns are packed with invective on all sides. At first, the negotiations proceeded smoothly between the Astronomer Royal and the Prince, but then—probably with Montagu's support—Newton created an opportunity for himself to intervene by electing Prince George a Fellow of the Royal Society. That smooth manoeuvre effectively put Newton in charge of the discussions, although he judiciously sheltered himself behind a Committee of Referees packed with his own supporters. For the next four years, vindictive letters flashed back and forth.

Fixated on obtaining the most recent observations, Newton repeatedly ignored Flamsteed's protests and made sure that all his requests for funding were turned down. Leaning on Queen Anne's authority when it suited him, he arranged that Halley would print a shortened version of Flamsteed's catalogue. When this appeared in 1712, the information had been tailored to suit Newton's requirements. The preface claimed (falsely) that Flamsteed had maliciously withheld observations, and also suggested (again falsely) that Halley had been obliged to correct many mistakes. Arranging that Halley should take over some of the work but be paid more than Flamsteed, Newton systematically eliminated references to Flamsteed in his revised *Principia*, even though he had relied on Greenwich astronomical data for his crucial comet calculations.[13] By exerting his authority as president, Newton had apparently vanquished Flamsteed, but many of their colleagues disapproved of his extraordinarily dictatorial behaviour. When Montagu died in 1715, Newton lost the protection of his patron, and Flamsteed took advantage of his own contacts to obtain most of the Halley catalogues that had been printed. Throwing them on a ceremonial bonfire, he 'made a sacrifice of them to *Heavenly Truth*'.[14]

At the Royal Society, as Newton aged he became increasingly unpopular, failing to win high numbers of votes in Council elections. And when it came to key appointments in the mathematical world, the positions often went to Flamsteed's supporters rather than Newton's. Eventually, Flamsteed's full catalogue was published after his death in 1719—and that was thanks to his widow, Margaret. Although women were banned from the universities and the Royal Society, at home they regularly participated in skilled crafts such as astronomy.

Margaret Flamsteed was a well-connected lawyer's daughter who had been only 23 at the time of their wedding, just half John Flamsteed's age. Perhaps he would have liked to marry earlier, but as his official salary was a meagre £100, from which he had to pay the costs of running the Observatory, he was obliged to wait until his father died and he inherited enough money to pay off outstanding bills. Like Newton and Hooke, Flamsteed also had a young niece tucked away in his residence. Ann Heming lived in Flamsteed's quarters at Greenwich Observatory for twelve years, where she provided company and help for his wife. Flamsteed also took on male apprentices, but they had the inconvenient habit of leaving once they had been fully trained. The advantage of dependent female relatives was their obligation to remain until married. And, of course, they also took care of the domestic responsibilities.

Margaret Flamsteed turned out to be an excellent choice as bride—an entertaining hostess who made their home inside the Greenwich Observatory an attractive meeting place where plans could be hatched round the dinner table. She was a co-founder of Greenwich Girls' Charity School, which was run by an all-female committee, and served as its treasurer for fourteen years, benefiting from the mathematics she had studied at home so that she could work with her husband. Like other female recruits—often known as computers—she carried out the tedious calculations needed to convert raw observations of stars into numerical coordinates that could be entered into catalogues of the heavens. She must have been an intelligent woman: her notebooks include several pages of calculations based on Newton's mathematical techniques.

Unlike Newton, Flamsteed wrote a will before he died in 1719. Although he carefully specified that his wife, Margaret, should inherit her own jewellery, along with the silver plate that she had been responsible for keeping polished, he left her less well endowed than he had intended. Unfortunately for her, he had invested £1000 in South Sea stocks, and after the Bubble burst some months later, her inheritance plummeted in value. When his successor as Astronomer Royal arrived—Newton's ally and her enemy, Edmond Halley—she was forced to leave Greenwich Observatory. Making her situation still more difficult, Flamsteed had failed to make provision for his instruments, and she became involved in a long legal tussle over their ownership.

Even so, Margaret Flamsteed was determined to complete Flamsteed's ambitious star catalogue with the splendour he had envisaged, and she spent years compiling data, commissioning expensive maps, and campaigning against a truncated version produced by Halley. No mere assistant or downtrodden wife, Margaret Flamsteed was an enterprising woman. After she had presented a full set of her three-volume catalogue to the Bodleian Library at Oxford, she was not embarrassed to approach the vice-chancellor of the university and ask him to get rid of Halley's edition: 'I most humbly entreat You will please to order that single volume to be removed out of Your Public Library, the greatest part of which is nothing more than an Erroneous Abrigment of Mr Flamsteed's Works.'[15]

Once Flamsteed had been successfully pushed aside, Newton set about demolishing another long-term antagonist, Gottfried Leibniz. This fight was not about who owned observations but about mathematical methods: who invented calculus first? In this era before protective legislation for intellectual property rights, priority was a hotly contested matter. For material possessions, the situation was brutally clear: the first-born inherited everything. One of Hogarth's contemporaries, Arthur Devis, painted his own Newtonian conversation piece, in which a plaque of Newton looks down from the wall of a London drawing room packed with scientific objects. On one side, the father of the family and his elder son are discussing a flute, an instrument deemed improper for women to play. On the other, a girl and another boy are building a house of cards, which symbolizes the fragility of fortune: this second male child knows that the entire estate will go to his twin brother, who was born a few minutes earlier.[16]

Claiming priority was tricky. While you were still developing an idea, how could you solicit advice and advertise your ingenuity without someone else stealing it? One solution was to write the crucial part in code—and that was what Newton had done many years earlier. In 1676, he sent a long Latin letter to Henry Oldenburg, then secretary of the Royal Society, purportedly outlining the calculus technique he called fluxions, but twice using encryption to hold back vital information. 'I have preferred to conceal it thus,' he warned: '6accdæ13eff7i319n4o4qrr4s8t12ux.' A knowledgeable reader would have recognized that this anagram referred to the Latin summary of Newton's theory, but be unable to work out the precise details.[17] In the meantime, Leibniz was independently carrying out similar research of his own. Because he saw Oldenburg's letters, and also corresponded directly with Newton, he knew that Newton was working on a closely related topic. When he published a paper in 1684 announcing his own very similar technique of differentiation, he failed to mention Newton. And for the next fifteen years, nobody—including Newton and Leibniz—seems to have worried about that.

But eventually, in 1699, apparently unprompted by Newton, Fatio de Duillier decided to attack Leibniz on Newton's behalf. In the prolonged battle that followed, his allies levelled increasingly vindictive accusations of plagiarism. Newton seemed to lie low, but behind the scenes he was orchestrating some anonymous ripostes. After a particularly vicious onslaught by an Oxford professor, Leibniz eventually snapped, firing off several letters of complaint to Hans Sloane, now secretary of the Royal Society. And this is when President Newton took advantage of his position to step in visibly, setting up a supposedly objective committee that was in fact packed with his own supporters. He leant on its members heavily, telling them which letters to look at and what conclusions to draw. Reporting back to the Society only six weeks later, in April 1712, under Newton's directions they went far beyond their original brief, not only exonerating him from being offensive but also confirming that he had invented calculus first. Before the end of the year, Newton had scrutinized, rewritten, and published the report in Latin—all paid for by the Royal Society, which distributed copies around Europe. His summary in English took up over fifty pages of the *Philosophical Transactions*, also produced under the aegis of the Society.

For Newton, this was no mere academic dispute but a personal fight to the death and beyond: he was once overheard remarking (boasting?) that 'He had broke Leibnitz's Heart with his Reply to him.'[18] Long after Leibniz died in 1716, Newton went over and over the details, fine-tuning his revenge until he had covered around 500 large sheets of paper. What neither of them could ever know was that, in a sense, Leibniz became the ultimate victor. During the eighteenth century, Newton's British inheritors obeyed his injunction to follow the example of the ancient Greeks by focusing on geometrical techniques rather than algebraic manipulation. Unconstrained by this embargo, Continental mathematicians developed Leibniz's version of calculus, which became particularly important in France and provided the basis for modern analyses. Eventually, Cambridge lecturers were reluctantly pushed into teaching calculus by a pressure group of undergraduates, who demanded to be kept up to date with what was happening in Europe.

Scientific Legacies

Newton took advantage of his position as president to promote the two books for which he is now most famous—*Opticks* and the *Principia*. Although the material in *Opticks* had never previously been gathered together into a single book, it predominantly comprised Newton's earlier work, some published in academic papers, some retrieved from notebooks going back to his student years. In contrast, the *Principia* had first appeared in 1687 while Newton still lived in Cambridge; once securely ensconced at the Royal Society, he generated revisions and additions for two further editions, daring—if tentatively—to make his theological position somewhat clearer.

Newton had only been in power for three months when, in 1704, he presented the Society with the first edition of his book on optics. Murmuring appreciatively, the Fellows deputed Halley to peruse it and prepare a summary for them (so much more convenient than reading it for themselves). Although Newton had finished a longer manuscript years earlier, it had languished in storage until after the death of Hooke, who could have been guaranteed to sabotage its publication by reviving his accusations of plagiarism. Still nervous about revealing his more extreme suppositions, Newton prudently sliced off a contentious introduction and final section, concentrating instead on producing an accessible version of experiments that he had first performed decades beforehand. Although for the Fellows there was little dramatically new, Newton's 1704 English *Opticks* had a large and immediate public impact. After this initial success, he launched several further editions, gradually gaining the confidence to include some of the controversial topics he had initially suppressed.

Opticks featured three major aspects. Most obviously, it brought together Newton's pioneering research into prisms, lenses, and the nature of light, including the discoveries he had presented at the Royal Society over three decades earlier, as well as work he had carried out since. Writing in English, Newton made his delicate experimental procedures sound like common sense, almost as if the family could gather around and perform them at home. This is how he opens his description of his seminal experiment on colours in light: 'In a very dark Chamber at a round Hole about one third of an Inch broad made in the Shut of a Window I placed a Glass Prism, whereby the beam of the Sun's Light which came in at that hole might be refracted upwards towards the opposite Wall of the Chamber, and there form a coloured image of the Sun...I turned the Prism slowly, and saw the refracted Light on the Wall, or the coloured Image of the Sun first to descend and then to ascend.'[19] In practice, this deceptively straightforward account proved as transparent as flat-pack furniture assembly instructions: so many details had been concealed that French researchers found it impossible to replicate his results. Newton relied on Desaguliers to sort out the situation by travelling to Paris and explaining more thoroughly how the experimental apparatus should be set up to produce the results claimed by Newton.[20]

Newton's relaxed narrative style contributed to his second aim: launching a disguised manifesto for the English method (the only right one, naturally) of carrying out scientific research. 'My Design in this Book', he announced in his first sentence, 'is not to explain the Properties of Light by Hypotheses, but to propose and prove them by Reason and Experiments.' Unprovable conjectures or entities had no place in Newton's vision of the cosmos: he demanded facts and hard evidence. The Royal Society promoted the ideology of Francis Bacon, who taught that theories must be built up from observations with an open mind, without making prior assumptions. It has always seemed to me that the only truly Baconian observers are new-born babies, and even they rapidly build up suppositions about how their environment works. For Newton and his followers, the bottom-up empirical approach provided a powerful rhetorical contrast with the rationalism of French philosophers who—allegedly—deduced their conclusions by working downwards from first principles.

The last section of *Opticks* is very different from the rest of the book. It comprises a series of 'Quæries' added at the end of the main text, which grew in successive editions from an initial sixteen to a final thirty-one.[21] Those at the beginning of Newton's numbered list ruminate about how light might behave, but the rest range over pretty well everything, including heat, gravity, magnetic attraction, the nervous system, chemical reactions, and electricity. Rhetorically, these Newtonian soliloquies were cleverly constructed, opening with a negative question anticipating a positive answer—'Do not Bodies act upon Light at a Distance...?' or 'Do not great Bodies conserve their heat the longest...?'—that Newton could then unpack, sometimes providing his own solutions at considerable length. This conjectural format enabled Newton to smuggle in a few of the wilder speculations from his notebooks without exposing himself to too much risk: posing a question did not imply the commitment needed to state a belief, and so would make it easier for him to retract in the face of opposition.

The first seven Quæries are only one or two sentences long, but some of the later ones cover several pages. At one level, they set out experimental information that investigators followed up after his death. By citing Newton's Quæries, relatively unknown researchers could gain prestige by sheltering beneath the master's reputation— and conversely, such acts of loyalty consolidated Newton's monolithic hold over English science. For example, the clergyman Stephen Hales was inspired by Newton's observation that while mercury rises only 60 to 70 inches (150 to 180 cm) in a barometer tube, water may reach a height of over 60 feet (1830 cm). By carrying out experiments on plants, Hales developed what is now known as the cohesion theory, exploring how the water lost by evaporation from a plant's leaves can be replenished by fresh supplies rising up through small capillaries in the stems.

Newton was also concerned to defend his contested conviction that light is composed of particles, not waves. By the time he got to

Quæry 29, he had found the courage to suggest this openly: 'Are not the Rays of Light very small Bodies emitted from shining Substances?' At some length, Newton considered one of the most problematic phenomena for him to explain, the double refraction properties of Icelandic spar (now identified chemically as calcium carbonate). When you look at writing (or anything else) through its crystals, every word appears twice, one diagonally displaced above the other. His conclusion in Quæry 26 does not sound terribly convincing: 'Every Ray of Light therefore has two opposite Sides, originally endued with a Property on which the unusual Refraction depends...' Newton had several eminent opponents, but despite their strong counter-arguments, he insisted that he was right—and in the early nineteenth century, this obduracy proved embarrassing when an English Newtonian demonstrated experimentally that he had been wrong.

By far the most famous Quæries are numbers 21 and 31, both of which raise metaphysical questions about the nature of the universe that seem out of place for an experimental book on optics. In fact, Quæry 31 is a longer version of an older draft that Newton had originally intended for the *Principia*. It opens: 'Have not the small Particles of Bodies certain Powers, Virtues, or Forces, by which they act at a distance... for producing a great Part of the Phænomena of Nature?' Such action from afar has now become the familiar mantra of Newtonian cosmology. However big or small—the earth and an apple, the sun and the planets—everything in the universe attracts everything else; this attractive force is stronger for objects that are near to each other, and stronger for heavy ones than for light ones (or more accurately, those of larger mass). Immediately after this Quæry was published, Newton panicked, trying but failing to recall that entire edition of *Opticks*. Getting hold of as many copies as he could, he cut out the final section of Quæry 31, in which he asked: 'Is not infinite Space the Sensorium of a Being incorporeal, living, and intelligent...?' But as he had anticipated, Leibniz took great delight in attacking this suggestion that God is eternally present throughout the cosmos.

In contrast, Quæry 21 proposes a totally different vision of how the universe is held together. Here Newton revives the ancient

Greek notion of an omnipresent ether that swirls around in what is apparently empty space. In his tentative, questioning style, Newton rhetorically presents its nature: 'And so if any one should suppose that Æther (like our Air) may contain Particles which endeavour to recede from one another...and that its Particles are exceedingly smaller than those of Air, or even than those of Light...' His hypothetical minute ethereal particles repelled each other but attracted ordinary matter, which brought Newton the great advantage that light could be transmitted by particles of ether but would exhibit wave-like features like sound travelling through air.

In postulating a ubiquitous ether, Newton had a still more fundamental goal. He was responding to those readers of the *Principia* who deplored action at a distance through empty space. Newton's opponents regarded remote attraction as a retrograde step, as a reversion to older mystical notions that had already been successfully eliminated. One critic derided it as 'a late Notion and Assertion in Philosophy, that every thing attracts every thing, which is in effect to say, that nothing attracts any thing'.[22] Newtonian gravity might now feel obviously valid, but what is taken to be knowledge often changes—after all, it used to be an incontrovertible fact that the sun travels around the earth. Nowadays, many people are happy to accept that we live in a universe consisting mainly of empty space and criss-crossed by invisible attractive forces. But for devout eighteenth-century Christians, this belief was sacrilegious because it entailed attributing power to inherently inert matter. In their dualist cosmos, there were basically two types of entity: lifeless objects such as pieces of metal or rocks; and some sort of undefined and possibly undefinable spirit able to endow matter with agency. Whereas a billiard ball is destined to lie on the baize for ever until it is struck by a cue, people and animals have been infused with a spark of life, assumed then to come from God, enabling them to control their own movements. Denying that difference would make it possible for an extreme materialist to dispense with the concept of a spiritual, immortal soul, thus threatening the basic tenets of Christianity.

Newton had already developed a more mathematical model of an ether, but the manuscript remained unpublished until almost twenty years after his death. His followers then adopted this proposal of a ubiquitous ether that is weightless, invisible, and undetectable. However weird that imagined entity might sound, during the nineteenth century it was deemed to be so real that scientists devised experiments to demonstrate its properties. Eventually, Newton's ether faded into oblivion after Albert Einstein's relativity theory of 1905 provided a different way of explaining the universe.[23]

None of the *Opticks'* cautiously framed suggestions featured in Newton's revisions of the *Principia*. Taking advice from other scholars, including Fatio de Duillier, he had begun planning a second edition almost immediately after the original version appeared in 1687, even preparing a special copy with blank sheets bound in between the printed pages so that he could note down corrections systematically (similar to Figure 6.1). Despite frequent reminders from colleagues, he continually procrastinated, repeatedly pleading the well-worn excuse that 'just one last experiment' was needed to make it perfect. It was eventually published in 1713 as a result of commercial pressures. Newton's colleague Richard Bentley, Master of Trinity College, was searching for profitable books to rescue the ailing University Press, and he recruited a young Cambridge mathematician, Roger Cotes, to take charge. Cotes leant over Newton, ruthlessly prodding him through the corrections and refusing to accept short-cuts or approximations. Progress was at best intermittent and ground to a complete halt while Newton was absorbed in his quarrels with Leibniz and Flamsteed. Newton rewarded Cotes with an engraving of his portrait as a visionary Roman senator.

Because of Cotes's frequent interventions, substantial changes were introduced throughout the *Principia*, but many readers noticed only two additions: an opening preface by Cotes defending Newtonian action-at-a-distance, and a General Scholium (scholarly commentary) by Newton at the end. He constructed this short appendix with great care, and it includes his famous phrase

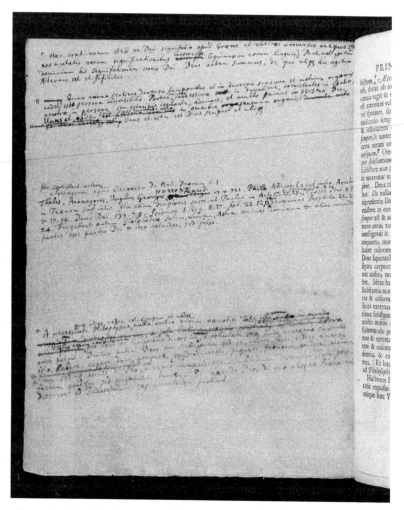

Figure 6.1 *Principia Mathematica* (1713) with hand-written additions and corrections; Isaac Newton, after 1713

hypotheses non fingo—I feign no hypotheses. This formed part of his insistence that he had no explanation for the cause of gravity, and was not prepared to make one up (a covert dig at the French). Newton was determined to keep theories as closely tied to facts as possible. Whether it concerned religion or natural philosophy, he believed that hard work was needed to control both the intellect and the imagination: just as temptation could draw a virtuous man

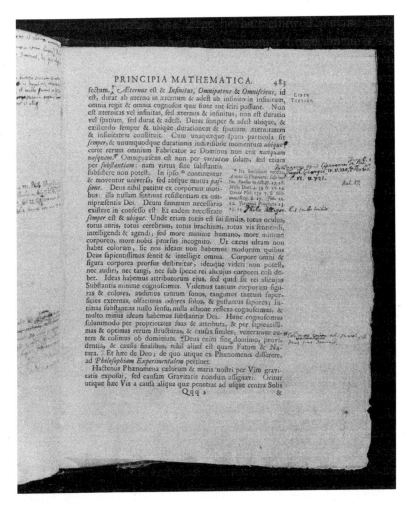

away from the straight and narrow, so, too, hypotheses could undermine his search for truth.

Based on private manuscripts compiled over many years, Newton's General Scholium was pitched at several audiences simultaneously. Even those unfamiliar with philosophical and theological subtleties would appreciate that Newton was attacking the ideas of his critics to defend his own belief that God is eternally present throughout His own creation. The General

Figure 6.2 Frontispiece of *Principia Mathematica* (1726); George Vertue after John Vanderbank, 1726

Scholium also carried concealed messages that could be accessed only by a privileged elite—for those in the know, Europe's greatest scientific treatise smuggled in a refutation of orthodox Anglican Christianity. Arguing that the orderly universe was itself testimony of God's power and independence, Newton suggested that God was defined by dominion over His servants, using terms reflecting his heretical Arian belief that Christ is not divine, but is subordinate to God.[24]

Newton began making further corrections to the *Principia* almost immediately, again ordering up a personalized copy with blank interleaved sheets for his annotations (Figure 6.1). This time the responsibility of goading Newton into completing his experiments and calculations fell to Henry Pemberton, a young medical doctor, although the revision process was carried out far less rigorously than before. The completed volume was produced in 1726, the year before Newton died. At least this time he included a proper tribute to Pemberton and rewarded him with 200 guineas (a guinea translates into £1.05, but it was always written non-decimally as 21 shillings, or £1.1s.0d.).

To make sure that this final work would preserve his memory, Newton liberally distributed luxurious presentation copies to influential colleagues at home and abroad. For the frontispiece, he chose a flattering picture of himself as an elderly scholar wearing a fitted jacket and white shirt, a tasteful costume that conformed to contemporary ideas of discreet masculine fashion for true English gentlemen (Figure 6.2).[25] Although the black-and-white printed engraving could not replicate the glowing crimson of his velvet coat, it did convey a sense of elegant dignity appropriate for the President of the Royal Society. An American visitor was not deceived. Defying the unspoken rules of Enlightenment politesse, he commented bluntly in a letter back home: 'by all those who have seen him of late, as I did, bending so much under the Load of Years as that with some difficulty he mounted the Stairs of the [Royal] Society's room. That Youthful Representation will I fear be considered rather as an object of Ridicule than Respect, & much sooner raise Pity than Esteem.'[26]

7
Hanover-upon-Thames

Distinguished from the rest of the audience by their special box, three royal children are central to Hogarth's conversation piece. From birth, they had been surrounded by family hostilities that matched the emotional intensity of the intrigues on stage. When Prince William insisted that this performance be repeated at the palace, his father may well have remembered the occasion, many years earlier, when he had cancelled his visit to watch The Indian Emperour *at the Drury Lane Theatre: his own father, George I, was conducting such a strong vendetta against him that he was concerned for the safety of any actors who dared to appear on stage in his presence.*

These three potential heirs to the throne had all been born in England, but an older Germanic brother is—as the cliché goes—conspicuous by his absence: Frederick. As the first-born son, Frederick was legally the next in line, but his parents—King George II and Queen Caroline—strongly preferred William, the boy shown here, who was fifteen years younger. These smaller siblings scarcely knew Frederick, whose family had left him behind to govern Hanover when he was only 7 years old. His mother, Princess Caroline, professed to be heart-broken, but there was little contact between mother and son for over a decade. When he did eventually rejoin his family, relationships were strained, and the royal parents continued to groom William, not Frederick, for the role of future king. While these three children were being painted by Hogarth, Frederick was living in his own separate palace, granted only a relatively meagre allowance.

Caroline never knew that her scheming failed: instead of her beloved William, it was Frederick's son who became King George III, long after her death.

* * *

Well before Queen Anne died in 1714, Newton knew that her successor would be one of the royal relatives from Hanover, selected mainly because they were Lutheran Protestants. The Hanoverian kings are not renowned for their intellectual ability, but there were some very smart women in the family. For several years, the most likely candidate as British monarch was Sophia, powerful matriarch of this extended Hanoverian family and, like Anne, a granddaughter of James I. Sophia's elder sister Elizabeth had been such an acute critic of René Descartes's theories that he dedicated his last book to her, crediting the young princess with understanding complexities that others had failed to grasp. Similarly, Sophia engaged in discussions with Newton's other main philosophical peer, Gottfried Leibniz, in a scholarly relationship that was perpetuated by her daughter Sophia Charlotte.

Admired as an unusually intelligent and well-educated woman, Sophia participated in the invisible Republic of Letters, a private correspondence network stretching across Europe. The Irish religious philosopher John Toland reported that she 'has long been admir'd by all the Learned World, as a Woman of Incomparable Knowledge in Divinity, Philosophy, History, and the Subjects of all Sorts of Books, of which she has read a prodigious quantity. She speaks five Languages...'[1] But Sophia suddenly died six weeks before Anne, and so Britain's next ruler was not her, but her son, who became George I. Even though there never was a Queen Sophia, her influence lived on. Thanks to her behind-the-throne negotiations, her grandson (who would later become George II) had already married her protégée Caroline of Ansbach, mother of the three royal children in Hogarth's picture. She, too, was an extremely clever woman—and after being transplanted to London's Hanoverian court in 1714, Caroline played a significant role in Newton's life and reputation.[2]

As Master of the Mint, Newton supervised the design and production of George I's coronation medal. He had been very keen to emphasize the Hanoverian's religious commitment, perhaps by an open Bible or a hand coming down from a cloud, but instead the final version showed a dour, fat-cheeked man being crowned by a voluptuous Britannia.[3] Newton tried to gain George's patronage by arranging to be presented at court, and by demonstrating his optical experiments to the king's long-term partner, a German aristocrat. But in general he allied himself with the next generation, the Prince and Princess of Wales, and maintained less contact with George I than he had enjoyed with either William or Anne. One difficulty was that his influential supporter Charles Montagu, the Earl of Halifax, died within a few weeks of George's accession. Moreover, throughout the thirteen years of his reign, the Hanoverian made little attempt to ingratiate himself with his new British subjects, shying away from public displays of regal splendour.

Newton and his allies welcomed George I not for himself, but because of who he was not—he was neither a Catholic nor a Stuart. Knowing little English, and speaking mainly in French, he surrounded himself with familiar Hanoverian courtiers. His court composer was yet another Hanoverian immigrant, George Handel, who had first come over to England while Queen Anne was on the throne. Following the traditional conventions of patronage, Handel had contributed pieces to her birthday festivities, and dedicated to her his new opera, *Rinaldo*, whose sensational staging featured water fountains and a flock of live birds. Herself a talented musician, Anne later granted him an annual pension of £200 as a reward. While George was still the Elector of Hanover, he had fired Handel for displaying his pro-British political allegiance, but he was now restored to favour, and arias from *Rinaldo* were performed during the coronation ceremonies.[4]

Taking up residence in St James's Palace, George I imported many—but significantly not all—members of his Hanoverian family. His wife, Sophia Dorothea, was left behind, having been despatched many years previously to near isolation in a small country village during their messy, acrimonious divorce. Although in his eyes she had sinned by conducting an adulterous affair, George did not believe in gender symmetry: his entourage included not only his father's illegitimate daughter but also three of his own, along with their mother, the Baroness Melusine von der Schulenburg. The couple never married, but lived together openly, effectively ruling as king and queen.

George I arrived with his son, and after a few weeks permitted his daughter-in-law, Caroline of Ansbach, to join her husband, accompanied by their three little girls (older than the ones in Hogarth's picture). Whatever his drawbacks or virtues as a monarch, there is no question that as a father-in-law he was insufferable. On top of separating Princess Caroline from her 7-year-old son Frederick, George I was soon embroiled in open warfare with his own son, her husband, who physically resembled the wife that he had so cruelly abandoned. He both loathed and admired Caroline: perhaps he felt threatened by this intelligent, beautiful woman? Following months of escalating enmity, the king banished George and Caroline from his court in St James's Palace, and forced their children to live with him. Eventually, they were all officially reconciled, but this rupture had a profound psychological impact that would ripple down through the royal generations.

Despite heading a dysfunctional family, when George I died of a stroke in 1727 he left behind him a stable royal dynasty with a clear line of succession. He also bequeathed a strong Whig government headed by Robert Walpole, often described as Britain's first prime minister. To mark a definitive break with his father's regime, George II indulged in a flamboyant, expensive coronation. One valid if flippant summary of this Hanoverian's long reign is this: George II spoke only broken English, was openly unfaithful to his wife, and died after drinking too much hot chocolate and collapsing in the lavatory. On the other hand, he was militarily and politically engaged in British affairs.

Most significantly, under Sophia's guidance he had had the good sense to marry Caroline of Ansbach, a shrewd and diplomatic woman who assembled around her London's leading intellectuals, including Newton. The ambitious Hanoverian princess and the elderly British knight took every opportunity to benefit from one another, and Caroline's patronage did much to boost Newton's metropolitan success.

Caroline of Ansbach (1683–1737)

From Newton's perspective, Caroline was an excellent choice as Princess of Wales. For one thing, there was no possibility of doubting her strong anti-Catholic sentiments. Before marrying

George, she had turned down a more prestigious proposal from Archduke Charles of Austria, son of the Hapsburg emperor, a star catch who was in line to become the king of Spain. But there was a cruel down-side: marrying him would entail converting to Catholicism. When this dazzling offer first arrived, Caroline had been very tempted. Orphaned at a young age, she had been brought up in various aristocratic households, but now 20 years old and with no fortune of her own, she knew that she needed to find a suitable husband. After months of private vacillation, she reneged on her initial acceptance and decided to reject the Archduke. Although she had anticipated criticism, after this agonizing period of soul-searching, she was widely praised for the sincerity of her Lutheran convictions and her independence of spirit.

Astutely playing to her strengths, as soon as she reached London Caroline began actively displaying her Protestant piety. She regularly and publicly attended church, adopted the recent tradition of religiously observing the anniversary of Charles I's death (by then described as 'martyrdom'), and dispensed charitable gifts to Christian causes. As time went by, she gradually converted her earlier refusal to marry a royal suitor into proof of her virtue: when the Bishop of London offered to discuss Anglicanism with her, she imperiously declared him 'very impertinent to suppose that I, who refus'd to be Empress for the Sake of the Protestant Religion, don't understand it fully'.[5]

Another great advantage for Caroline was her evident fertility, and she worked hard to acquire her nationwide reputation as an exemplary mother, an icon of maternal domesticity. After the uncertainties about succession during the reigns of William and Anne, she inspired confidence that the British monarchy would remain both stable and Protestant into the future. She already had four healthy children when she arrived in London, and she went on to have three more who survived—the three in Hogarth's picture. Whatever her psychological shortcomings as a mother, she ensured they were well cared for physically and was—most unusually for this period—so obsessed with hygiene that the family acquired over twenty wooden bath tubs, some with wheels for moving them from room to room.

0.1 *The Indian Emperor. Or the Conquest of Mexico. As performed in the year 1731 in Mr Conduitt's, Master of the Mint, before the Duke of Cumberland &c. Act 4, Scene 4*; William Hogarth, 1732

0.2 *Sir Isaac Newton*; Godfrey Kneller, 1702

The Hotel St. Martins Street. Leicester Fields,
Formerly the Residence of Sir Isaac Newton.
Engraved by Lacy for the European Magazine from an original drawing by Meredith.
London Published by J. Asperne, Cornhill, 1st Nov.r 1811.

1.1 *Newton's House, 35 St Martin's Street*; C. Lacy after Edward Meredith, 1811

1.2 *David Le Marchand*; Joseph Highmore, 1724

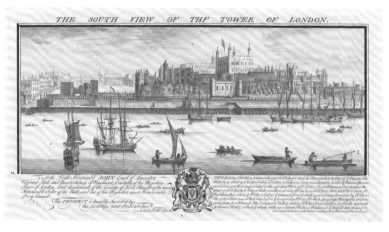

2.1 *Tower of London*; Samuel and Nathaniel Buck, 1737

2.2 *Queen Anne's coronation medal*; Isaac Newton and John Croker, 1702

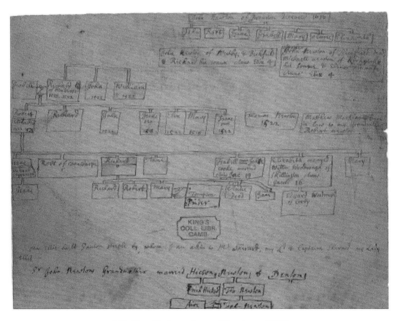

3.1 Family tree; Isaac Newton, 1705

4.1 Medal of John Conduitt; designed by Gravelot, engraved by John Sigismund Tanner, 1737

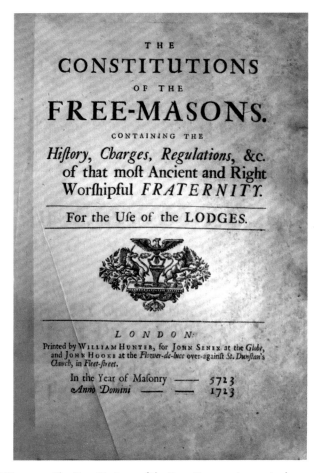

5.1 Title page, *The Constitutions of the Free-Masons*; James Anderson, 1723

5.2 Frontispiece, *The Constitutions of the Free-Masons*, 1723; engraving by John Pine

5.3 *A New & Exact Map of the Coast, Countries and Islands within ye Limits of ye South Sea Company*; Herman Moll, 1711

6.2 Frontispiece of *Principia Mathematica* (1726); George Vertue after John Vanderbank, 1726

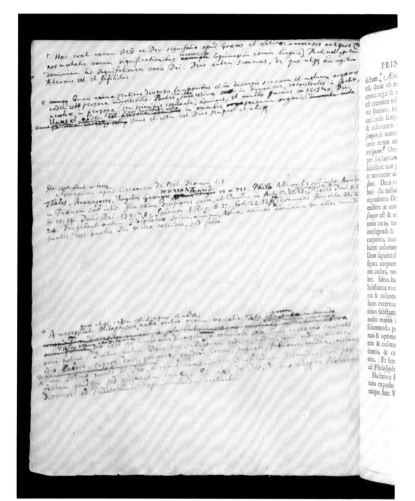

6.1 *Principia Mathematica* (1713) with hand-written additions and corrections; Isaac Newton, after 1713

sectum. ¶ *Æternus* est & *Infinitus, Omnipotens* & *Omnisciens*, id
est, durat ab æterno in æternum & adest ab infinito in infinitum,
omnia regit & omnia cognoscit quæ fiunt aut sciri possunt. Non
est æternitas vel infinitas, sed æternus & infinitus; non est duratio
vel spatium, sed durat & adest. Durat semper & adest ubique, &
existendo semper & ubique durationem & spatium, æternitatem
& infinitatem constituit. Cum unaquæque spatii particula sit
semper, & unumquodque durationis indivisibile momentum *ubique*,
certe rerum omnium Fabricator ac Dominus non erit *nunquam*
nusquam. ¶ Omnipræsens est non per *virtutem* solam, sed etiam
per *substantiam*: nam virtus sine substantia
subsistere non potest. In ipso * continentur
& moventur universa, sed absque mutua *pas-*
sione. Deus nihil patitur ex corporum moti-
bus: illa nullam sentiunt resistentiam ex om-
nipræsentia Dei. Deum summum necessario
existere in confesso est: Et eadem necessitate
semper est & *ubique*. Unde etiam totus est sui similis, totus oculus,
totus auris, totus cerebrum, totus brachium, totus vis sentiendi,
intelligendi & agendi; sed more minime humano, more minime
corporeo, more nobis prorsus incognito. Ut cæcus ideam non
habet colorum, sic nos ideam non habemus modorum quibus
Deus sapientissimus sentit & intelligit omnia. Corpore omni &
figura corporea prorsus destituitur, ideoque videri non potest,
nec audiri, nec tangi, nec sub specie rei alicujus corporei coli de-
bet. Ideas habemus attributorum ejus, sed quid sit rei alicujus
Substantia minime cognoscimus. Videmus tantum corporum figu-
ras & colores, audimus tantum sonos, tangimus tantum super-
ficies externas, olfacimus odores solos, & gustamus sapores; In-
timas substantias nullo sensu, nulla actione reflexa cognoscimus, &
multo minus ideam habemus substantiæ Dei. Hunc cognoscimus
solummodo per proprietates suas & attributa, & per sapientissi-
mas & optimas rerum structuras, & causas finales; veneramur au-
tem & colimus ob dominium. ¶ Deus enim sine dominio, provi-
dentia, & causis finalibus, nihil aliud est quam Fatum & Na-
tura. ¶ Et hæc de Deo; de quo utique ex Phænomenis disserere,
ad *Philosophiam Experimentalem* pertinet.

Hactenus Phænomena cælorum & maris nostri per Vim gravitatis exposui, sed causam Gravitatis nondum assignavi. Oritur
utique hæc Vis a causa aliqua quæ penetrat ad usque centra Solis

Qqq 2   &

* Ita sentiebant veteres:
Pythag. apud *Cicer.* de Nat.
Deor. l. 1. *Virgil. Georgic.* IV. v. 220, & *Æneid.*
VI. v. 721.
Aet. 17.
Arans in Phænom: sub ini-
tio. *Paulus* in Act. 17. 27, 28.
Moses Deut. 4. 39 & 10. 14.
David Psal. 139. 7, 8. *Solo-*
mon I Reg. 8. 27. *Job.* 22.
12, 13, 14. *Jeremiæ* Propheta 23.
23, 24. *Philo Allegor.* l. 1 sub initio.

7.1 *Caroline Wilhelmina of Brandenburg-Ansbach*; Jacopo Amigoni, 1735

8.1 'The Art of Coining', *Universal Magazine*, 1750

8.2 Gold assay plate, 1707

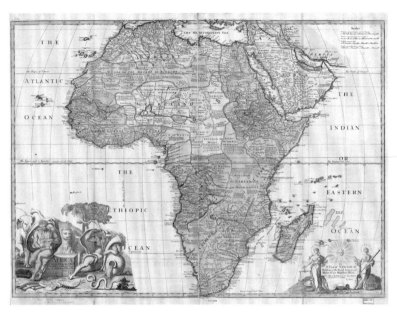

9.1 *Africa: Corrected from the Observations of the Royal Society at London and Paris*; John Senex, 1725

9.2 Company of Royal Adventurers Trading into Africa, coat of arms, 1663

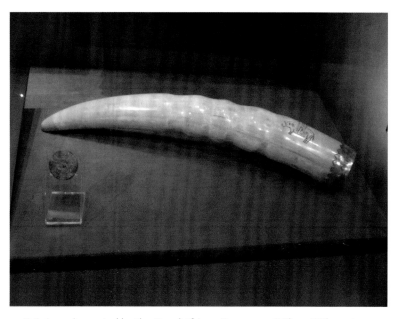

9.3 Ivory imported by the Royal African Company, 17th or 18th century

9.4 Cape Coast Castle

Quel est le droit du plus fort?.. c'est... ce qui
fait que je te mange

10.1 Newton in Senegal, 1770; from Jean Delisle de Sales, *Philosophie de la nature*, 1770

Female monarchs were regarded as being handicapped by two innate shortcomings. Their bodies were (supposedly) frail and subject to their emotions, and married queens were legally subordinate to their husbands. Elizabeth I had dealt very effectively with both those problems by emphasizing her sexual power while remaining single. Anne made it clear that she ruled over her husband, and focused on her appeal as a nursing mother, striving—but ultimately failing—to guarantee the succession. Alexander Pope wrote admiringly in the *Dunciad*, 'O! She was All a Nation could require / To satisfie its Hope, or large Desire.'[6]

Caroline surpassed these predecessors by effectively running the Court, producing seven potential heirs, and being acclaimed as a buxom beauty (Figure 7.1). Only a couple of years after Hogarth finished *The Indian Emperor*, Caroline commissioned the renowned Italian artist Jacopo Amigoni to paint her own portrait as a gift for the royal physician, Richard Mead, who treated Newton in his final years. Amigoni made a point of including putti in his pictures, and by Caroline's left foot he showed two particularly chubby cherubs holding up a cornucopia brimming over not only with flowers but also with seven baby heads. These were a tribute both to Mead's medical skills and to her own fecundity.

Amigoni's picture also includes two larger putti hovering above her head bearing a crown and a wreath to symbolize her intellectual interests. As a small child, Caroline had received only a patchy education, and her handwriting remained poor throughout her life. When she was 13 years old, she went to live with Sophia Charlotte, sister of the future George I, whom she adored and emulated. Under her tutelage, Caroline was introduced not only to the delights of dancing, theatricals, and taking snuff, but also to the conversation of leading Enlightenment scholars. One of these remained significant throughout her life: Gottfried Leibniz, who introduced her to Newtonian physics.

Although less immediately obvious as a catch than the rejected Archduke Charles, George was already third in line to the British throne when Caroline married him in 1705. Apparently he slept through the wedding sermon, but the marriage proved a great success—or perhaps it would be more accurate to say that she

Figure 7.1   *Caroline Wilhelmina of Brandenburg-Ansbach*; Jacopo Amigoni, 1735

excelled at making it run smoothly. Sophia Charlotte may have passed on Sophia's excellent advice that a marital quarrel should never escalate into a crisis—or, as she put it, 'don't make a thunderclap out of a fart.'[7] From the outside, George and Caroline appeared genuinely attached to each other, and she bore plenty of children while quietly tolerating his sexual affairs. As cynics observed both in Hanover and later in London, it was clear who was in power:

> You may strut, dapper George, but 'twill all be in vain;
> We know 'tis Queen Caroline, not you, that reign...
> Then if you would have us fall down and adore you,
> Lock up your fat spouse, as your dad did before you.[8]

For her first married decade in Hanover, Caroline had little to do except produce children and wait patiently until the older generations had died off. With prudent forethought, she began to train herself for the future that very probably lay ahead. Christened Wilhelmina Caroline, she dropped the first name, and welcomed English visitors to Hanover, who were naturally delighted to win favour by teaching her the language and serving her tea, that essential component of British life. Sycophantically, she called her first daughter Anne, although the British queen systematically rebutted such overtures from Hanoverian hopefuls.

Arriving in London soon after Anne's death, Caroline immediately began implementing Continental customs of intellectual patronage and support for the arts. An avid collector, she sought out books by the intellectual men attending her court (but was challenged by anything in Latin), as well as accumulating gifts and patronizing London booksellers. Like many immigrants, she was concerned to make herself seem more English than the English. Her protégé Desaguliers was so keen to demonstrate his new national allegiance that he declared a horse could pull the same weight as either five Englishmen or seven Frenchmen. Similarly, although Caroline never lost her heavy Germanic accent and felt more comfortable speaking in French, when she sent three of her children to watch a play by John Dryden and be painted by William Hogarth, she knew she was endorsing two prominent defenders of her adopted country's superiority.

Newton at Court

As part of her plan to embed herself within the nation's affections, Caroline strategically cultivated leading figures such as Newton, pressing him to visit her at court and consulting him about educating her children. Their mutually beneficial relationship was publicly recognized: poetic references to Caroline as a source of light who 'darts her Beams' were allusions to Newton's *Opticks*.[9] Left behind in Hanover, Leibniz became increasingly concerned by her tantalizing hints that she was being converted to Newtonian ideas. 'I am in on the experiments, and I am more and more charmed by colours,' she wrote to him; 'I can't help being a little biased in favour of the vacuum.'[10] Newton naturally encouraged her royal patronage, which helped him to promote the interests of the Royal Society and also lent him status among his colleagues. He quietly boasted about his grandiose connections by dispensing instructions to other Fellows about where and when to arrive for an official reception at court.[11]

Caroline was, remarked John Conduitt, 'the Minerva of her age'. Such patent flattery was crucial for social survival but can make it difficult to discern genuine feelings. In the first draft of his Newton memoirs, Conduitt reported that 'The Queen…frequently desired to see him, & always expressed great satisfaction in his conversation. She was graciously pleased to take part in the disputes he was engaged in during his life, & has shown a great regard for every thing that concerned his honour & memory since his death.' As Conduitt repeatedly revised his manuscript, he first added and then deleted these words: '& yet [the Queen] had the goodness in his [Newton's] later years to forbear laying her commands frequently upon him in consideration of his age'.[12] Had Conduitt simply been complimenting Caroline on her thoughtfulness? Or did he recognize that she might be bored with accommodating a doddery old man?

Newton was delighted to discover that—whether sincerely or from self-interest—Caroline manifested fascination in his chronological studies, enjoyed theological debates, and was willing to take his side in arguments with Leibniz, her Hanoverian mentor. From her perspective, her father-in-law George I and Leibniz were both obstinate, elderly men rooted in Hanoverian culture; Newton was also obstinate and elderly, but at least he was English and hovered round the court of the younger royal couple. Clearly exasperated, she reprimanded the two scholarly rivals: 'But great men are like women, who never give up their lovers except with the utmost chagrin and mortal anger. And that, gentlemen, is where your opinions have got [you] to.'[13]

Caroline was determined to ensure that her husband, George, appeared very different from his father, even though both of them were in many ways stereotypical royals. They enjoyed being soldiers, slept with other men's wives, had few intellectual interests, ate too much, and attended church out of duty rather than devotion. Both Georges were also arrogant, obstinate, and hot-tempered: when George II was angry, he kicked his wig round the room like a football. Thanks to Caroline's manoeuvres, before long she and her husband had endeared themselves to London's elite by hosting lavish and lively entertainments, while George I was publicly maligned for retreating into the security of his private rooms.

Hostilities between the two generations intensified rapidly. In July 1717, the younger couple failed to attend George I's spectacular première of Handel's *Water Musick*, played by fifty musicians in barges processing along the Thames. That November, cannon fire announced the arrival of a second royal grandson, but George I insisted on selecting the new arrival's godparents. This superficially trivial provocation had disastrous consequences. Relationships between the generations had already reached breaking point, and after several violent shouting matches, George I presented Caroline with a bleak choice: she could either follow her husband into exile from St James's Palace and her children, or she could stay behind on her own with her three little girls and the baby. An agonizing decision—but she plumped for the option of following her husband.

After her new-born son died in the king's household three months later, her father-in-law remained intransigent, making himself still more unpopular with his new subjects.

Conveniently for Newton, during their banishment the Prince and Princess of Wales set up their own court in Leicester House, very near to his home in St Martin's Street. Since George I refused to deal with anybody who visited the younger royals, by frequenting Caroline's court Newton was making a strong statement about his loyalties. Carried across in his sedan chair, he became a regular visitor at Caroline's assemblies, to which she also invited London's other literati and glitterati—Mary Wortley Montagu, John Gay, Joseph Addison, Jonathan Swift, John Evelyn—for discussions on philosophical and religious topics. By importing fashionable European salon culture, Caroline sought to gain popularity, although her plan backfired to some extent because Pope and other visitors she hoped to attract were suspicious of such overt royal patronage, and circulated scathing comments about her intellectual pretensions. Swift initially paid several visits to his 'freind [sic] her Royal Highness' but, when the anticipated royal rewards failed to materialize, he began openly criticizing her.[14] Aware that consorting with royalty brought advantages, Newton let himself be enticed.

Newton died shortly before Caroline came to the throne, and—as so often happens—promptly acquired still greater glory posthumously. She immediately set about recruiting this iconic Englishman for her own campaign to confirm her acquired national identity. First, she commissioned the Royal Mint's engraver to create commemorative medals in gold, silver, and bronze, priced at three levels to suit different budgets; three years later, she included Newton's bust with those of other national heroes inside a fashionably whimsical retreat designed by William Kent, the architect who planned Conduitt's monument to Newton in Westminster Abbey. Located in what is now Kew Gardens, this pseudo-ancient Hermitage nestled among rocks and shrubbery at the end of a tree-lined walk; adding to the conceit, she even installed a resident poet. Inside, the main room was an octagonal chamber with niches eventually holding the marble heads of five men—including Newton—described in a newspaper as 'the glory of their country: they stampt a dignity on human nature: they were all well-skill'd in those arts which naturally tend to improve and exalt the mind, mend the heart, or reform the life.'[15]

If only Newton had still been alive to bask in the glory! Later demolished by Capability Brown, this building advertised Caroline's intellectual credentials. Perhaps more importantly for her, she was lauded for abandoning Leibniz, her former friend from Hanover, and instead installing Newton. If she happened to read this adulation from a journalist, she would have felt a flush of achievement: 'she built herself a Temple in the Hearts of the People of England.'[16] On the other hand, by then she had lost control over the vengeful pen of Jonathan Swift. Sceptically comparing her to Louis XIV of France, the Sun King who bolstered his prestige by dispensing munificent patronage, Swift accused Caroline of economizing by commemorating the dead instead of supporting the living needy (he was, of course, thinking of himself):

> Lewis the living genious fed,
> And raised the Scientific Head;
> Our Q—, more frugal of her Meat
> Raises those heads which cannot eat.[17]

Theological Differences

Newton's first three marble companions inside Caroline's Hermitage were British philosophers renowned at the time, if not now, for their engagement in theological debates—Samuel Clarke, John Locke, and William Wollaston. The prominent central niche, decorated with a sunburst of golden rays, was later occupied by Robert Boyle, whose painted portrait dominated Caroline's picture gallery. Although Newton and Boyle are today celebrated as scientific pioneers, it was their religious commitment that prompted Caroline to award them a place in her hall of fame. In his will, Boyle had left money to fund eight church sermons a year, with the intention of consolidating the links between traditional Christianity and the latest innovations in natural philosophy. Many of these lectures reinforced Newtonianism by making it compatible with the teachings of the scriptures. Naturally, Newton was a keen supporter of this initiative.[18]

Caroline enjoyed dramatic Newtonian demonstrations, and she splashed out on expensive instruments later put on display in the Queen's Gallery at Kensington Palace, notably a large orrery whose internal clockwork rotated to display the movements of the planets. But when it came to serious salon conversation, she preferred to focus on religion. Her personal copy of Kneller's 1689 Newton portrait showed him not with a telescope or a prism, but with the biblical Book of Daniel, to which he devoted great attention in the final decade of his life; this picture was, she declared, one of her favourite possessions. According to Conduitt (presumably choosing to gloss over the fracas with Conti), Newton had 'often had the honour to hear Her Majesty say before the whole circle, that she kept the abstract of Chronology Sr Isaac gave her written in his own hand among her choicest treasures & that she thought it a happiness to have lived at the same time, & have known so great a man.'[19]

Caroline's interest stemmed from her former life in Hanover, when, as well as wrestling with the distinctions between Catholicism and Lutheranism, she had become preoccupied with the difficulty of explaining how a benevolent, perfect God can tolerate the existence of evil and suffering. She often discussed this thorny problem with Leibniz, who was such an expert that he even invented the topic's formal label—theodicy—for the title of his 1710 book, which he wrote in French, the international language among scholars and aristocrats.

Leibniz never married, but three powerful women played crucial roles in his scholarly life and reputation. The first was Sophia (mother of George I), followed by her daughter Sophia Charlotte (Prussia's first queen), and then finally Caroline, the aristocratic orphan the older women took into their care. While Sophia was still alive, Leibniz tried to bolster his insecure position in the Hanoverian court through Sophia, who recommended him to her influential friends. Their bond turned out to be far stronger than a conventional patronage arrangement: they exchanged over 300 letters, which reveal not only her support but also their shared interest in philosophical debate (they also swapped snippets of gossip they thought might come in handy). In his position as the Elector's librarian, Leibniz travelled around Europe collecting information for his history of the royal family, an unwelcome task he never completed, mournfully comparing himself to King Sisyphus, who was eternally condemned to push a boulder up a hill and watch it roll down again just before reaching the top.

From the next generation, Sophia Charlotte also proved a loyal and influential patron. After persuading her husband, the king of Prussia, to found a scientific academy, she made sure that Leibniz was appointed as its first president. More confrontational than her mother, she often invited Leibniz to stay at her palace, where she continually pushed and probed further on theological questions, forcing him to clarify his thoughts. After she died suddenly— poisoned, according to the rumours—Leibniz retreated into depression, repeatedly recycling their conversations in his head. Eventually, he hauled himself together by converting them into his book on theodicy, the only one he ever published.[20]

By then, Caroline had moved to Hanover, but she had first met Leibniz in 1703, when she was living in Berlin with Sophia Charlotte. Confronted with the possibility of marrying Archduke Charles, it was to Leibniz that Caroline turned for advice about converting to Catholicism. After she left for London in 1714, Leibniz hoped for a strong ally right inside the English court, although he soon felt that her loyalty was fading under Newton's influence. Where Handel had succeeded, Leibniz failed. He did visit London, but George I despatched him back to his job as the Elector's librarian, a dismissal that suited Newton perfectly. It was very much in his interests to keep Leibniz out of this transplanted Hanoverian court next to the Thames so that he could maintain his own supremacy as the royal scientific expert.

When Caroline tried to find an English translator for Leibniz's *Théodicée*, she was introduced to one of Britain's leading theologians, Dr Samuel Clarke, and he soon became a regular visitor to her court. A clergyman and former Boyle lecturer, Clarke held unorthodox views about the Trinity and leaned towards Arianism—so in some ways he resembled Newton, although less extreme and more diplomatic. Unusually, he understood the *Principia* so well that he could debate its metaphysical concepts with Newton himself. Clarke belongs on the very short list of people who could be described as Newton's close friends—although 'paid acolyte' might be a better label, since Newton rewarded him with £500 for translating *Opticks* into Latin.

While Princess Caroline was debating theology in her correspondence with Leibniz, she was also engaged in conversations with Newton and Clarke. In 1715, puzzling over her beliefs, she wrote to ask Leibniz for advice about a point in Clarke's theology, a step that launched five rounds of angry letters between the two men. Acting as intermediary, Caroline did far more than just watch from the sidelines: she monitored the exchange and influenced its conduct. Newton realized that he had an excellent opportunity for pursuing his vindictive quarrel with Leibniz while staying out of the direct line of fire. As soon as an answer arrived from Hanover, Caroline would send it round to Newton for consideration, and she also invited Newton to visit her privately with Clarke.

Torn between loyalty to Leibniz, her protector in Hanover, and her desire to cultivate his arch-rival, Newton, Caroline knew that any association with the British hero would help her broader project of endearing herself to her future subjects. Sensitive to her internal tussle, Leibniz watched sadly as she slipped away from his side to fall under the influence of Newton, Clarke, and their allies. The exchange came to an end when Leibniz died, and soon Clarke published an annotated, pro-Newtonian version of the entire correspondence. Effectively a piece of propaganda, this book greatly boosted Newton's reputation. Many people assumed that Newton was the sole author of Clarke's replies, whereas this was a joint production in which Caroline had played a crucial role while Newton remained concealed back-stage.[21]

God, government, and the cosmos were inextricably tied together, so that, as Leibniz commented, the quarrel was not only a personal one between him and Newton but also a national one between Germany and Britain. It was impossible to disentangle metaphysical controversies from political differences, whether concerning Newton *v* Leibniz, or the Tories *v* the Whigs, or the French *v* the English, or non-Conformists *v* Anglicans *v* Catholics. Because the central question concerned God's involvement in the cosmos, the debates resonated across Europe. As Newton saw it, God and the universe are inseparable: God constantly intervenes in its operation and somehow (a one-word euphemism that here stands in for reams of scholarly exegesis) pervades the whole of space and time. Leibniz (and many others) found that view impossible to accept, partly because it is hard to understand how a purely spiritual being such as God can interact with material, worldly objects that are inherently lifeless. Ostensibly attacking Clarke, but really aiming at Newton, in his first response to Caroline Leibniz delivered a beautifully formulated but insulting challenge: 'Sir Isaac Newton, and his followers, have also a very odd opinion concerning the work of God. According to their doctrine, God Almighty wants to wind up his watch from time to time: otherwise it would cease to move. He had not, it seems, sufficient foresight to make it a perpetual motion.'[22]

Leibniz was referring to the familiar image of a clockwork universe, which—like all metaphors—operated in two directions. The first cathedral clocks were constructed not primarily to tell the time, but more to advertise God's splendour in creating a universe with steadily circulating planets. Reciprocally, natural philosophers designed theoretical models in which planets circulated with the mechanical regularity characterizing an accurate clock. Leibniz was only too aware that, in real life, machines are intrinsically imperfect, that ordinary clocks break down and have to be repaired. During any time left over from arguing with Newton and fulfilling his library responsibilities, Leibniz was struggling with the physical problems of constructing an arithmetical calculator. As his assistant kept purloining parts to mend a clock, Leibniz despaired of ever getting his machine to work properly.

While he accepted the imperfections of human-made instru-ments, Leibniz judged it sacrilegious to imply that God could not design the eternally rotating cog-wheels he so longed to create for himself. By building his calculator from clock components that his assistant so annoyingly appropriated, Leibniz was following standard practice in a culture that relied on renewal. Materials were constantly being used over and over again to repair what was broken or had worn out, and to supply what was needed for making something new. Recycling was so ingrained that the word had not been invented, and the concept permeates Newton's life and cosmos. He ordered that old coins be melted down to make new ones; he converted a child's toy into an experimental prism; he economically used the heat from horse dung to warm his alchemical crucibles. Contemplating the earth, Newton envisaged a repetitive cycle of terrestrial airs ascending and turning into aether before tumbling down again for reconversion, speculating that the world resembles 'a great animall or rather inanimate vegetable, draws in aethereall breath for its dayly refreshment & vitall ferment & transpires again wth grosse exhaltations'. Extending that notion of constant circulation to the entire universe, he suggested that comet tails consist of vegetative matter, as if they were energy-laden repair kits sent in by God to correct gravitational discrepancies.[23]

Leibniz accused Newton of positing a fallible God who had created an imperfect universe, but there were advantages to a God who is immanent throughout the universe and can affect how it operates. A truly clockwork universe, one that never needs adjustment, is ordained to rotate for ever, but in principle such determinism precludes the possibility of free will. Newtonians argued that a perfect God who is worshipped from afar is like a human sovereign who rules with total authority and denies freedom to his subjects. The liberty of the people depends on having a wise and loving ruler whose interests coincide with their own—a resident God, as it were—so that any decisions are mutually advantageous.

Both men were poker-faced players in the international game of patronage. While Newton stayed out of sight in his house near Leicester Square, Leibniz tried to exert action-at-a-distance from Hanover by reminding Caroline that he intended to dedicate the English translation of *Théodicée* to her. More ambitiously, Leibniz hoped to unite several different non-Catholic sects and, as one of his tactics, he bracketed together Locke, Newton, and Clarke, accusing them of following a heretical creed called Socinianism.

These three men found themselves ranked together in Caroline's Hermitage, her demonstration of Anglo-Hanoverian loyalty to Great Britain. As the editor of the *Free Briton* rejoiced, 'not even her own Leibnitz is allowed a place there'.[24]

Desaguliers and the Royal Family

While he was working on his large picture for Conduitt, Hogarth was given permission to paint the royal family, although the commission was cancelled after he had completed only two oil sketches, which are essentially identical.[25] The more finished of these, still in the Royal Collection, shows George II and Queen Caroline supposedly relaxing with all seven of their children next to an ersatz temple in the gardens at Richmond. The project may well have been prematurely cancelled because Hogarth's design painfully reveals the rifts ripping the family apart: if this outdoor conversation piece had been made public, it would only have emphasized the absence of polite Enlightenment communication amongst the royals. In the front, the two youngest girls are teaching tricks to a spaniel, while their parents sit apart from them on an ornate throne, gazing out into the middle distance. Close to the king stands a small ungainly boy—William, the favourite child—formally dressed as a miniature adult and apparently protecting them all with his outstretched sword. Far over on the other side of the picture stands Frederick, the outcast technically due to inherit the throne but separated from his parents by the next three daughters.

As girls, Frederick's five sisters represented a burden that had either to be supported for life, or else negotiated over until a sufficiently rich and influential husband could be persuaded to assume responsibility for them. In a grand climax to many stormy, tearful rows, the oldest—Anne—declared she would rather marry a baboon than stay with her parents, and after a sumptuous wedding she disappeared to Holland. The other two older siblings remained trapped in the stultifying daily routine of silk embroidery, demure walks, and mild gambling over card-games; succumbing to ill-health and parental obstinacy, they never escaped into even an unhappy marriage. Of the two little ones in Hogarth's picture, Louisa became very popular as Queen of Norway and Denmark, but died in her twenties of horrific complications resulting from repeated childbirth. Her slightly older sister, Mary, soon moved in to look after the babies, delighted to be freed from an abusive marriage and determined to stay away from England.

When she was their age, Queen Caroline had been forced to obey her father-in-law's diktat that Frederick should be left behind in Hanover. For over two decades, this first son was spurned by both parents as if they were somehow obliging him to re-enact their own painful childhood experiences. Caroline was an orphan, and George II probably never saw his divorced exiled mother after he was 11 years old; similarly, Frederick was forced to live in a different country from Caroline for fourteen years. There are no surviving letters between them, and he was not invited to his parents' coronation in 1727—and another full year went by before they grudgingly offered him a cool reception in London. Courtiers found Frederick to be very different from George II—artistic, shy, and withdrawn, with no inclination towards military activities (although he did like women and gambling). In London, he moved into his own residence at Kew, and after a few years of contact and public displays of unity, relationships broke down more or less completely. One possibility is that he was not really their son: at his birth, rumours circulated that the healthy boy of a Turkish footman had been secretly substituted for a sickly royal girl.

Caroline and Frederick did, however, share an interest in Newtonianism, and Desaguliers slipped in and out of both households as he searched for patronage. His first official commission seems to have been to lecture at Hampton Court in 1717, shortly before the two generations of Georges became estranged.[26] Perhaps hoping to alleviate the family tensions, Desaguliers entertained the royals with spectacular experiments designed to impress as much as to educate. Typical items in the repertoire of such scientific salon performances were (literally) shocking spectators with an electrical machine, displaying large clockwork models of the planets revolving around the sun, and silencing a ringing bell inside a glass dome by sucking out the air. His presentations must have gone down well, because he successfully persuaded the Prince and Princess of Wales to join George I in subscribing to his influential book on Newtonian physics.

Desaguliers knew that his major royal prospect for obtaining funds was Caroline. It is impossible to be sure how many times he actually met her, because those seeking patronage had few qualms about exaggerating the significance of minor events. Taking every opportunity to demonstrate his allegiance, Desaguliers even made public their shared birthday of 1st March—such a bore, he remarked, having to wait an extra day every leap year—and possibly it was under his influence that she donated some communion plate to a Huguenot church in Westminster. To celebrate George II's coronation, he organized a firework display at Edgware, near the estate of Lord Chandos, when 'all the Inhabitants of the Town rode out with Trumpets and Musick... the Reverend Doctor Desaguliers at their Head, who play'd off a very handsome firework at Night, to conclude the Rejoicings.'[27]

Desaguliers could hardly have expected Caroline to hear about his Edgware performance, but as part of his bid to secure her continued support, the following year he published a long allegorical poem that flatteringly likened the enlightened new monarchs to the powerful sun at the centre of a Newtonian universe. In *The Newtonian System of the World, the best Model of Government*, he portrayed the royal couple as liberated rulers radiating love. As well as being self-serving, Desaguliers's poem was simultaneously scientific and theological and political, those three inseparable strands that threaded through so many texts of the time. Implicitly contrasting the British model of government with top-down regimes, Desaguliers praised the king and queen for guiding rather than controlling the freely moving citizens of a democratic society.

> That *Sol* self-pois'd in *Aether* does reside,
> And thence exerts his Virtue far and wide;
> Like Ministers attending e'ery Glance,
> Six Worlds sweep round his Throne in Mystick Dance.
> He turns their Motion from its devious Course,
> And bends their Orbits by Attractive Force;

His Pow'r, coerc'd by Laws, still leaves them free,
Directs, but not Destroys, their Liberty...
ATTRACTION now in all the Realm is seen
To bless the Reign of GEORGE and CAROLINE.[28]

Desaguliers's poem was published belatedly in 1728, the year after the coronation, because he insisted on completing copious astronomical explanations to accompany it. When Frederick was at last recalled from exile in Hanover, Desaguliers began cultivating this new source of royal patronage. Formally, he was employed as one of Frederick's chaplains, but by the time Caroline died in 1737, he had ingratiated himself sufficiently well to become an established member of Frederick's household at Kew, helping him to soak up the long, idle hours by teaching him natural philosophy. During the mourning period for his mother, reported a lady-in-waiting, 'The Prince lives retired, seeing no company. We have a new amusement here, which is both very entertaining and instructive. Dr Desaguliers has a large room fitted up at the top of the house, where he has all his mathematical and mechanical instruments at one end and a Planetarium at the other... The Doctor reads lectures every day which the Prince attends diligently.'[29]

By aligning himself with Frederick, Desaguliers alienated himself from George II. But when Frederick's son became George III, he inherited his father's instrument collection—now preserved in London's Science Museum—and remained interested in science throughout his reign. Newton and Desaguliers both set out to further their own immediate interests, but by picking such powerful royal patrons, they also influenced the sciences of the future.

ACT III

THE PLAY

ISAAC NEWTON AND ENGLISH IMPERIALISM

Restoration playwrights jettisoned melodramatic heroes to create more realistic, complex characters whose failings laid bare the underlying nature of human life; like William Hogarth's paintings, the mirror world of the stage reflected realities of human existence and held them up for inspection. First performed in 1665, John Dryden's The Indian Emperour *remained a perennial favourite for decades, even though literary critics delighted in identifying grammatical slips and dramatic shortcomings.*[1]

Restoration theatre was political theatre, and this story about love, honour, and the Spanish conquest of the Aztec Empire was also a commentary on current affairs—the splendour of the royal court, England's commercial and territorial battles against Dutch rivals, the decline and fall of once-mighty empires. Lacking accurate knowledge, and conflating various interpretations of 'Indian', theatrical designers applied Eastern stereotypes to depict American peoples with little concern for verisimilitude. Early productions featured the king's lover Nell Gwyn (not one of her best performances, according to Samuel Pepys) as well as an exuberant feathered coat from Surinam contributed by the playwright Aphra Behn.[2]

Even if later repeats were less exotic, the script included sufficient plot twists, musical interludes, and macabre incantations to grip generations of spectators. By the time of its performance in Conduitt's drawing room, Dryden's play seemed rather old-fashioned. Restoration drama was being increasingly parodied, and that year Henry Fielding's Tragedy of Tragedies *opened, watched by two older* sisters of the small royal children shown here. Fielding's play—published with a frontispiece by Hogarth—satirized Dryden's poetic style and addressed more modern themes by mocking women as ferocious consumers both of commercial products and male suitors.[3]

Yet, politically reinterpreted, The Indian Emperour had become freshly relevant in the early eighteenth century, when the South Sea Company was promising huge rewards from trading in the southern Americas. In its first four lines, some Spaniards arrive on the Central American coast. Setting out their plans to conquer the land and its riches, they marvel at the unspoilt abundance lying around them, an obvious parallel to the lucrative opportunities for British adventurers in Africa and other distant parts of the globe:

> On what new happy Climate are we thrown,
> So long kept secret, and so lately known;
> As if our old world modestly withdrew,
> And here in private had brought forth a new?[4]

Playing fast and loose with the historical facts, Dryden's convoluted plot explores the tussles for power between the Mexican emperor Montezuma, an equally fictionalized version of the Spanish conqueror Hernán Cortés, an anachronistic Francisco Pizarro, and some largely imaginary subsidiary protagonists. Basically, all the key characters are in love with and/or loved by two people, but not always recipro-cally. Few of them come out of it well. Montezuma commits suicide rather than receive Spanish charity, Cortez follows the flawed orders of his distant king, and the Indian princess Almeria stabs both herself and her rival for Cortez's heart. The details of these conflicts are less important than the moral dilemmas confronted by the characters, who are repeatedly forced to choose between honour, love, and lib-erty—ideals as important in Conduitt's time as in Dryden's.

As its name suggests, The Indian Emperour is permeated with what now seem to be racial slurs and stereotypes of indigenous peoples, although it was then standard to regard non-Europeans as primitive. Even so, at times Dryden's Indians display high moral standards and theological sensitivity, while the major villain of the piece is ruthless, rapacious Pizarro. In Cortez, Dryden presents an appealing hero who honourably subordinates his own desires to the greater interests of king and country. In comparison with Pizarro and the other Spanish characters, he is civil and magnanimous, innocent of the horrendous torture that is imposed by a Roman Catholic priest.

Following French fashions, to explore his imperial and religious themes, Dryden decided to compose a poetic tragedy in heroic couplets. During the eighteenth century, these pairs of rhyming lines in iambic pentameter (five stressed syllables) became a particular favourite for English poets. This typical example is spoken by Montezuma, who (in contrast with the European invaders) insists that he places less importance on being the Emperor of Mexico than on his love for Almeria, daughter of the late Indian queen:

> But of my Crown thou too much care do'st take,
> That which I value more, my Love's at stake.[5]

While the younger children in Conduitt's living room could relish the rapid twists and turns of fortune, the older ones might have contemplated the moral questions being posed. Should a leader surrender or let his people starve? Should a young woman save the life of the brother she loves by agreeing to marry the one she loathes? Is it better to die for your country or to marry the person you love? Should you kill the person who deserts you for somebody else? How can a woman revenge herself on the ardent older suitor who killed her mother? These were extreme versions of dilemmas encountered by young British aristocrats in their lives outside this temporary theatre.

Revered as a great national poet, Dryden composed a feel-good play for English audiences, although his rivals criticized him for exaggerating New World wildness. 'This Zany of Columbus', wrote the poet Richard Leigh, 'has discover'd a Poeticall World of greater extent than the Naturall, peopled with Atlantick Colony's of notional creatures.' By deliberately emphasizing South America's exoticism, Dryden strengthened his exposure of Spanish barbarism and cruelty. The play opens with an Aztec mass sacrifice, but that takes place discreetly off-stage; in contrast, the final act directly confronts the audience with *a horrific spectacle of Montezuma being stretched on a Spanish rack by a relentless Catholic priest. Leigh regretted that Dryden's heroes were 'more lawless than their Savages,' but that was one of the playwright's aims. By making the Spaniards appear as uncivilized as the Aztecs, he flattered his English audiences, who could feel cultured and honourable. No English people appear on the stage, an absence implying their refusal to participate in such depravity. After watching this play, Conduitt and his colleagues could vaunt themselves as intrinsically superior.*[6]

Dryden excelled at making the English look special. A couple of years after The Indian Emperour *first appeared, he published the long poem—1216 lines—that made him famous:* Annus Mirabilis *or* The Year of Wonders, *which endorsed mercantile capitalist expansion and predicted a prosperous future for England under a strong monarch. Following the twin scourges of the Plague and the Great Fire, London would, he optimistically predicted, become the centre of global trade:*

> Now, like a Maiden Queen, she will behold,
> From her high Turrets, hourly Sutors come;
> The East with Incense, and the West with Gold,
> Will stand, like Suppliants, to receive her doom.[7]

By the time his imperial drama was performed in Conduitt's drawing room almost seventy years later, Dryden's ambitious dream was in the process of being realized. European leaders had split the world into three areas to colonize, exploit, and fight over: Asia, the Americas, and Africa. For Conduitt's chauvinistic friends, the metropolis was the lynchpin not only of Great Britain but also of the entire globe. By commissioning Hogarth to paint The Indian Emperour, *Conduitt was advertising his pride in being British and also his loyalty to the Whig ideals he shared with Newton and the government.*

The Whig buzzword 'liberty' appears throughout the play and becomes crucial towards the end, when Alibech proudly rejects Cortez's offer of power—'Our Liberty's the only gift we chuse,' she declares.[8] *Yet freedom is a problematic ideal. 'The word Liberty', commented one eighteenth-century theatregoer at another play, 'never failes of a Whigg Clap but more especially in one Place where Cato laments the Loss of Rome & Liberty more than that of his son who lyes dead before him.*[9] British liberty could also be interpreted by Whig merchants as the freedom to pursue profit for their own benefit, regardless of the consequences to others.

The Whigs that Newton helped put in power aspired not to global harmony but to British supremacy, openly embracing slavery in the interests of commercial profit. Queen Anne scored a diplomatic coup by signing the Treaty of Utrecht, which included a political sweetener transferring trading rights from the French to the British in the Americas. As she explained, the 'Contract for furnishing the Spanish West-Indies with Negroes shall be made with Us for the Term of Thirty Years, in the same manner as it hath been enjoyed by the French for Ten Years past.' Thomas Tickell—the poet whose party loyalty earned him the nickname 'Whigissimus' (the most Whiggish), succinctly (if not very elegantly) summarized his party's attitudes:

> Fearless our Merchant now may fetch his Gain,
> And roam securely o'er the boundless Main.[10]

8
Making Money

When the royal children and their aristocratic elders watched the performance in Conduitt's drawing room, Dryden's play was almost seventy years old, but it reiterated a familiar fantasy—that inexhaustible supplies of gold lay across the oceans waiting to be discovered by European adventurers. In the opening scene, Vasquez expresses the collective wonder of the Spanish travellers:

> Methinks, we walk in dreams on fairy Land,
> Where golden Ore lies mixt with common sand;[1]

Like Englishmen arriving on the coast of West Africa, the intruders assume that God has given them—privileged Europeans—the right to take whatever they desire from countries that are waiting to be possessed, despite being already inhabited:

> Heaven from all ages wisely did provide
> This wealth, and for the bravest Nation hide,
> Who, with four hundred foot and forty horse,
> Dare boldly go a New found World to force.[2]

Dryden gives Vasquez the lines of an arrogant colonialist perceiving a Primitive Other:

> No useful arts have yet found footing here,
> But all untaught and savage does appear.

Cortez is rather more sophisticated. For him, the Indians are indeed different, but they possess the innate nobility of those who have not yet been corrupted by civilization:

> Wild and untaught are Terms which we alone
> Invent, for fashions differing from our own:
> For all their Customs are by Nature wrought,
> But we, by Art, unteach what Nature taught.[3]

Conduitt's guests watched this scene only a decade after Newton and other unwary British investors had poured money into the South Sea Company, which predicted great dividends from exploiting the southern Americas. That scheme's failure did little to dampen expectations. Attention now focused on Africa, whose natural resources—people, minerals, ivory—circulated around the globe in a triangular trading loop that promised to produce endless profit for wealthy Londoners.

That concept of perpetual productivity was appealing and metaphorically familiar. Faith in paper money relied on believing that wealth can always be generated, resembling the machinery of Newton's cosmos that never winds down but is maintained in constant motion by God. At the Mint, Newton recycled old coins into new ones, a continuous process that the economist Adam Smith deemed 'somewhat like the web of Penelope; the work that was done in the day was undone in the night. The Mint was employed not so much in making daily additions to the coin as in replacing the very best part of it which was daily melted down.'[4] Nicholas Barbon, the ruthless entrepreneur who grew rich from shoddy housing schemes, maintained that 'the Stock of a Nation [is] infinite, and can never be consumed; For what is Infinite, can neither receive Addition by Parsimony, nor suffer Diminution by Prodigality.'[5]

The spectators in Conduitt's drawing room could also interpret Dryden's play to confirm their chauvinistic prejudices about British superiority over the lazy and imprudent Spaniards. Landing in the southern Americas, they had seized the precious ores that were readily available and then spent the profits. In contrast, British imperialists congratulated themselves on not simply grabbing the gold but behaving industriously and sensibly by improving natural resources. Governed by what Max Weber much later termed the Protestant work ethic, they concentrated on getting rich through virtuous labour. In the northern Americas, which lacked valuable minerals, settlers developed their new territory's agricultural potential. Similarly, astute *financiers with global ambitions maximized the benefits of African gold by using it to boost Britain's flagging economy.*

* * *

In June 1696, a couple of months after Newton arrived at the Mint, two men in a draper's shop on London Bridge embarked on one of those familiar conversations about everything in the country going downhill. A customer, Robert Morgan, began moaning about the widespread economic hardship that he—like many others—attributed to the Glorious Revolution. Coins were in short supply, he complained, and he only had a few old clipped shillings in his pocket. 'Was not the tradeing better when King James was here than now?' he demanded of Edmund Baker, the apprentice behind the counter. '[T]hen our Lives must have paid for it', replied Baker, who rated freedom from royal tyranny higher than wealth. But 'our Livelyhoods & Lives goes now,' grumbled Morgan, who suspected that the new government had ruined trade while establishing networks of spies and informers to stifle opposition.[6]

Newton would have sided with Baker in this argument, but Morgan did have a point: those who had already been poor were suffering more than the wealthy. After a relatively prosperous and peaceful era under the Stuarts, the new government had begun imposing heavier taxes to replenish the nation's depleted coffers and finance a series of expensive wars. In addition, poor harvests were causing food shortages, immigrants were being blamed for unemployment, and chaotic attempts to reform the currency had precipitated a financial crisis that resulted in many wages being stopped. Money, tax, and trade became the three buzzwords that dominated coffee-house conversations and journal articles. This was the situation that Newton inherited at the Mint and spent the following three decades trying to sort out.

Newton's long-term economic influence was significant globally as well as nationally. During his lifetime, heading the Mint was a government appointment that commanded more wealth, prestige, and influence than any of his scholarly activities. How else could he have met Czar Peter of Russia? Newton was responsible for manufacturing coins efficiently and accurately, but he also monitored the country's economy, taking on a role somewhat comparable to governing the Bank of England today. Benefiting from the influx of African gold, he earned nearly £3500 during his fifth year as Master of the Mint, whereas his salary as Lucasian Professor had been £100, and the presidency of the Royal Society was an unpaid position.

The Royal Society was less important than its Fellows would have liked it to be, and it was only in the nineteenth century that they became powerful players on the national stage. It was at the Mint, not the Royal Society, that a wrong prediction by Newton had international consequences. Thanks to the policies he implemented, in 1717 Britain became the first country in the world to adopt gold as its standard. Remaining in power until he died, Newton took decisions that affected Britain's international trade, reputation, and imperial expansion.

Recoinage

Modern theories of economics are extremely sophisticated, yet, as demonstrated by financial collapses, they do not always produce the right answers. Newtonian mathematics can predict the date of an eclipse or the path of a comet with spot-on precision, but—as Newton found out for himself during the South Sea Bubble— stock-market fluctuations are harder to confine within an algebraic formula. When he started work at the Mint in May 1696, the country had been wracked by financial problems for several years, but no mathematical models of supply and demand, or of inflation and depression, were available. The implications of making interventions had to be thought through from scratch, and bitter disagreements repeatedly culminated in procrastination. By the mid-1690s, Parliament had finally accepted that doing nothing was not going to resolve a situation spiralling downwards out of control. Newton was called in to implement a remedy with which he disagreed—and despite his ruthless thoroughness, it failed to work.[7]

The non-decimal and mutually incompatible currencies of seventeenth-century Europe now seem arcane, although the British system survived until 1971. Newton covered many, many pages with calculations, and this brief extract from one eight-page hand-written memorandum is a typical example: 'From Decemb. 31 1689 to Decemb. 31 1699 there has been coyned in Gold 2059384. 06. 07. If an eighth part thereof be subducted as weighty guineas culled out & sent back to the Mint & to the remainder be added the French & Spanish Pistols & Guineas which came hither from abroad {w}hen Guineas were at 30s a piece & afterwards at 22s & all which (considering that above a million has been coyned here out of forreign Gold monies & that Pistolls are here at a higher value then Guineas) I'le reccon at about a million & an half....'[8]

In this extract, Newton refers to the value of guineas—recently invented coins minted with gold from the African region of Guinea—in shillings, which he abbreviates as s. For understanding the challenges he faced, the modern unfamiliarity of shillings and guineas is relatively trivial: what really matters is that coins were conceptually different. Instead of being tokens with no intrinsic value, they were made of precious metal: in principle, although often not in practice, a coin labelled 'pound' was worth a pound after being melted down and converted into bullion. As an added complication, coins were not all made of the same metal. Traditionally, international values were based on silver, but now African gold was being used for large purchases, which led to still more difficulties. As the Council of Trade reported, 'For it be impossible, that more than one Metal should be the true Measure of Commerce; and the world by common Consent and Convenience [has] settled that Measure in Silver; Gold...is to be looked upon as a Commodity [whose] value will always be changeable.'[9]

Another problem was crime. Years before Newton arrived at the Mint, the system had already begun breaking down because coins were tampered with by clippers, criminals who filed away slivers from the edges and compensated by hammering the metal thinner. When an abandoned bag of silver coins was dug up in Bristol some 250 years later, it weighed only two thirds of what it should have done. Ironically, modernization had made the problem worse. Under Charles II, French equipment had been installed to replace the skilled craftsmen hammering by hand. The precise design of

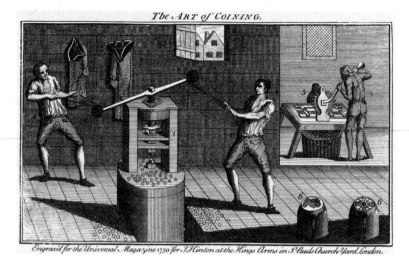

The ART of COINING.

Engrav'd for the Universal Magazine 1750 for J.Hinton at the Kings Arms in S.Pauls Church Yard London.

Figure 8.1 'The Art of Coining', *Universal Magazine*, 1750

this imported machinery was guarded as a state secret, and this engraving of 1750 (Figure 8.1) seems to be the earliest British illustration of operations hidden away behind the Tower's stone walls. Heavy screw presses, controlled with rotating levers by two strong men, stamped the coin's pattern on to blanks put in place by a third man (plenty of opportunity for squashed fingers). When Newton was vetting performance, the strike rate shot up to almost once a second. Another machine, shown at the back right, created milled edges that were virtually tamper-proof.

Because the precious-metal content of these machine-tooled coins was guaranteed, people either saved them in case of future need or melted them down to make an immediate profit by selling the bullion abroad. As a consequence, everyday transactions were increasingly being carried out with older, damaged, hand-made money. Nothing was fixed in this shifting monetary arrangement, which reached crisis point in 1695. Golden guineas were worth far above their face-value, while silver coins were in short supply, either hoarded away as an investment or shipped abroad as melted-down bars to pay for luxuries. Clipped money remained in circulation, but good coins were effectively dead cash, unavailable for public use. Agricultural prices were rising, the exchange rate was falling, and the new Bank of England was spending around £200,000 a week just to support the army. Even ordinary shopping could involve long processes of bargaining, because traders were 'necessitated first to settle the Price of the Value of the very Money they are to Receive for their Goods; and if it be in Guineas at a High Rate or in Bad Moneys they set the Price of their Goods accordingly.' People began carrying portable scales to weigh the money they were being offered.[10]

The Secretary of the Treasury, William Lowndes, decided to consult some experts, including Christopher Wren, John Locke, and Isaac Newton. Their opinions differed. Still based in Cambridge, Newton agreed with Lowndes that there should be parity between bulk metal and minted money—that the silver (or other precious metal) in a coin should be worth the same as its face-value, neither more nor less. As he explained, if the silver content were too high, then traders would melt down the coins to sell the raw metal, and the Mint would be losing money by buying expensive silver and converting it into less valuable coins. 'It seems reasonable that an Ounce of Bullion should be by Parliament Enacted of the same Value with a Crown-Piece of Milled Money,' he wrote in response to Lowndes's questionnaire, 'thereby to prevent the Melting or Exporting it, and to make the Milling of Bullion Practicable without Loss.'[11]

There were, and there still are, ardent debates about the pros and cons of the various remedies proposed, which had political as well as financial implications. For Whig supporters of King William such as Newton, defacing the currency was symbolically equivalent to harming the monarch, and the financial crisis could be interpreted as a Tory conspiracy. Some modern economic historians argue that Newton was right, and they vaunt him as a prescient advocate of devaluation, even though that term was not introduced until the early twentieth century, when markets operated differently.

Although Newton recommended reducing the silver content of coins, he was outvoted in Lowndes's advisory group, notably by Locke, who contended that the value of silver could not in itself rise or fall: an ounce of silver was an ounce of silver, and was worth only what people were willing to exchange for it. He maintained that there should be a complete recoinage—that all the clipped money in the country should be melted down and reissued in coins that contained the same amount of silver as their face-value. This strategy was adopted, although modified by Newton's insistence that the procedure should take place gradually rather than instantaneously.

At last, after yet more prevarications and hesitations, in December 1695 Newton's patron Charles Montagu persuaded Parliament to vote for all clipped coins to be recalled, made illegal as tender, and converted into new money. The chaos was immediate, despite several pieces of emergency patch-up legislation. One immediate difficulty arose because the timetable for withdrawing the clipped silver coins was unrealistically rapid and scheduled in complicated steps. Uncertainty reigned right from the beginning, so that nobody would accept old money as payment in case it soon proved to be worthless. All over the country, tradesmen were unable to settle their bills or buy raw materials because their money had in effect lost its purchasing power. Even those lucky enough to own valuable golden guineas found them of little use for paying a daily wage of thirteen pennies or buying a pound of beef for three.[12] In contrast, rich metropolitan merchants knew how to offload their coins rapidly at face-value, even gaining rather than losing in the process.

And then there was the question of paying for the recoinage, which was an extremely expensive operation entailing not only the administrative costs of collection and production but also the replacement of all the silver that had been literally shaved away from the currency by clippers. Normal Mint expenses were covered by charging duty on imported liquor, but to deal with this exceptional case, Parliament imposed an ingenious sliding-scale tax on windows, to be paid not by a house's owners but by its inhabitants. That tax lasted for well over a century, and its legacy can still be seen in the bricked-up windows that helped people avoid payment but did little for their health and their eyesight.

Even though he had argued against recoinage, Newton gratefully accepted Montagu's offer of taking over as Warden of the Mint, moving to the Tower in April 1696. Despite disagreeing with official policy, he threw himself into salvaging the situation. From the outset, this job provided him with ample opportunities to adopt the same approach as for star positions or dynastic reigns—to scrawl over sheet after sheet drawing up tables, copying out memoranda, adding up numbers. At first, there was little visible progress: in June, John Evelyn worried that riots would break out, provoked by the 'Want of current money to carry on the smallest concerns, even for daily provisions in the markets…and nothing considerable coin'd of the new and now onely current stamp…'[13] Newton piled on the pressure. For twenty hours a day and six days a week, three hundred men and fifty horses operated ten mills at the Mint. By personally monitoring worker performance and scrutinizing quotations from external contractors, Newton ensured that production rates shot up and costs went down. He did, however, insist on an increase in his own salary.

By the summer of 1698, the recoinage had been completed, although what should have been a success proved to be a failure. Nearly seven million pounds' worth of silver coins had been minted, but they disappeared almost immediately, melted down to buy foreign imports or privately hoarded as security against an uncertain future. International financiers agreed that, in principle, it was silver that should be the invariable standard for conducting trade, with gold and other metals shifting in value against it. But over the next couple of decades, the cost of gold soared and silver coins remained scarce. The fate of English money, Newton explained repeatedly, was tied to the demands of international trade, especially with China.

East Asians valued gold and silver not for currency, but for creating beautiful objects that would display the owners' wealth and power, while also acting as a portable insurance policy in the case of disaster. Although delighted to sell luxuries such as spices, tea, and silk, Chinese merchants had no interest in trading them for European iron, wool, or furs, let alone clocks or other instruments that were less sophisticated than their own. What they mainly wanted in exchange was silver. This demand acted as a constant drain on the British economy, because if a coin had less symbolic purchasing power at home than the international value of its physical metal, merchants would melt it down for export as bullion.[14]

Asked to help rectify the unforeseen and unprecedented emergency, Newton repeatedly compiled reports in which he compared the world's major currencies against gold and silver. Perhaps he relished the time-consuming arithmetical challenge of converting various non-decimal systems of weights and money between one another: he certainly performed the task meticulously. In 1717, he issued his most momentous recommendation—that the value of a guinea should be set by Parliament at twenty-one shillings, even though it had originally been introduced as a sovereign (a pound) of twenty shillings. Just as he did for the natural world, Newton assumed that the future would behave like the past. The guinea had recently been coming down in value from its peak of around thirty shillings, and he predicted that this decrease would continue. 'If things be let alone,' he declared confidently, 'the gold will fall of it self.'[15] But he was wrong: for over 200 years, until 1931, while gold remained steady at £3 17s. 10½d. per troy ounce, the price of silver fluctuated violently.

In Pursuit

Persuading gullible investors to buy risky stocks may have been morally reprehensible, but lying to obtain money was not in itself a criminal offence. Responsibility lay with the victim, a principle first officially laid down in a key trial of 1703, when an unfortunate Mr Jones borrowed £20 from a friend, and later returned it to a third man whom the friend had sent to collect the debt. At least, that is what the third man claimed: in reality, he was perpetrating a con, and kept the money for himself. In a landmark decision, the judge dismissed Mr Jones's case, arguing that he should have been more sensible; it is wrong, he said, 'to punish one Man because another is a Fool'. A deceit, he decreed with long-lasting influence on unwary share purchasers, should be deemed a crime only if it was 'such a Cheat as a Person of an ordinary Capacity can't discover'. From then on, individuals were responsible for protecting themselves, so that it became legal to market wrongly labelled products, to steal from someone who was asleep, or to sell a horse with only three legs.[16]

Fake coins were different. Unlike a three-legged horse, their deficiency was not immediately apparent, and with Newton at its head the Mint pursued forgers and clippers remorselessly, however pitiable their status. Before the recoinage, Parliament had tried to stem the collapse of England's currency by passing increasingly ferocious legislation, and when Newton came to power, counterfeiting a coin was regarded as high treason, punishable not merely by hanging at Tyburn Gallows (near where Marble Arch was later relocated at the top of Oxford Street), but also by being eviscerated while still conscious. Harsh punishment—but such crimes threatened to undermine an established hierarchy based on birth and wealth. Because the right to vote was restricted to male landowners, forgery signified not only defacing the monarch but also revolutionizing society by giving power to the poor.

Initially, Newton tried to avoid the dangerous, time-consuming task of tracking down offenders, even though it was specified in his job description. Three months after arriving at the Tower, he was summoned before a special committee and officially ordered to investigate the mysterious case of the missing dies—moulds for making coins that had been stolen from right inside the Mint. Once he had agreed to take on the search for fraudsters, Newton pursued the hunt assiduously, characteristically starting by compiling all the relevant documents he could find and writing a history of Mint prosecutions. Over the next eighteen months, he cross-examined 200 informers and suspects, including many who were struggling on the breadline, themselves the victims of crime and poverty. False accusations were encouraged by rewarding witnesses and despatching potential informers to spend a few weeks in Newgate. This notorious prison had been rebuilt after the fire of 1666, but the elegant Wren façade concealed a cramped warren of cells resembling the hold of a slave ship. The corrupt and poorly paid warders demanded money to provide food and a bed, or to have manacles and neck collars removed. Even within the protected confines of Newgate, wealthy prisoners fared better than the poor.[17]

Newton later told Conduitt to burn many of the depositions he recorded, but enough survive to indicate that many thousands of illiterate men, women, and children suffered hardship during the recoinage. Desperate for survival, petty criminals attacked the Mint's agents, abused their own families, and turned in everybody they could to save themselves. For instance, Ann Pillsbury had already been manhandled and body-searched in a bread shop when she was taken to Newton's office with her small daughter. After he ordered them both to be examined again, a few coins were found hidden in the child's clothing. Her mother's crime? She had tried to pass on to the baker a counterfeit sixpence palmed off on her by the butcher, who then refused to take it back.[18]

The Mint records reveal that Newton also dealt with more professional criminals—gangsters who thrived on forgery, pimping, and extortion rackets. Capturing them cost money as well as time, and Newton charged the Treasury well over £600 for a couple of years' work. He kept his accounts meticulously, at one stage calculating his expenditure to be exactly £56 5s. 8¼d. more than his income from melting down forged coins sent in by agents placed around the country and in Newgate. Because these crooks were sharp dressers, Newton spent £5 on a smart new suit for Mint employee Humfrey Hall, who was sent out in disguise to scour the local taverns. Other expenses included paying for travel to places as far away as Wales and Worcester, as well as many small sums for informers who may well have technically been criminals themselves. As just one example, over several months Newton committed almost £30 to securing the services of John Gibbons, a porter at Whitehall Palace, who acted as a double-agent and specialized in terrorizing women.[19]

Newton the scientific sleuth soon discovered that he had his own Professor Moriarty, a serial offender whose ingenuity rivalled his own and whom he pursued with the same vengeful ferocity that he unleashed on Hooke, Leibniz, and Flamsteed. William Chaloner first learnt to forge small coins as a nail-maker's child apprentice in Birmingham, but after walking to London, he acquired further skills—making dildoes, japanning (imitating Asian lacquer work), gilding silver coins to look like guineas. These various activities proved so profitable that he bought a large house in Knightsbridge and passed himself off as a loyal citizen, a guise that enabled him to collect large rewards from the government by betraying Jacobite supporters. For several years, Chaloner was simultaneously counterfeiting coins, publishing proposals for rescuing the rapidly declining currency, and printing forged Bank of England £100 notes. To protect himself, he collected payments for denouncing his colleagues and other informers, who were then sent to Newgate and/or the gallows.

By early 1695, Chaloner had ingratiated himself into political circles so successfully that King William authorized him to be paid £1000, but a few months later, he was himself in Newgate. Eventually, after a series of inspired manoeuvres, he secured his release by condemning the Mint for internal corruption and denouncing its chief engraver as a Jacobite. For the next couple of years, Chaloner embarked on increasingly audacious schemes, even suggesting that he should be employed by the Mint to produce unforgeable coins. Repeatedly buying himself out of trouble with large bribes until he ran out of money, he also accused Newton of negligence and lies. Meanwhile, Newton plodded on indefatigably, collecting around fifty witness statements and—mirroring Chaloner's own tactics—planting informers, who warned him of his target's plans and reported verbatim his threat that 'he would pursue that old Dogg the Warden to the end so long as he lived...'[20]

Chaloner was tortured and hanged for high treason on 17 March 1699. Having ignored his pleas for mercy, Newton continued to assemble evidence against other informers who had helped him to secure Chaloner's execution, but had now switched sides to pursue their own careers as counterfeiters. That year, he also welcomed another long-anticipated death—the Master of the Mint, Thomas Neale, the former 'Lord of Lotteries' who had received bonuses totalling £20,000 for the recoinage implemented by Warden Newton. On Christmas Day, his fifty-seventh birthday, Newton was promoted to the Mastership of the Mint, and for almost three decades received an annual salary of £500 on top of a handsome fee for every pound of metal that was coined.

The Master's Trials

Managers who weed out corruption, fire employees, and increase efficiency are rarely popular. During his three decades at the Mint, initially as Warden and then from 1699 as Master, Newton became involved in a succession of vitriolic controversies. With opportunities for deceit at every stage, everybody associated with making coins had to demonstrate not only their expertise but also their honesty. Newton aimed to clean up the Mint but he was dealing with traditions going back four centuries, when two main centres were established to manage London's money manufacturing trade: the Royal Mint inside the Tower, and Goldsmiths' Hall on Maiden Lane (now in Covent Garden), near the dense network of city workshops.

Since his own income depended on the quantity and quality of coins that were minted, Newton was in a vulnerable position. Some abuse was straightforward: one imprisoned victim of his campaign to expunge forgery swore that the new Warden was 'a Rogue and if ever King James came again he would shoot him and the s^d Ball made answer God dam my blood so will I and tho I don't know him yet Ile find him out.'[21] Other accusations were more subtle, such as this witty but anonymous verse insisting that nobody is immune from the internal gravitational attraction of personal greed:

> The *Principles* by which Men move,
> Are private interest, base Self-Love;
> So far their Love or hate extends
> As serves their own contracted Ends.[22]

As President of the Royal Society, Newton was proud of being regarded as an elite natural philosopher. But as Master of the Mint, he operated not only as an administrator, but also as a practitioner: like goldsmiths and other skilled craft workers, he belonged to an extended experimental community stretching throughout the city and straddling social hierarchies. The processes of refining and testing precious metals involved the same chemical procedures and knowledge as isolating new elements, or producing drugs, or searching for the philosopher's stone. The main textbook on metallurgy, published at the same time as Newton's *Principia*, was written by John Pettus, a distinguished politician and Fellow of the Royal Society for twenty years. Despite such links, Newton condescendingly declared that 'the Assaymaster acts only as a manual Artificer', even though his effectiveness as Master depended on an intimate knowledge of the skills that he was so ready to dismiss as merely manual. When four men applied to become assay master at the Mint, Newton supervised 'a Comparative Trial before the officers they made each of them Eight Assays of Gold in four successive Fires, two in artifice, and as many of silver...'. To pick the right candidate, he needed practical experience to judge how well they performed and how much they knew.[23]

One major production problem was to determine which coins were valid—the right size, the right weight, the right metal. Small variations were permissible. The tolerance, confusingly called the remedy, was 3.5 parts per 1000, and it was needed because precious metals contain traces of other substances; in any case, completely pure gold and silver would be too soft for repeated financial transactions. Newton inherited a system originating in the tenth century, when it was agreed that coins should comprise 925 parts of silver to 75 parts copper, although by his time the precious-metal content had been reduced to 916.6. A pound weight of this sterling mixture was sliced into 240 pennies, making a total of a pound in money. Newton still followed this format when he recommended to Parliament not that a sovereign should weigh a particular amount, but that a weighed piece of metal should be divided into a certain number of coins.

Newton was responsible for making sure that the nation's coins matched up to agreed standards. Whether at the Mint or in Goldsmiths' Hall, opportunities for fraud occurred at many different points in the process—measuring the quality of the metal, weighing the coins, and tallying the accounts of income and expenditure. For example, goldsmiths or bankers who brought in bullion were recompensed in golden guineas, but up to a quarter of these coins were heavier than they should have been; they were called 'Come-again Guineas', because they could be melted down to generate still more profit. Newton insisted that close and potentially combative scrutiny was required at every stage: 'it's easy for an Assayor to give a Turn to the assay of a quarter of a Grain, or an half penny weight or above for or against the Master. And if any such thing be expected, the Assayer must Repeat his Assay, till the Officers of the Mint are satisfied of his acting with skill and candour.'[24]

By tightening up procedures, Newton reduced deficits at the Mint, but antagonized those who lost their profitable sidelines. His probity was at stake, but so, too, was the value of the national currency, a matter of great state importance. Every year, independent tests were carried out publicly during a ceremony that dated back to 1282. In this 'Trial of the Pyx' (which still takes place), a fifteen-man jury from the Worshipful Company of Goldsmiths assessed a random sample of the year's coins that had been collected in the special Pyx Chest. They were compared against part of a golden trial plate (Figure 8.2) that was stored in the Chapel of the Pyx; one made under Newton's supervision on 25 June 1707 was inscribed 'This Standard comixed of XXII Carretts of Fine Gold and II Carretts of Allay [sic] in the Pound w^t Troy of Great Brittain.'[25] As an additional check against cheating, the original plate was distributed in six rectangular sections with zig-zag edges that had to fit together at the Trial like jigsaw pieces.

During Newton's reign, the ritual remained essentially the same, although the Treasury trimmed back the entertainment allowance. Early on a summer morning, the Pyx Chests—accompanied by sheaves of documents as well as charcoal for melting selected

Figure 8.2   Gold assay plate, 1707

coins—were rowed by two boatmen wearing velvet jackets and scarlet stockings from the Tower to Palace Yard at Westminster, the traditional site of executions. Newton and other Mint officials followed behind, while a similar but grander boat transported the jury from the wharf near St Paul's Cathedral. By 9 o'clock, they were all in place waiting for the Lord Chancellor to deliver a speech and swear in the jury. Watched by Mint officials, the goldsmiths completed their analyses and gave their verdict. Finally, the Mint paid for a lavish dinner at a nearby inn, afterwards often pleading poverty and recouping the cost from the Privy Purse.

In 1710, the serenity of this annual ceremony was noisily disrupted when the jury announced that the year's coins were sub-standard. Violent arguments broke out, and the Mint officials were angrily ejected from the assaying chamber. Naturally, Newton was incensed at this slur on his competence, but it turned out that the new assay plate he had authorized three years earlier was made of finer gold than usual. When measured against the old plate, the coins passed the test, but they failed to meet the requirements imposed by this new one. Newton's alchemical expertise came in handy for carrying out his own refining experiments, which led him to blame the assayers and tell them where they were going wrong: 'If this aqua fortis be poured off & fresh aqua fortis be poured on, this second water (especially if it be a little stronger then the former) will eat away a little more of the silver & leave the Gold finer than before. And a third water will leave it still finer, & a fourth still finer. But Assaymasters & Refiners proceed no further then to two waters.' And so on. The 1707 plate was never used again, but recent tests have shown that Newton's recorded measurements were faulty.[26]

Trips along the Thames or through the streets of London were probably Newton's only journeys on Mint affairs, although he did take responsibility for some distant outposts. To speed up the recoinage, five temporary Mints were established around England, each with their own staff. Following the unwritten rules of patronage, Newton made sure that Edmond Halley was rewarded with a lucrative position in Chester, where the local infighting turned out to be even more savage than in the Tower. After a clerk threw an ink-stand across the room, Halley asked Newton for help in sorting out fraud and absenteeism. An official warning from London headquarters indicates how far the situation had degenerated: 'the Mint will not allow of the drawing of Swords, & assaulting any, nor ought such Language, Wee hear has been, be used any more amongst You.'[27]

With Newton in charge, Mint business was political business. He avoided undertaking a still longer journey to Edinburgh in 1707, when Scotland was fused with England and Wales into a new kingdom, Great Britain. This Act of Union confronted him with a diplomatic problem, because it stipulated that Scottish money should be made under Tower rules. Newton delegated his mathematical ally, the Scot David Gregory, to oversee the tricky transition from Scottish pounds to English ones, which looked different and were worth about twelve times as much. After spending eleven days on the road from Oxford, Gregory discovered that essential machinery had not yet arrived, but—despite several other glitches—the unpopular recoinage was eventually completed. This time, Newton found himself out-manoeuvred. Even when the work had been completed, Edinburgh officials continued to draw their salaries—and when Scottish customs officers refrained from collecting import duties on liquor, the Tower had to foot the bill.[28]

Britain remained defined by the seas around its edge rather than any internal unity. Even negotiating with Cornwall entailed political expediency. The distant county returned more MPs than London, so in the hope of gaining political influence Queen Anne had agreed to buy a substantial amount of tin every year at an unusually high cost. Unsold supplies rapidly built up at the Mint, and Newton found himself negotiating sales all over Europe, while worrying about being undercut by competitors. As Newton explained, when interest and freight charges were taken into account, the crown was losing hundreds of thousands of pounds by buying Cornish tin at an unreasonable rate; on the other hand, lowering the price too far would ruin the miners. This was a problem he never managed to resolve, and the piles of surplus tin continued to grow until his death.[29]

Newton became more publicly (and humiliatingly) involved in demands for Irish autonomy. After the Act of Union, Ireland remained a separate country, although it was ruled from London. A fresh controversy arose in 1722, when, without consulting Dublin, the British crown granted the request of an Englishman, William Wood, to mint 360 tons of copper coins and ship them over. To help secure this licence, Wood had bribed Baroness Melusine von der Schulenburg, George I's illicit partner from Hanover, and accusations of corruption soon began circulating. This was a sensitive topic. The Tower had already quashed several demands from Dublin for its own Mint, at least once on Newton's own recommendation.[30] Moreover, in 1698, the English Parliament had condemned as seditious a forceful argument for the legal independence of Ireland by William Molyneux, Newton's near equivalent in Ireland.

A close friend of John Locke, Molyneux was a Fellow of the Royal Society, a renowned expert on eclipses, mathematics, and optical instruments, and had founded Dublin's Philosophical Society. Like Newton, Molyneux was a thorough man who undertook extensive historical research to support his case. He was particularly angry about recent restrictions on wool exports, which were ruining Irish cloth manufacturers, and he insisted that Ireland should not be bound by laws enacted in London. Following his well-established habit, Newton copied out long sections of Molyneux's tract, but he reached the opposite conclusion—that London over-ruled Dublin: 'it lies in the breast of an English Parliament,' he wrote, 'to interpret & declare the meaning extent & force of all the Irish laws not excepting those by which they claim any power to themselves.'[31]

When Wood's patent was announced, Jonathan Swift fanned Irish resentment by railing against Britain's imposition of a non-Irish manufacturer. Newton laid himself open to further criticism by refusing to inspect Wood's factory, instead asking him to send a selection of coins to test at the Tower. Even though there was a distinct possibility that Wood had submitted an unrepresentative sample, Newton decreed the coins to be valid. In retaliation, Swift stepped up his campaign, and critical Irish pamphlets began appearing, claiming 'how Visible and Plain must it appear to all the World, That Mr Wood and his Friends have Imposed upon Sir *Isaac Newton* [and his staff], by bringing them Specimens of said Coyn, and Tryall-Pieces so different in Value and Weight from what is daily seen in *Ireland*.'[32]

Swift continued to slate Newton for unfairly backing an English colleague, and laced his next satire—*Gulliver's Travels*—with hostile invective. For example, during his visit to the imaginary Academy of Lagado and the flying island of Laputa, Gulliver professes himself mystified that other-worldly astronomers should keep interfering in politics, to which they are so clearly ill-suited. Gulliver remarks that he had 'observed the same Disposition among most of the Mathematicians I have known in *Europe*' (Newton is an obvious candidate here); they seem to think—wrote Gulliver/Swift—'that because the smallest Circle has as many Degrees as the largest, therefore the Regulation and Management of the World require no more Abilities than the handling and turning of a Globe.'[33] A few chapters later, Swift imagines the ghost of Aristotle predicting that gravity will go the way of all once-fashionable doctrines: '*Attraction*, whereof the present Learned are such zealous Asserters...would flourish but a short Period of Time, and be out of Vogue when that was determined.'[34]

Over the following years, Swift published further scarcely veiled attacks. Since Newton died only a few months after *Gulliver's Travels* was published, he presumably never realized that Catherine Barton's former friend was undermining her husband's sustained promotional activities. While Conduitt's iconographic agenda identified Newton as a unique genius, Swift's literary campaign questioned Newton's intellectual reputation as well as emphasizing his political and economic motivations.[35]

9
Knowledge and Power

Women dominate the plot of The Indian Emperour *and have some of the best lines. Yet like the biblical Eve, they are blamed for causing the downfall of their men. In the scene portrayed by Hogarth, Montezuma's daughter Cydaria believes that she has caught her admirer Cortez in the act of declaring his love for another royal woman, Almeria. Dressed in pink, Almeria stands in front of the diminutive handcuffed Cortez; her pose is reflected by Cydaria, clad in white satin and in real life Caroline Lennox, the oldest daughter of the admiring Richmond couple to the left of the picture, the only adults watching the play. The girl standing behind her is the Conduitts' daughter Kitty, included even though, according to Dryden's script, no third woman should be present on stage at that point.[1]*

The scenery portrays a grim prison cell, but authenticity is limited: the Aztec royal women are wearing Spanish-style costumes with a token feather in their hair, while following thespian conventions Cydaria addresses the audience rather than the other actors—and because this is a play, they all declaim in English heroic couplets. The triangular tussle on stage is a reprise of the scene Hogarth had recently chosen to depict in The Beggar's Opera. *There, the rival lovers Lucy and Polly were both pleading for the life of handcuffed Macheath, while now, Almeria and Cydaria are vying for the chained Cortez. In both scenarios, the man echoes Hercules, forced to choose between Vice and Virtue.*

Woven through The Indian Emperour *is a sub-theme about another woman, the Indian queen Alibech, who vacillates between two suitors, Guyomar and Odbar, both sons of Montezuma. Two scenes earlier, Alibech has temporarily rejected Guyomar's insistence on honourable patriotism and turned towards her more ardent lover (naturally, she chooses the more virtuous man in the end). In a 'Does the end justify the means?' dialogue, she maintains 'That ill is pardoned, which does good procure.' Guyomar immediately objects: 'The good's uncertain, but the ill is sure'. This interchange forms the prelude to a discussion about the rights of monarchs, a sensitive topic in those early years of the Restoration, when royalists were trying to obliterate the previous twenty years from public memory and behave as if nothing untoward had happened.*

Seventy years later, when children performed this play in Conduitt's drawing room, the political situation was very different: the Stuarts had been deposed in the Glorious Revolution, and the country was governed by Hanoverians with a reduced amount of power. But, however much rulers liked to ordain collective oblivion of the past, there were strong continuities as well. Presumably this couplet by Alibech stirred spectators' reservations about the current monarch, George II:

> When Kings grow stubborn, slothful, or unwise,
> Each private man for publick good should rise.[2]

*   *   *

In 1725, a new map of Africa was published by the printer John Senex, already one of London's most successful cartographers and soon to become a Fellow of the Royal Society (Figure 9.1).[3] On the lower right, Senex pays homage to an elderly British knight, Sir Isaac Newton. Taking his inspiration from Renaissance iconography, Senex portrays Newton as an eternal star amidst a halo of golden rays, honouring this semi-deity with his full panoply of titles: 'Sr ISAAC NEWTON Kt, President of the Royal Society and Master of her Majesties Mints'. Queen Anne had died more than a decade earlier, but following regular money-saving practices, for this cartouche Senex has recycled an earlier plate engraved when he was her royal map-maker.

This map looks very different from one that Senex had published in a large atlas only four years earlier, although no major new discoveries had been made since then. His revised version not only emphasizes Newton's importance for Britain's imperial ambitions, but also uses colours to show how the African continent was being carved up and appropriated by European powers. In the cartouche

Figure 9.1 *Africa: Corrected from the Observations of the Royal Society at London and Paris*; John Senex, 1725

on the bottom left, Africa is visualized as an exotic land inhabited by unfamiliar beasts, dangerous snakes, and muscular men. The cornucopia, ivory, and golden pieces of money indicate that, for invading Britons, the continent is a land of plenty—and that is one of the reasons why the Royal Society was interested in being linked with imperial cartography. Most of the place names lie along the coast, because voyaging across the ocean was easier than hacking out new paths overland: this is not a map designed to help explorers travel around the continent, but one that displays its riches. A large inland tract, coloured yellow, is labelled Negroland to indicate a mysterious place rarely entered by foreign travellers. To its south lies Guinea, which was artificially divided into territories named not after their local inhabitants, but for the plunder to be found there: gold, ivory, slaves. Politicians promised that, under the new Whig freedom, these African imports would revive England's flagging fortunes.

When Newton became President of the Royal Society, he took over an organization that professed itself dedicated to discovering truths of nature—but it was also committed to promoting Britain's global interests. Like Newton, many Fellows supported Whig ideals and invested in the new trading companies that depended on transatlantic slavery to sustain the national economy. Newton did not settle permanently in London until 1696, but he had already embraced the global attitudes that he implemented throughout the course of his metropolitan career. Even in the 1660s, he was soliciting information from English merchants overseas, and his involvement in imperial enterprises continued to strengthen. Once at the Mint, he relied on securing the most advantageous deals in African gold. Privately, he invested in companies promising enormous profits from trafficking people. And at the Royal Society, he reigned over an institution that had encouraged overseas exploration and exploitation since its foundation.

The growth of Enlightenment science was rooted in the Royal Society's Restoration origins. Conventional versions of its history feature the Fellows' supposedly disinterested search for knowledge about the natural world, but reappraising Newton's activities during his three London decades entails telling a different story about the Society's origins and uncovering still further links between Hogarth's picture, Newton, and imperial Britain.

The Early Royal Society

At the end of Dryden's play, a messenger from the gods appears on stage to deliver an epilogue in rhyming couplets. *The Indian Emperour*, he declares, is an entertainment designed for everybody, whether man or woman, 'of Court, of Coffee-house, or Town'.[4] In Restoration London, coffee houses were not just familiar places for refuelling or mitigating a hangover. Instead, they were a recent innovation that fostered a substantial shift in English society. Open to any man with loose change in his pocket, they provided unprecedented opportunities for exchanging ideas, hatching plots, securing patronage, and effecting introductions—they helped to make public opinion important. Charles II felt so threatened that he tried to ban coffee houses, but the crown's authority was shrinking in the face of increasing government power. Defying the royal will, these hot-houses for democracy survived, regulated by a state-run licensing system.[5]

Dryden was a leading actor in this new sphere of urban conviviality. London's most popular playwright, he was the star attraction of Will's, a leading coffee house on Russell Street, a key location between the City and Westminster. Samuel Pepys described the novelty of dropping in to Will's on his way home from work, where he met Dryden and other London wits gathering together over newspapers and drinks (hot chocolate was a favourite for fashionable gentlemen). Negotiating with coffee-house colleagues, Dryden tried to establish a college for improving the English language, modelled on the French *Académie* in Paris. Although that project never came to fruition, Dryden and his allies—notably John Evelyn, Thomas Sprat, and Abraham Cowley—soon became influential in a Restoration product that had a long life ahead of it: London's Royal Society.

According to the standard story, the Royal Society was born in 1660, when Charles II reclaimed the throne. Symbolically, that year became enormously significant for his supporters as they competed to demonstrate their enduring loyalty. In reality, several had rapidly switched allegiance. Within the space of a year, Dryden wrote poems celebrating both Oliver Cromwell and Charles II—and Pepys cannot have been the only professed monarchist who sat miserably through a dinner-party agonizing that an old school-friend might reveal his childhood jubilation at the beheading of Charles I.[6]

The metropolitan roots of the Royal Society have now been traced back to well before the Restoration, but the conventional account begins in royalist Oxford, a buzzy city where England's first coffee house had opened in 1650, two years earlier than in London. Several of the Royal Society's future Fellows—young researchers such as Christopher Wren, Robert Boyle, Robert Hooke, and Thomas Willis—met there regularly, gradually shifting their discussions to London's Gresham College, where Wren was appointed professor of astronomy in 1657. A recent graduate, he was building up a reputation as a mathematician and experimenter, but had not yet become a famous architect: nobody knew that St Paul's Cathedral would burn down less than a decade later. It was apparently in Wren's rooms, on 28 November 1660, that the friends decided to establish an experimental society.

However high their expectations may have been, they had no way of foreseeing that their enthusiastic speculations at Gresham College would later be viewed as a key turning-point in the history of science and technology. They knew nothing of the future, and had no idea that they would later be celebrated as scientists, a word that was not in common use until the early twentieth century. There were no university degrees in science, no professional organizations, no journals, no ready-made career ladders for young graduates to climb. Experimental investigations were still far from prestigious, and one of the Society's major problems was mockery: Pepys reported that Charles II laughed at them 'for spending time only in weighing of ayre, and doing nothing else since they sat'.[7]

The first Fellows of the Royal Society were laying ambitious plans for the future, but they were also concerned about their own immediate problems of earning money, remaining politically safe, and persuading sceptics that this new style of research would yield dividends—both economic and factual. For years, the Society's function remained unclear, its survival uncertain. Should the Fellows set up a college, regulate inventions, aim to make a profit? Many such possibilities were proposed but abandoned.[8] People in power gave priority to other objectives—accumulating money, dominating world trade, and gaining global territory. To flourish, the Royal Society needed to demonstrate that it, too, could contribute towards those goals.

The Society got off to an inauspicious start. In 1662, Charles II agreed to award it a Royal Charter, but he soon started complaining about the lack of visible progress. When the Fellows realized that the king's initial spark of interest was fading and that no financial support would be forthcoming, they decided it was time to generate some publicity. The main driver seems to have been Dryden's coffee-house friend John Evelyn, now most famous for the revealing diary that he kept for over sixty years. But that was only published posthumously, and among his contemporaries he was known as a staunch royalist who was also an expert on trees and coins.

The Fellows' bid for self-promotion was temporarily stymied by committee hiccups, authorial procrastination, and the Plague, but eventually Thomas Sprat—a rather stolid clergyman who had been involved in Dryden's failed language academy project—published his *History of the Royal Society* in 1667. Writing sporadically and under pressure from different factions, Sprat proved an unreliable narrator whose text reinforced the concept of sudden birth in 1660. Diplomatically flattering the king, he emphasized the importance of his royal patronage and glossed over experimental activities that had been taking place during the previous regime. Sprat's book did indeed contain prescriptions for experimental research, but it was also a self-serving document that reflected the immediate desires of the Society's members to placate the king, gain influence, and replenish the nation's empty coffers.[9]

One striking feature of Sprat's long, digressive account is that he wrote relatively little about the content of scientific knowledge. Instead, a major concern was to win over critics by persuading them that the Society would help to make the country rich and powerful. Since the organization had only received its Royal Charter five years earlier, his book was more of a manifesto than a historical account, although he did reproduce several research papers to demonstrate that—despite the king's scepticism—the Fellows were capable of obtaining results. Recruited for his writing skills rather than his scientific expertise or influential contacts, Sprat produced a persuasive narrative that was idiosyncratic but must have been vetted to some extent by Evelyn and other senior fellows.

While Sprat was putting the final touches to his *History*, Newton was isolated in a Lincolnshire farmhouse, reputedly absorbed in carrying out crucial experiments with prisms and wondering why apples fell from the tree in the garden. Five years later, in 1672, he dazzled the Royal Society (and antagonized Robert Hooke) with his first paper on optics, which overturned previous theories by showing that the colours of a rainbow are already invisibly present in the light coming from the sun. By the time he was elected president in the early eighteenth century, Newton was becoming a major player in metropolitan society. Like the country and the Society, he had absorbed the policy expressed by Sprat and his mentor Evelyn: 'whoever commands the trade of the world, commands the riches of the world, and whoever is master of that, commands the world itself.'[10] English gentlemen, Sprat preached, have a moral responsibility to spread the benefits of civilization to other parts of the world by exporting material benefits as well as their Christian religion. Trade was the best way not only to make individuals rich but also to expand England's imperial possessions.

Many historians have glossed over those messages, preferring instead to scour Sprat's text for the roots of modern science. And they have unearthed what they were looking for: Sprat does indeed also describe a dedicated group of experimenters committed to the precepts of Francis Bacon. At one time England's Lord Chancellor, Bacon had died half a century earlier, but the Fellows declared allegiance to his ideology as if he were a patron saint. Their guiding motto was *nullius in verba*—take nothing on authority or, to put it more colloquially, don't believe everything you read in books. Theories should, Bacon insisted, be built upwards from raw data, rather than be derived by arguing logically from premises that might or might not be valid. For him, there was only one route to true knowledge: observation, observation, observation.

Modern scientists credit Francis Bacon with inventing 'the scientific method', but in practice its principles are rarely followed. He is also famous for declaring that 'Knowledge is power', but although he expressed the concept, he did not himself coin that neat aphorism. Sprat's *History* strongly endorsed Baconian method, while also exhorting its readers to promote England's commercial and imperial ambitions. Sprat proposed that the entire nation—farmers, sailors, surveyors, miners, physicians—should collect all the information that they could find and send it up the social scale for processing by the elite group based in London.

From its foundation, the Royal Society vaunted itself as a Baconian organization that would base knowledge on facts—but the Fellows were also hungry for the power that came with it. As expounded by Sprat, Baconianism entailed scientific projects— mapping the world, collecting specimens, recording physical phenomena—but it also aspired to gaining wealth and global influence. '*Trafic*, and *Commerce* have given mankind a higher degree than any title of *Nobility*,' Sprat exhorted his readers, 'in those Coasts, whither the greatest *Trade* shall constantly flow, the greatest *Riches*, and *Power* will be establish'd.'[11] Playing to contemporary arrogance, Sprat maintained that the English were God's chosen people: 'So that even the position of our climate, the air, the influence of the heaven, the composition of the English blood; as well as the embraces of the Ocean, seem to joyn with the labours of the *Royal Society*,' he enthused; 'Nature will reveal more of its secrets to the English, than to others; because it has already furnish'd them with a Genius so well proportion'd, for the receiving, and retaining its mysteries.'[12]

Twin Sisters of the Restoration

Naturally, Sprat reserved his more flowery eulogies for Charles II. Comparing him to King Solomon (creator of the temple admired by Newton), Sprat congratulated the restored monarch on improving the nation's financial situation 'with great vigour, by the *Foundation* of the *Royal Company*'. He was referring to the Company of Royal Adventurers Trading into Africa, which originated in 1660, the same year as the Royal Society, and was already reaping huge profits by marketing gold, ivory, and people. This company was, Sprat wrote sycophantically, 'the Twin-Sister of the *Royal Society*' to which 'we have reason as we go along, to wish all *Prosperity*. In both these *Institutions* begun together, our *King* has imitated the two most famous *Works* of the wisest of antient *Kings*: who at the same time sent to *Ophir* for *Gold, and* compos'd a *Natural History*, from the Cedar to the Shrub.'[13] Rather like golden El Dorado, Ophir was a mythical land, but travel writers competed to give it a precise location. 'Royal Adventurers Trading into Africa' readily identified Ophir with Guinea, regarding their Royal Society colleagues as the modern-day counterparts of Solomon's natural historians.[14]

For its first few years, the Royal Adventurers flourished. Plantation holders in the West Indies welcomed African labourers, who were cheap to feed and clothe, and lacked the social cohesion that enabled imported English servants to rebel. After plague reduced England's population, it seemed even more important to deter emigration and encourage the mass transfer of captives from elsewhere. But the Dutch Wars had been expensive, and as debts mounted, the Adventurers put up their prices. Pressure on the royal monopoly came from two sides: private merchants, who resented being excluded; and the plantation owners, who claimed to con-template ruin unless they could buy forced labour at a low cost. In 1670, the Company of Royal Adventurers Trading into Africa was obliged to wind down, but only two years later, it re-emerged as the Royal African Company, which was essentially the same organiza-tion, although with diminished royal involvement.

The twinned royal sisters were linked together by their political leaders and their global aims. To gain knowledge was to gain power—and that was a national aspiration. The Royal Society was packed with men who were ambitious for themselves as well as for England. Around a third of the early Fellows were aristocrats, courtiers, and politicians dedicated to promoting the interests of England's landed classes. They absorbed from Sprat's *History* the messages they wanted to hear. Some of them were probably convinced that knowledge is worth acquiring for its own sake, but many were swayed more strongly by the rhetorical, almost prophetic, tenor of Sprat's chauvinistic predictions that England could achieve a glorious destiny by following Baconian prescriptions.

The Royal Society has outlived its twin sister, but it remained the weaker sibling for decades. By using the imagery of birth, Sprat reinforced the notion that these two organizations had sprung out of nowhere, as if created solely through the king's initiative. He also cleverly boosted the Fellows' importance by linking the two together, even though, as a modern-day Solomon, Charles had already manifested far more interest in the Ophir-company promising gold than in its poor relation who could only offer learned information about cedars, shrubs, and other marvels of nature. Whereas Louis XIV, the French Sun King, hoped that liberally funding scientific research would enhance his glory and strengthen Parisian control over his nation, the English monarch awarded little to London's Royal Society beyond a regal label.

One apparent exception was the king's creation in 1675 of a new post, the Astronomer Royal, to be based (with a meagre salary) at an Observatory on top of a hill in Greenwich. This ostensibly scientific initiative illustrates how Charles's primary goal was to augment English power by improving navigation, trade, and military strength. Charles was persuaded into the project by a woman, his long-term lover Louise de Kérouaille (the grandmother of Charles Lennox/Duke of Richmond in Hogarth's painted audience), who made him realize that the French king might be gaining a strategic advantage from astronomical research at his new Paris observatory. Charles commissioned a London equivalent to be built by the Tower's Ordnance Office, which, in the absence of realistic royal funding, was forced into thrifty economizing. Paid for by selling off some decayed gunpowder, the building was constructed by recycling bricks and metal from a disused fort in Tilbury, supported by timbers retrieved from an old Tower gatehouse.[15] The new telescopes, clocks, and other essential equipment were all paid for privately, not by the crown—and the building was unhelpfully aligned at an angle of thirteen degrees to the line of longitude.

The Royal Society and the Royal Adventurers were founded during the Restoration, but their trajectories were fashioned by earlier events, and their influence continued into the future. Both these organizations were crucial to Newton's metropolitan success. His name is indelibly linked with the Royal Society, but in addition he relied on the trade networks established by the Royal Adventurers and other commercial companies (notably the East India Company), benefiting from them in three major ways: collecting worldwide data from international merchants; importing the African gold for which he was responsible at the Mint; and building up his own personal fortune.

During Charles's reign, England's major enemies were the Dutch, a long-lasting hostility that permanently penetrated the English language with expressions such as 'Dutch courage' (gin allegedly induced belligerence). Both powers wanted to trade in gold and intervene in the lucrative spice and textiles trade dominated by Asian merchants. Even in the interludes when officially at peace, they fought on African battlegrounds to retain the overseas monopolies that they both presumptuously claimed as their own. Recognizing the value of Dutch financial initiatives, England strengthened its resources by emulating its enemy, and when Newton arrived in London, the English economy had already been boosted by public–private enterprises from which everybody was supposed to benefit. The Bank of England and London's major Companies—East India, South Seas, Royal African—were based on financial strategies imported from Holland.

Before the twin sisters were founded, Charles had been carefully planning his return, and the Company of Royal Adventurers Trading into Africa received a Royal Charter almost straightaway, two years earlier than the Royal Society. In October 1660, Pepys 'heard the Duke speak of a great design that he and my Lord of Pembrooke have, and a great many others, of sending a venture to some parts of affrica to dig for gold=ore there. They entend to admit as many as will venture their money, and so make themselfs a company. 250*l* is the lowest share for every man. But I do not find that my Lord doth much like it.'[16] Despite his Lord's reservations, the plans went ahead. Three successful years later, the Royal Charter was extended, giving permission for the Company to trade in human captives as well as gold, ivory, and other goods.

Royal Charters were awarded for ventures combining private and public gain, but they needed to be renewed and could be revoked; the British Broadcasting Corporation is one of the few surviving examples. Although Charles never did come through with the last £6000 of the capital he had originally promised, he offered generous support by leasing to his Adventurers a large tract of his West African territory (well, he said it was his…) for 1000 years at an annual rent of two elephants. He also gave the Company the exclusive privilege of trading in wood, ivory, and other materials, as well as one third of the rights to the gold mines. And on top of that, the Charter gave the Company unusually strong powers by authorizing it to appoint governors, train military forces, and administer martial law.[17]

Like the Royal Adventurers and other international trading companies, the Royal Society contributed to an undefined experimental community that spread across London. Whether motivated by accumulating knowledge or making their goods more profitable—or both—its participants shared an interest in collecting and analysing information and materials from around the world. Benefits accrued in every direction. For example, the Royal Society invested money in the East India Company and elected some employees as Fellows; conversely, when Edmond Halley wanted to set up an observatory on St Helena, he travelled on a company ship.[18] Similarly, the Royal Society was well placed to cooperate with its sister, and stressed the links between them. Like several other aristocratic directors of the Royal Adventurers, the Duke of York was a Fellow of the Royal Society. The twins also had some more active personnel in common. Of the sixty-six people named in the second Charter endorsing slavery, nine were (or became later) Fellows of the Royal Society. These included the Duke's private secretary, Sir William Coventry of the Admiralty—and he was succeeded in that post by Henry Brouncker, the brother of the Society's first president, William.[19]

As fervent Baconians, the Fellows were keen to garner information from around the globe, and trading networks provided ideal opportunities for them to achieve that aim. Advertising for contributions to its own stated project of improving natural knowledge, the Royal Society issued 'Directions for Sea-men, bound for far Voyages', and over the years, travellers sent in reams of information about flora and fauna, winds and tides, magnetic and astronomical phenomena. Whatever individuals might have thought privately, collectively the Society tapped into the king's search for wealth and imperial power. Sailing under the flag of knowledge, the fellows of the Royal Society could regard the entire globe as a giant cabinet of curiosities waiting to be retrieved for display in metropolitan showcases.

Their enquiries reflected the imperial interests that the Royal Society held in common with the Royal Adventurers. For example, Robert Boyle was eager to learn about other peoples—'their Stature, Shape, Colour, Features, Strength, Agility, Beauty (or the want of it), Complexions, Hair, Dyet, Inclinations, and Customs that seem not due to Education'.[20] In addition, the Society maintained personal links with individual Royal Adventurers based in African trading posts. A letter to a Mr Floyd of around 1670 was packed with rumour. Is it true that new-born African babies are a yellowish-white colour? Do Africans regard stinking fish and rotten elephant meat as great delicacies? But Floyd was also requested to send concrete information about the location of the best gold mines. The writer was clearly well informed, demanding details of internal routes from Acania to Assingrad and on through Alance to Accabel.[21]

The Society's mercenary interests were protected by the wealthy merchant Abraham Hill, who was an elected official—including treasurer—for twelve years, but made no contributions to scientific knowledge. He did, however, compile a questionnaire designed specifically for travellers to Guinea, which reveals not only the curiosity of the Fellows but also the unreliability of information based on hearsay. Is the rain, he asked, so hot that it rots cloths and generates worms? Is an African's eyesight far keener than that of a European? Are the people different shades of brown and black? More practically, Hill also wanted to know how to find the best gold, prepare poisoned arrows, and distil grain alcohol—no coincidence that this Royal Society Fellow later became a Commissioner for the Board of Trade.[22]

At the beginning of Sprat's *History*, an emblematic frontispiece displays a multitude of Baconian instruments. One of the most prominent is a triangular sea-clock, which the Fellows hoped would keep time so accurately that it could be used to measure a ship's longitude at sea. After some preliminary trials, the Society used its contacts at the Royal Adventurers to send two experimental versions on an expedition to Africa led by Robert Holmes (the flamboyant naval officer who later had an affair in the Isle of Wight with Hooke's niece Grace). His official military orders, drafted by Coventry of the Royal Society, were to defend the Company of Royal Adventurers and build a fort, but he was also told privately that he should look for a rumoured mountain of gold. Holmes surpassed royal expectations by taking the opportunity to claim territory, blockade ports, and seize enemy ships. 'I hope I have nott exceeded my instructions, they being to concerve our commerce,' he protested with mock innocence.[23] Continuing to follow Coventry's guidelines, Holmes embarked on further aggressive campaigns against the Dutch and, despite some calamitous setbacks, ended up being a royal favourite.

The Fellows were proud to associate themselves with such imperial success, especially when they could make money from it. The very first issue of their new journal, the *Philosophical Transactions* of 1665, carried an article describing how well their clocks had performed on Holmes's voyage. The inventors were, the author boasted, both Fellows of the Royal Society and the experiment had been arranged by 'some of our Eminent *Virtuosi*, and Grand Promoters of Navigation.'[24] But the Society's future existence was still uncertain. The main instigator had been Hill, who in his position as treasurer helped to boost the Society's financial situation by giving his name to patents for profitable inventions, including not only the longitude clock but also carriages, guns, and pistols. By registering these patents to Hill, continuity would be ensured, should the Royal Society collapse.[25]

But the neophyte society did survive. Four decades later, when Newton took over as president, its activities were still closely tied to the nation's global trading ambitions.

Into Africa

The African Company's motto made Charles's motives clear—*Regio floret patrocinio Commercium, commercioque Regnum*: Business flourishes with royal patronage, and the kingdom flourishes with business. One of the king's main advisers was George Downing, Treasury Secretary and spy-master who acquired so much power that he gave his name to a London street as well as a Cambridge college. Brought up in America, he was widely mocked as the 'Judas of Downing Street' who had launched his career under Oliver Cromwell but after the Restoration contrived to reinvent himself as a wealthy royalist. The spitting is audible in the diaries both of Samuel Pepys—'perfidious rogue...most ungratefull villaine'—and of John Evelyn: 'Sir George Downing, one that had been a great...against his Majesty [his dots], but now insinuated into his favor; and, from a pedagogue and fanatic preacher, not worth a groate, had become excessively rich.'[26] It was through Downing that Dutch influence remained strong from Cromwell to William and beyond. His reforms were crucial for enabling the credit-driven economy that characterized England during Newton's regime at the Mint—he stressed the importance of commerce, strengthened the position of the Treasury, and established a state based on credit and indirect taxation.[27]

As a joint-stock company, Charles's Royal Adventurers Trading into Africa was a new financial invention (there is much scholarly debate about whether it deserves the accolade of being England's first). Before the Restoration, there were two major types of commercial organization. Oldest were the guilds, associations of merchants that could acquire a monopoly by giving money to the monarch. Next came chartered companies. Named after different parts of the world, such as Hudson Bay or East India, they enabled merchants to exploit newly discovered areas by obtaining exclusive trading rights from the crown. Although definitions vary, the new joint-stock companies brought together the interests of court and city: the crown had substantial control, but private investors could buy and sell shares. This concept of trading shares in a combined royal and commercial enterprise had been introduced by the Dutch East India Company at the beginning of the seventeenth century, but it was only later that the English India Company adopted the structure.[28]

Chartered in 1660, the Company of Royal Adventurers Trading into Africa exemplified England's mercantile policy—to maximize exports under a government that controlled the economy and sought to enhance its international strength. Joint-stock companies seemed like a win–win proposal: the great appeal to investors lay in promising high returns but at the same time spreading risk; for Charles II, strongly swayed by Downing, the main lure was gaining revenue and reducing his dependence on a Parliament that was reluctant to finance all the crown's ambitions. With a profitable base in Africa, the king could develop lucrative trade deals with the cash-rich Spanish Americas—and at home, he hoped to tighten his grip by gaining the allegiance of grateful financiers as well as of politicians who would guarantee his security in order to advance their own careers.

The Royal African Company, which was active during Newton's regime at the Mint, retained the same heraldic insignia as its predecessor (Figure 9.2). During a session at Whitehall, Pepys 'saw a draught of the armes of the company, which the King is of and so is called the Royall company—which is, in a field argent a Elephant proper, with a Canton [a heraldic term] on which England and France is Quartered—Supported by two Moores; the Crest, an Anchor Winged I think it is...'[29] The ancient symbol of a war elephant carrying a castle-like howdah on its back can still be found in some medieval churches, and it long predates the Elephant and Castle area of London. Although very few Europeans encountered this animal from Africa's inland regions, the iconic elephant was engraved onto imported ivory (Figure 9.3), guns, golden coins, and company ledgers. It came to provide familiar evidence of England's increasing imperial strength.

Figure 9.2 Company of Royal Adventurers Trading into Africa, coat of arms, 1663

Standing on either side of the shield in the Royal Adventurers' coat of arms, two supporters conform to English stereotypes of fierce chieftains, made widely available in a 1670 book by John Ogilby, which remained the standard source of misleading information about Africa for decades. This former dancer reinvented himself several times, first endearing himself to Charles II by orchestrating the coronation festivities, followed by a spell working as a surveyor with Wren and Hooke. Next, Ogilby was appointed royal cosmographer, but—like many self-styled authorities—never travelled himself to the remote regions of the world that he described so evocatively. Creatively translating and plagiarizing older works, he reinforced prejudices about naked savages who needed to be tamed and civilized by English settlers.

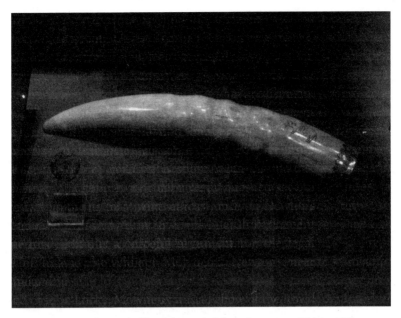

Figure 9.3 Ivory imported by the Royal African Company, 17th or 18th century

Ogilby and his readers would have been astonished to learn that some African kings worked in offices decorated with Dutch tapestries, Indian cloths, and silverware made from New World ores. During the sixteenth century, local rulers along the western coast had become rich and powerful by playing off two major trading networks—Atlantic and Saharan—that were seeking access to gold. In a sophisticated market economy, valuable imports—iron, fruit, copper, maize—were being exchanged for gold, whose commercial value rose as demand increased. Much of it was carried to the ports from inland areas by enslaved Africans, who were then forced to undertake the return journey laden down with purchases. The entire region flourished as its small independent kingdoms profited by trading with India, Brazil, Portugal, and each other. But in the middle of the seventeenth century, this mutually beneficial stability rapidly deteriorated after Europeans intervened. They introduced guns as a new form of currency, and—like golden coins—African people became tokens of exchange for desirable goods. Deprived of their labour force and now armed with lethal weapons, local leaders stopped cooperating and began fighting internal wars that were stoked by Europeans hoping to obtain more human captives for export.[30]

The guineas made from African gold carried the Royal Adventurers' elephant and castle symbol on their reverse. Even before Newton left Cambridge for his metropolitan career at the Mint, he must have been familiar with that royal sign of an elephant and castle inscribed on the nation's currency. There is no evidence that he ever met Charles or James, but he was familiar with both kings' faces, which appeared on the golden coins next to the motto *Dei Gratia*—by the Grace of God—as if English monarchs were divinely sanctioned to plunder gold or convert people into slaves. The physical or melted-down value of these guineas soon soared to well over twenty shillings (which made a pound), and eventually in 1717—during Newton's regime at the Mint—the guinea was fixed as a new unit of currency at twenty-one shillings. This arithmetically inconvenient amount still featured in legal documents and primary school arithmetic questions a quarter of a millennium later.

The Door of No Return

When Lemuel Gulliver was at last safely home from his travels, he parodied Whig-speak by describing how the king's global plans might have played out: 'the *British* Nation…may be an Example to the whole World for their Wisdom, Care and Justice in planting Colonies; their liberal Endowments for the Advancement of Religion and Learning; their Choice of devout and able Pastors to propagate *Christianity*…to crown all, by sending the most vigilant and virtuous Governors, who have no other Views than the Happiness of the People over whom they preside, and the Honour of the King their Master.'

Actuality had, of course, been different. Swift's account may be jaundiced and exaggerated, but it sounds horribly authentic: 'A Crew of Pyrates are driven by a Storm they know not whither; at length a Boy discovers Land from the Top-mast; they go on Shore to rob and plunder; they see an harmless People, are entertained with Kindness, they give the Country a new Name; they take formal Possession of it for the King…Here commences a new Dominion acquired with a Title by *Divine Right*. Ships are sent with the first Opportunity; the Natives driven out or destroyed, their Princes tortured to discover their Gold, a free Licence given to all Acts of Inhumanity and Lust; the Earth reeking with the Blood of its Inhabitants.'[31] Operating in the king's name and with exclusive legal access, when Newton became Master of the Mint the Royal African Company alone had sent over 500 ships, built eight coastal forts, transported 100,000 prisoners to plantations in the Americas, imported 30,000 tons of sugar, and provided gold for 500,000 guineas.[32]

In *Gulliver's Travels*, Swift included diagrams, navigational specifications, and anthropological descriptions that were patently fictitious, but the geographical accounts on which real monarchs and traders relied were often low on facts. Seventeenth-century maps of West Africa were even vaguer than Senex's Newtonian tribute (see Figure 9.1), their labels indicating what Europeans could purloin for their own benefit—Grain Coast, Gold Coast, Slave Coast. England was far from being the only European country that assumed a God-given right to settle in other places and seize other people to exploit as slaves. In 1661, Portugal simply transferred Tangier and Bombay (now Mumbai) to Charles II as part of a marriage deal that also included rights to Portuguese ports in Africa then occupied by the Dutch. It was Tangier, not Bombay, that was the jewel in Charles's crown, a thriving port only a fortnight's sail away, compared with three months to the American colonies or six to India. Strapped for cash, Charles immediately leased Bombay to the East India Company, but built up a military garrison at Tangier to protect the Mediterranean, which then remained more lucrative for British trade than distant continents. This commercial profit came at a human cost: during Newton's lifetime, around 6000 Britons were captured by Mediterranean pirates for forced labour, many of them dying young from disease or the hardship of enduring twenty-hour days shackled to the oar of a galley-ship. That figure may sound high, but of course it was minuscule compared to the numbers of enslaved Africans.[33]

By the time the Royal Adventurers began operating, some permanent trading settlements had already been established in West Africa, although tropical diseases and dense vegetation deterred the more intensive colonization taking place in America and the West Indies. English ships had been intermittently travelling to and from Africa for over a century. The first documented voyage was in 1533, but by the end of the seventeenth century, England had already shipped almost half a million human beings from Africa to the Americas. Precise figures are hard to establish, but they continued to rise steadily.[34]

The long western coast of Africa was strung with European settlements, many of them within sight of each other, although the highest concentration lay in what is now Ghana, 7500 kilometres almost due south of London. Forts were built both to protect their European occupiers from the land-based attacks of resentful locals, and also to provide defence against the ships of foreign invaders. British trade centred on Cape Coast Castle (Figure 9.4), perched on a rocky headland and originally a mud-brick Swedish trading base; after being claimed by both the Dutch and the Danish, it was seized by Holmes and his English troops in 1664. By 1721, when Newton

Figure 9.4 Cape Coast Castle

had been in charge of the Mint for over twenty years, the Castle encompassed 'a Smith's Shop, a Cooperage, Store-houses, a Chappel, and Houses for the Officers and Servants...A Bastion runs out from it that has a very pleasant Prospect to the sea, discerning with a Glass the Ships coming down the Coast...'[35] Upkeep was expensive. African rulers charged high rents and handsome rewards were necessary to ensure political cooperation; daily survival depended on maintaining smooth relationships with local suppliers and labourers. Malaria and yellow fever were rife, the iron guns immediately went rusty, and frequent lightning strikes melted the gold in its bags and the soldiers' swords in their scabbards (fortunately, the gunpowder in the basement was so damp that it never ignited).

Restored after Ghanaian independence from Britain in 1957, Cape Coast Castle is now a UNESCO World Heritage Site: the vultures still circle, but the tropical diseases have vanished. Although resembling a powerful coastal fortress, the Castle functioned as a warehouse used for storing goods and people in transit. Inside, it felt like an ocean-going ship, structured in a vertical hierarchy with luxurious upper-deck cabins for the senior officers, ranging down to cramped slave holes below the waterline, where a thousand captives could be conveniently stashed at a time. Tourists can now visit these gloomy dungeons, still pervaded by stinking fetid air. Most of the early captives were men, thrown down through a small opening to share a single damp space. Women were crammed into smaller cubicles enabling guards to ogle them through holes in the wall, while the tiny condemned cell temporarily housed prisoners being starved to death after trying to escape. Nearby lay the one-way exit to the Americas through 'The Door of No Return'.[36]

African trade in people, gold, cotton, and other resources was a global concern: events along the Guinea coast sent ripples round the world and, conversely, were affected by affairs elsewhere. Because sugar plantations in the West Indies were rapidly expanding, European owners demanded more slaves to run them, and private profiteering flourished. Robinson Crusoe was a fictional character, but his experiences were closely based on those of real-life adventurers who were making small fortunes. After borrowing £40 to buy the standard assortment of trinkets, Crusoe set off for Guinea and 'brought Home *L. 5. 9 Ounces* of Gold Dust [worth] almost 300 *l*. Scaling up again, he took a cargo of English manufactured goods to Brazil, selling it for four times his original stake—and 'the first thing I did, I bought me a Negro Slave, and an *European* Servant also....'[37]

Defoe had carried out his historical research thoroughly—indeed, his hero insists on the authenticity of his tale and 'the real Facts in my History'. In August 1651, Crusoe embarked on a slave-trading voyage, only to be shipwrecked a month later on the island that became his kingdom. These dates accurately mark the period when Charles II was preparing to take back the throne.[38] The restored king started by awarding a Charter to the Royal Adventurers for trading in goods, but then—like Crusoe—upsized three years later to include humans, even lending the Company three royal ships. Steered by Downing, he promised the Company that it 'shall for ever hereafter have use and enjoy all mines of gold and silver which are or shall be found in all or any the places above mentioned, and the whole entire and only trade [to those parts] for the buying and selling bartering and exchanging of for or with any negroes slaves good wares and merchandises whatsoever to be vented or found at or within any of the Cities.'[39]

This new Charter had far-reaching consequences for captured Africans, and promised large profits for a select group of wealthy Englishmen who could afford to buy subscriptions at £400. Although the Royal Society was enthusiastic about its twin-sister company, private traders were incensed, because under Downing's directions the crown squeezed out the Crusoe-style merchants who had been operating independently. In 1667, the same year as Sprat's *History*, a group of merchants petitioned Parliament to remove the royal monopoly on enslaved Africans. They protested unsuccessfully that enhancing the king's revenue would damage their own livelihood and put plantation owners out of business: 'That formerly there hath always been a freedom of Trade for all His Majesties Subjects for *Negroes* on the whole coast of *Guiney*, by reason whereof the said Plantations have been plentifully supplied with *Negroes* of the best sort, and at an indifferent rate, to the great encrease of the said Plantations, and the advantage and profit of this Crown and Nation.'[40]

Instead, Charles appointed his brother James, later king but then the Duke of York, as the governor of the Royal Adventurers. James spread his dukedom around the world by ousting the Dutch and converting New Amsterdam into New York. The initials DY were permanently branded with a burning iron on the right breasts of people shipped across the Atlantic from West Africa to the Americas—over 100,000 during the twenty-eight years he was in charge. Every year, thousands of captive Africans—women as well as men—were confined in the dungeons of holding stations such as Cape Coast Castle and Gorée to be haggled over between local traders, European merchants, and African rulers. Like ivory tusks and nuggets of gold, they became branded Company commodities that could be bought in exchange for European guns or iron bars and sold at a profit.[41]

Sprat gave the twin-sister societies a common birth, and links continued to be forged between them. When the Royal African Company was founded, one of its first participants was the philosopher John Locke, fellow of the Royal Society and secretary to the Council of Trades and Plantations. By the time Newton became President of the Royal Society, the crown's direct powers had been further curtailed, and the government had instituted financial controls that enabled private enterprise to flourish by buying and selling human beings. As head of the Royal Mint as well as of the Royal Society, Newton was in a strong position to promote the interests of the Fellows, the nation, and himself. He knew that trade, war, science, and empire were inextricably tied together.

10
Going Global

The children in Conduitt's drawing room are dressed to resemble adults, but they must have found The Indian Emperour rather heavy going at times. They were probably paying most attention at the beginning, when the Spanish invaders marvel at the treasures promised by this newly discovered land:

> Each downfal of a flood the Mountains pour
> From their rich bowels rolls a silver shower.[1]

Any spectators (young or old) who dozed off as the play progressed through its five acts must surely have woken up during the final scene, which takes place in the prison cell. Although—bar a few corpses— there is a moderately happy ending, before that the audience had to watch a long session of physical torture. Hardly suitable for children, one might think, but given the harshness of their upbringing, perhaps the small royal spectators were so inured to cruelty that they enjoyed seeing somebody else suffer.

Stretched in agony on a rack, Montezuma emerges as a noble hero who will neither convert to Christianity nor reveal where his gold is to be found. Dryden depicts this Mexican emperor as being more civilized than his Spanish conquerors, whom he denounces for engaging in primitive behaviour by indulging their craving for wealth:

> The gods will Punish you, if they be Just;
> The gods will Plague your Sacrilegious Lust.

Similarly, the Catholic priest exhibits the savagery more commonly attributed to indigenous peoples, mercilessly ordering his men to slaughter the honourable Indian leader:

> *How wickedly he has refus'd his wealth,*
> *And hid his Gold, from Christian hands, by stealth:*
> *Down with him, Kill him, merit Heaven thereby.*[2]

As the plot unfolds, Montezuma comes to resemble a true-blooded Englishman who values his liberty above all else, opting for suicide rather than captivity by the Spanish conquerors:

> *If either Death or Bondage I must chuse,*
> *I'll keep my Freedom, though my life I'll lose.*[3]

There is no way of knowing what impact this performance had on the lives of its young performers and spectators, but perhaps it did persuade some of them to reflect on Britain's international conduct towards subjugated peoples. Outside the protected confines of this domestic theatre, different standards ruled. During the seventeenth and eighteenth centuries, many thousands of Africans were shipped across the Atlantic, forced to work as slaves on British plantations. Like Montezuma, they placed great emphasis on personal honour, but when they replicated his high moral stance by jumping overboard or starving themselves to death, they were despised for displaying cowardly, criminal behaviour.

The young actors may also have contemplated the slave-like conditions that European gentlemen imposed on their womenfolk. In the scene depicted by Hogarth, Cydaria (dressed in white) is denouncing Cortez as a philanderer, blending imagery of male domination over women and over empire (no coincidence that, in English, countries are gendered female in a predominantly neutral language):

> *More cruel than the Tyger o'er his spoil;*
> *And falser than the Weeping Crocodile:*
> *Can you add Vanity to Guilt, and take*
> *A Pride to hear the Conquests which you make?*
> *Go, publish your Renown, let it be said,*
> *You have a Woman, and that lov'd, betray'd.*[4]

Confined by his chains, Cortez protests his fidelity, and—in an unusually symmetrical mixed-ethnicity relationship—both Cortez and Cydaria declare that they would rather die than live without the other. These may be the defiant lines that Hogarth captured Cydaria/ Caroline Lennox in the very act of pronouncing:

> No, let me dye, and I'le my claim resign;
> For while I live, methinks you should be mine.[5]

Some ten years later, this heartfelt moment was perhaps recalled by Lennox and her parents when she eloped with the politician Henry Fox and was cut out of her father's will.

*   *   *

'Freedom is Slavery' ran Big Brother's second slogan in George Orwell's *Nineteen Eighty-Four*. Three centuries earlier, post-Revolution England was far from being Oceania's Airstrip One, but some powerful Britons voiced the same sentiment. Individual liberty, they argued, included the right to behave like the king and profit from trading in enslaved people. Newton lived through three major upheavals—the Civil War, the Restoration, and the Glorious Revolution. In all three, the question of individual rights had been an underlying theme, but all three failed to achieve the ideals they aimed at. After 1688, the Whigs succeeded in diminishing the absolute control of the monarchy, but wealth and influence still lay in the hands of a privileged few. British liberty brought personal freedom to pursue property and profit without worrying unduly about the long-term consequences.

Orwell's Oceania was ruled by an elite Inner Party comprising only 2 per cent of the population, and Newton hovered around the outer edges of its Georgian equivalent, unctuously ingratiating himself with members of the next tier up in the hierarchy. Like many of his wealthy colleagues, Newton gained financially from international slavery, protectionist taxation policies, and industrial espionage. The value of his investments relied on privately backed credit schemes and profits derived from people trafficking; collectively, their long-term effects included disrupting the economic and political stability of Western Africa, and squeezing Asian competitors out of the global market.

Totalled over several hundred years, Britain shipped more captive Africans across the Atlantic than any other nation. Towards the end of the seventeenth century, this trade in people escalated during the political shift away from absolute monarchy towards greater state control and supposed democracy. In order to supervise the country's finances more closely, after the Glorious Revolution the government gave the king a budget, refusing to sanction the crown's traditional practice of replenishing its private coffers by monopolizing markets. In 1694, while Newton was feeling restless in Cambridge and sounding out other possibilities, new Whig legislation claimed to enhance individual freedom by removing the royal monopoly on people trafficking.

Private merchants had long campaigned for free trade. While James II and the Royal African Company openly profited from importing gold and selling people, their own lucrative activities were technically illegal. Their mounting frustration erupted in colourful invective directed against the former regime: 'Through the Countenance of the then Duke of *York* their Governour, and the strong Influence of the Beams of the then Prerogative, a Brood at length came forth to engage in a Design so apparently opposite to the Laws of the Land, so destructive of the Native Liberty and Freedom of the Subjects of *England*, and so contrary to the true Interest of the Nation, with respect to its Commerce.' But now that all lay in the past: the new Act would restore their 'Native Liberty' by abolishing the royal monopoly. That might sound like a positive step towards a more democratic society, but it meant that private companies—not just the monarchy—were entitled to trade in people as well as in goods. Profiting from slavery had become an English citizen's right, and the national economy soared during the eighteenth century, maintained at the cost of long-term suffering throughout Africa and the Americas.[6]

Confidence in the value and virtue of international trade became a national declaration of faith in Christian capitalism. Josiah Child, a key director of the East India Company (EIC), declared that 'Foreign Trade produceth Riches, Riches Power, Power preserves our Trade and Religion; they mutually work one upon and for the preservation of each other.'[7] During the 1690s, Child and his colleagues were found guilty of extreme corruption, and after a series of public protests about high profits and low wages, the company plunged into financial crisis. When it proposed to rescue itself by unifying its Indian and Chinese branches, Newton and many others objected, but the controversial merger went ahead. To disillusioned supporters of the Glorious Revolution, it seemed 'strange after all our battles for liberty that this monster, monopoly, should lift up its horns and shake his chains to the terror of the honest trading subject'.[8] Newton valued the parliamentary regime that reduced royal power but enhanced state control, and he strongly opposed this creation of a mainly private mega-EIC: 'Divide them that you may govern them,' he advised. Apparently living by his principles, he never invested in the joint EIC, although he had bought a holding in one of the original companies.[9] This mammoth commercial organization came to dominate world trade, effectively governing India by the end of the eighteenth century.

Trusting the Facts

Ever craving certainty, Newton sought refuge in the security of incontestable facts. Reluctant to publish until he had checked and double-checked and triple-checked, he was repeatedly confronted by the unpalatable reality that evidence can be unreliable. Each piece of data had to be scrutinized with the same care as a financial note of credit: could it be trusted? When studying the natural world, Newton discovered that instruments disagreed, that observers made careless measurements, that natural phenomena inexplicably changed from day to day or even hour to hour. Investigating the past generated still further frustrations: dating systems were vague, writers favoured metaphorical allusive language, manuscripts flatly contradicted one another.

Identifying trustworthy facts is not always easy. Imagine yourself sitting in a hushed reading room at the British Library, two eighteenth-century items placed on the wooden desk in front of you: a map and an illustration. Meticulously drawn, the map shows Central and Southern America—the '*Coast, Countries and Islands within ye Limits of ye South Sea Company*' (see Figure 5.3). Next to it lies a black-and-white picture: also finely executed, it depicts Isaac Newton perched on a rock near a young African albino at the mouth of the River Senegal, eavesdropping on a conversation between a merman and an oyster (Figure 10.1). Naturally, you place more faith in the map than in the picture. Yet both of them are fallible—and both of them are also informative about reality.

The 1711 map (see Figure 5.3) comes with impeccable credentials. It was drawn by Herman Moll, a distinguished Dutch cartographer who lived in England and moved in the same circles as some of Newton's colleagues—John Locke, Robert Hooke, Jonathan Swift. Commissioned by the South Sea Company, it advertises the enormous expanse of land and ocean over which the company claimed exclusive trading rights. The detailed outlines and precise nomenclature proclaim its authenticity, although there is no guarantee that it faithfully replicates actuality. However authoritative a map's origins might be, everybody knew that a fair amount of creative thinking was involved, especially for the interiors of continents. Even Newton got it wrong, mistakenly moving Baghdad on his map of the Middle East from the right place to the wrong one.[10] Swift's scepticism was justified:

> So Geographers in *Afric-maps*,
> With Savage-Pictures fill their Gaps;
> And o'er unhabitable Downs
> Place Elephants for want of Towns.[11]

Geographical knowledge had to be gleaned second-hand from merchants and navigators who rated survival and profit more highly than accuracy. Since Moll had never ventured to the southern hemisphere, he had to depend on unverifiable visual evidence—earlier maps, secret logs stolen from captured enemies—as well as verbal testimony from people who had at least passed through the region. Their information was neither complete nor trustworthy. Travel was expensive, dangerous, and not primarily aimed at

Quel eſt le droit du plus fort?.. c'eſt... ce qui
fait que je te mange

Figure 10.1 Newton in Senegal, 1770; from Jean Delisle de Sales,
Philosophie de la nature, 1770

broadening the mind: there were always ulterior motives, such as lucrative trading or ferreting out political information or converting foreigners to Christianity. Diplomatic missions provided cover for industrial espionage, while research expeditions doubled up as opportunities to claim land and seize valuable resources, including human captives as well as samples of minerals or plants.[12]

Fortunately for Moll, he had an illustrious predecessor in Newton's ally Edmond Halley, who had sailed across the Atlantic some ten years earlier to compile magnetic data. Yet even Halley could not be depended upon. To cover areas he had not visited himself, he incorporated the reports of a seventeenth-century buccaneer, hardly a reputable source. When his charts were criticized, he candidly admitted that he had drawn smooth curves through only three points. As Halley had done, Moll included Pepys Island just off the coast of what is now Argentina, helpfully adding an enlarged inset revealing prominent features such as Mount Charles (named after the king) and Secretaries Point (Samuel Pepys was Chief Secretary to the Admiralty). Published when the South Sea Company was touting for investment, Moll's map offered valuable reassurance that British ships could stop for fresh supplies on friendly non-Spanish territory before embarking into the unfamiliar Pacific. Eventually, Pepys Island proved as illusory as the South Sea Bubble, although it was only in 1764 that this imagined island was finally declared to be non-existent.[13]

Through cartography, the South Sea Company confirmed its ownership of inhabited land, although naturally the directors had not thought to consult the people who lived there. Pepys, one of Newton's predecessors as president of the Royal Society, had never ventured anywhere near the island named after him, but he was deeply involved in the financial arrangements of London's trading companies. The members of the Royal Society and of the Royal Exchange collaborated to benefit each other, reaping both knowledge and profits at the expense of England's imperial possessions.[14]

In contrast, the apparently bizarre scene of Newton with an albino, a merman, and an eloquent oyster was patently fictitious, yet metaphorically revealing. Produced after his death, it reflects enduring associations of Newtonianism with global concerns of slavery and trade. Just off the coast of Senegal lies the island of Gorée, now a World Heritage Site but during Newton's lifetime a key holding post for enslaved people awaiting shipment across the Atlantic. Originally Dutch, but repeatedly passed back and forth by French and English aggressors, the island became symbolically significant. In London, an Old-Mr-Gory was seventeenth-century slang for a gold coin, while in the Gold Coast, people had themselves been converted into a form of currency. Like paper notes or metal coins or guns, their value depended on what they could be exchanged for, on what credit they could muster. In well-established trading ports, they were worth more than in new ones, where African traders had not yet realized how much value Europeans would attribute to them, what price they would pay per head.[15]

This maritime sketch of Senegal originally illustrated an episode in a satirical playlet of 1777 composed by a French Enlightenment radical, Jean Delisle de Sales, and was included in later editions of his ever-expanding *Philosophy of Nature*. A banned text, like many similar works it was published abroad as a small pocket-sized book ideal for clandestine circulation. Ranging over many topics, it included the scandalous view that living beings are essentially collections of chemicals. Brandishing his pistol to protect himself, Newton features as an icon of rationality, identified here as a vegetarian at the top of an intelligence ladder who is adjudicating about the moral dilemmas posed by eating a creature that thinks, loves, and may have a soul. Towards the end of Delisle's scenario, Newton draws on his intellectual powers of logical argument to conclude that although the albino African is inferior to a European, he is fundamentally different from the oyster and the merman because he understands the concept of God.[16]

The question of what it meant to be human was central to debates about the rights and wrongs of slavery. When Robinson Crusoe is thrown overboard, he saves himself from being drowned beneath giant waves—the mindless power of nature—by applying his intellect to 'pilot' his non-reasoning body towards the shore. Similarly, Newton came to be regarded as a disembodied genius who formulated abstract laws for governing the universe. After being stranded for a quarter of a century as the solitary monarch of a desert island kingdom, Crusoe at last acquires a loyal subject, Friday. Vaunting himself as a civilized European, Crusoe simply assumes he has the right to rule over other people just as he had the power to overcome the challenges of the natural world. Initially, Crusoe perceives Friday as a slave, but then upgrades his status to servant after recognizing him as a fellow human being, a creature endowed with sufficient powers of reason to 'pilot' (Defoe's repetition of this image) them both off the island.[17]

Delisle and his readers were aware that, according to eighteenth-century evolutionists, marine creatures had not been originally placed on earth by God as a separate creation, but were an early ancestor of human beings. In contrast, some slave-owners justified themselves by arguing that black Africans were animals and hence basically different from Europeans, who had the right to own them and also the duty to protect them. The caption beneath Delisle's picture is '*Quel est le droit du plus fort?...c'est...ce qui fait que je te mange*', which translates loosely as 'Which is the strongest right? The one that allows me to eat you.' Victory goes not to the most morally worthy but to the most powerful, to the European men of reason like Newton.

Although Newton has the reputation of being a lone worker, he took advantage of a global correspondence network to obtain data from informants based along the routes of trading ships participating in the international transfer of goods, gold, and people that underpinned the British economy. In this imaginary visit to Senegal, he is holding a large open tome, presumably his book on gravity. Perched on a coastal rock, he seems to be acting out one of the most famous remarks attributed to him: 'I know not what I may seem to the world, but as to myself, I seem to have been only like a boy playing on the sea-shore and diverting myself in now and then finding a smoother pebble or a prettier shell than ordinary, whilst the great ocean of truth lay all undiscovered before me.' John Conduitt was so impressed by this seaside metaphor that he pasted an early version from a Jacobite magazine into his biographical scrapbook.

In real life, there is no evidence that Newton ever ventured outside his comfort zone of Lincolnshire, Cambridge, and London, let alone abroad: his most adventurous journey by water seems to have been a voyage up the Thames to Hampton Court. Just as Moll had relied on informants to carry out his virtual tour of the South Seas, so Newton vicariously visited ports in West Africa and other coastal areas by taking advantage of travellers stationed along the trade routes. For the second and third editions of the *Principia*, he solicited data from East India Company personnel so that he could revise his gravitational calculations. What is now revered as the world's greatest book on physics incorporated information that had been gleaned from British colonizers who were both exploring and exploiting the globe.[18]

William Wordsworth immortalized Newton as a lone genius voyaging through strange seas of thought alone, but Newton relied on a virtual crew of observers who really did sail around the globe. That had been the case since he was in his twenties: the very first letter of his that survives, from 1669, discusses how information could be collected from voyagers overseas. Some thirty years later, when he was revising the *Principia* for the second edition that eventually came out in 1713, Newton recruited a young mathematician at Cambridge, Roger Cotes, to do much of the arithmetical hard work. For his calculations on the pull of the moon, Newton needed observations of tides—and the best people to ask about that seemed to be officials based in foreign ports and employees of the East India Company.

Newton collated information from about thirty locations scattered around the globe along trade routes converging on Britain from China and India, from West Africa and the West Indies. At a time when even readings of the local London tides failed to agree, little confidence could be placed in measurements finding their way back from the other side of the world. Could he believe what these distant observers reported? For one thing, perhaps they were insufficiently gentlemanly to be trusted. Moreover, they were naturally more concerned to maintain the safety of their ships and their men than to worry about the niceties of gravitation, and so might well exaggerate numbers in whichever direction suited their own interests. This was a general problem, not just Newton's. His rival Robert Hooke pointed out that, paradoxically, the more readings you got sent, the worse off you were: 'the greater the Collections of Observations are, the more trouble and difficulty is created to the Examiner; they not only confounding one another, but perplexing those also which are real and perfect.'[19]

The accuracy of the data was crucial, and in principle Newton was ruthless about eliminating observations that failed to meet his high standards. But that is where the circular arguments begin. How can you tell when a measurement is right? If you trust the reporter, then you should feel reassured that his number is correct. But suppose it contradicts the predictions of your theory? Do you ignore that particular reading, or do you abandon your conclusions and start again? In other words, do you blame your equations or your informant? And what if two apparently proficient observers disagree? Do you average their results—or do you follow Newton's example, and sometimes yield to the temptation of picking the one that suits you? Trying to salve Cotes's conscience while also getting his own way, at one stage Newton advised him that 'your scruple may be eased (I think) by relying more upon the observations of the tide' at one port than another.[20]

And then there was what Cotes and his friends called 'the French dilemma'. Working in different parts of the world, French experimenters examined pendulums that swung at exactly one-second intervals. Disconcertingly, although their lengths should theoretically have been the same, they seemed to vary, which might suggest that gravity was stronger in some places than others, or that the earth bulged slightly at the equator. On the other hand, since the measurements were being made to tiny fractions of an inch, it was impossible to eliminate simple errors or the effects of temperature. Perhaps Frenchmen were just generally incompetent? Between them, Newton and Cotes decided that some observers were more reliable than others, and that readings from Gorée were particularly divergent and therefore suspect. In the end, Newton essentially resorted to inventing reasons for the scatter of observations and flatly rejecting new readings that he could not accommodate within his theory. He knew that there is no simple route from data to theory: the conversation runs in both directions.

While Newton was revising the *Principia* to establish that the laws of gravity are universal, in his position as head of the Mint he was also struggling to establish an international standard for gold. Similar problems of calibration arose, because samples from different places produced different measurements. How do you know which one is true gold? Or even if there is such a thing? And how much of the apparent variation can you attribute to faulty instruments or to careless observers? Unsurprisingly, everybody involved with gold accused everybody else of cheating. English traders arrived in Africa convinced that all sorts of fraud were being perpetrated, but were disconcerted to find experienced local negotiators who spoke several languages, demanded high prices, and were knowledgeable about European instruments. A French expert made it clear to Robert Boyle, eminent chemist at the Royal Society, that there were two basic problems: 'The gold varies, Sir, not only inasmuch as it is varyingly adulterated by the natives, but also because it naturally differs in the form which it leaves the mines.' In addition, there was yet another challenge: Europeans as well as Africans were trying to turn a quick profit.[21]

Trying to ensure that coins were equivalent in England, Wales, Scotland, and Ireland, Newton was plagued with the same issues of reliability as he encountered for the length of a one-second pendulum: who can you trust, how consistent are the instruments, what is the true value? He was not above bluffing and bludgeoning his way through inconveniences. Reigning over the Mint, Newton candidly admitted that no procedure was 100 per cent reliable: 'I cannot undertake absolutely that...there shall be no faulty barrs which may escape the assays, but I am safest in people that are afraid of me.'[22] This may have been the Age of Reason, but personal power still mattered.

Newtonian Imperialism

Unlike other global empires, Britain's was never ruled by an emperor, but perhaps Sir Isaac Newton comes close to justifying the title. He is internationally celebrated for founding a new version of physics, but his ideas also came to underpin a world view characterized by central control, uniformity, and mathematization— Newtonian imperialism.

The simplest and the most common Newtonian parallel was to describe control from the centre. Britain was visualized as lying at the midst of a global system that exported the benefits of civilization—manufactured goods, Christianity, Newtonian science—while importing unprocessed materials such as sugar, cotton, and gold. Writing to commemorate Newton's death, the Scottish poet Allan Ramsay exhorted the Fellows of the Royal Society to bestow the benefits of British culture on less enlightened peoples:

> May from your *Learned Band* arise,
> *Newtons* to shine thro' future times,
> And bring down knowledge from the skies,
> To plant on wild *Barbarian* climes.
> 'Til nations, few degrees from brutes,
> Be brought into each proper road,
> Which leads to wisdom's happiest fruits,
> To know their Saviour and their God.[23]

This was the same centralized imagery that Desaguliers had outlined in his poem to George and Caroline, which described courtiers circling around their king as if held captive by his radiating power. Information flowed into the metropolis from observers stationed around the country and abroad, while conversely, the science created by the Fellows was transformed into marketable commodities—books, lectures, instruments—for global distribution. Put bluntly, data in, knowledge out. The East India Company regularly sent 'fishing fleets' to India, exporting cargoes of young English women as suitably cultured potential wives for their employees. Those still single at the end of the season were 'returned empty', as if they had been drained of value and learnt nothing while overseas. Similarly, children born abroad were shipped back to school in Britain so that they could be filled up with civilized habits.

According to the self-flattering myth that is still beloved by chauvinistic Britons, this small offshore island came to dominate the world through its innate superiority. This arrogant vision of Britain as a Newtonian centre, as an exporter of civilization and an importer of raw products, was consolidated during the eighteenth century. The Church of England raised huge sums of money to free the relatively small number of enslaved Britons captured in the Mediterranean, but sent out missionaries to convert Africans destined to work on colonial plantations. The most famous hymn to British imperialism appeared in 1740, five years before the first performance of the National Anthem:

> 'Rule, Britannia! rule the waves:
> 'Britons never will be slaves.'

So ran the original refrain of *Rule, Britannia!*, first composed for a court masque (a one-off private musical entertainment) celebrating the third birthday of Princess Augusta, Queen Caroline's granddaughter, who was thus taught at a young age that slavery is fine as long as it happens to other people. The song's author was a Scottish poet and loyal Newtonian, James Thomson, who earlier in his career had taught Newtonian mathematics at a London academy; his most famous work, *The Seasons*, is laden with Newtonian imagery.

Patriots celebrated the imperial success of a small Newtonian island lying at the hub of a two-way global trade, but this appealing metaphor of centrality collapses under scrutiny. In principle, Newtonian equations show symmetry: the attractive force between two masses is exactly the same for each one. But very often, one mass is substantially larger than the other—the earth and an apple, for example—so that the force appears to operate in one direction only, from the larger to the smaller. As an added complication, all objects act mutually on everything else, although as Newton discovered, the mathematics soon becomes horrendously complex. Even dealing with three bodies—the sun, the moon, and the earth—presented intractable difficulties.

A more realistic version of international commerce would have featured mutual gravitational attractions reverberating through the strands of a giant network wrapped right around the globe. Britain reacted to world events rather than initiating them, or even being involved. Rice became a staple crop in the Americas after enslaved Africans brought across seedlings and agricultural expertise; Indonesian coffee savoured by metropolitan Enlightenment gentlemen originated as cuttings sent from Yemen to Jakarta by a

Dutch governor in India; demand for silver in China led to financial crises in Europe; quinine extracted from South American bark came to flavour the gin cocktails of Indian settlers; when sugar merchants in the West Indies increased their prices, the Dutch undercut them by converting much of Java into a plantation. And so on.

Another legacy of Newtonian ideology was universality. According to older conventional models of the cosmos inherited from Aristotle, there is a fundamental split between the eternally smooth circulation of the planets in the heavens and the chaotic environment of the terrestrial sphere. Building on the work of his predecessors, Newton introduced mathematical laws that dispensed with that separation and governed the entire cosmos. But theories were not enough: he needed precise observations to confirm that his ideas were justified. From his presidential base at the Royal Society, Newton sent off requests to global travellers for information about tides, pendulum oscillations, and other natural phenomena. As he tried to match these measurements with his theories and with each other, discrepancies kept cropping up. Accepting them at face-value pointed towards a frightening conclusion—that his bid to unify the universe was invalid. Newton is famous for spurning hypotheses, yet establishing his version of gravity depends on a fundamental assumption—that nature is uniform, that the laws governing the fall of an apple are the same whether the tree is growing in York or in New York, that a person on earth is subject to the same equations as a space voyager to Mars. If that were not true, the entire edifice would collapse.

In his introduction to the second edition of the *Principia*, Cotes spelled out this underlying assumption: 'For if gravity be the cause of descent of a stone in *Europe*, who doubts that is also the cause of the same descent in America? If there is a mutual gravitation between the stone and the earth in *Europe*, who will deny the same to be mutual in America?'[24] Under Newton's guidance, Cotes's persuasive rhetoric was placed at the beginning of this second edition. For the conclusion, Newton composed his General Scholium, in which he deployed theological rhetoric to justify Cotes's pronouncement that stones behave in the same way all over the world. Buttressed by these two book-ends, the main text of the *Principia* could argue that if a pendulum bob seemed to be heavier at the poles than at the equator, the reason lay not in the variability of gravity but in the shape of the earth—rather than being perfectly spherical, it was slightly squashed at the north and south (a shape known technically as an oblate spheroid).

The ultimate validity of Newton's gravitational physics is supported not by observations but by his declaration of faith in an all-powerful deity. A crucial but short appendix of under 1500 words, the General Scholium was designed to cement together religion and natural philosophy and so counter what Newton perceived with dismay as a growth in disbelief. Much of it is deliberately opaque, but like Cotes, Newton made his basic message crystal clear, insisting that the 'most beautiful System of the Sun, Planets, and Comets, could only proceed from the counsel and dominion of an intelligent and powerful being.'[25] There is only one true God, Newton argued—and that God is in charge of the cosmos, constantly present and ensuring the uniformity of nature. Smuggling in that crucial supposition meant that a convenient circular argument became feasible. (1) Nature is uniform because God is omnipotent; (2) Natural laws are universal; (3) Therefore, an omnipotent God must exist.

Above all, Newton's gravitational model is a mathematical one. Traditionally, natural philosophy and mathematics had been distinct from one another. In ancient Greece, philosophers had searched for causes, for answers to questions about why the cosmos operates as it does. In contrast, mathematicians were interested in building models that did not necessarily replicate reality but had the great advantage of producing the right numerical results. When Nicolaus Copernicus suggested that the sun rather than the earth lies in the middle, many astronomers agreed that his version made the calculations work far better. But in the absence of clinching physical evidence one way or another, they preferred to continue believing that we live in a geocentric universe.

Newton's *Principia* was an extremely influential book, but it did not suddenly spring out of an intellectual desert like an apple falling from a tree. By the time Newton went to Cambridge, most educated people believed that the earth goes around the sun. And natural philosophers such as Johannes Kepler, Galileo Galilei, and René Descartes had already introduced measurements and equations to supplant qualitative Aristotelian ideas expressed as tendencies, humours, and occult forces. Newton's physics incorporated mathematics, but that was no single giant step for mankind: quantification was already becoming important. Using instruments such as thermometers, barometers, and magnetic compasses, experimenters were trying to regulate the natural world through numbers.

During the eighteenth century, the entire nation became increasingly controlled through quantification. In laboratories, experimenters relied on measurements rather than descriptions to keep tabs on how the universe operated, and similarly the government set up a network of inspectors who monitored percentages of alcohol in order to calculate the correct taxes. A brewery may be a very different place from the Royal Mint, but diluted beer and adulterated gold presented similar challenges of detection and proof. At the Treasury, as well as in private companies, accountants developed meticulous and supposedly objective systems to record how sums of money were being allocated and moved around the globe. When Africans were shipped across the Atlantic, they were counted up as units in merchant ledgers and stacked as freight in the ship's hold. Their breathing space was carefully measured to maximize the numbers that could be packed in, with an expected loss calculated for the natural wastage by deaths during transit.

Newton's mathematical gravity contributed to this quantifying process. He originally formulated his inverse-square law to account for the movements of comets and planets, but before long it was being applied to the living world. Mathematical models were created to describe the transmission of nervous signals through the body, the action of drugs on fevers, even the loss of belief over time in the existence of Christ. One Newtonian legacy is today's fundamental faith that mathematical laws reign supreme, that economic activity can be explained by equations, that achievement and personality can be measured quantitatively, that numbers are what count.

Gold Matters

Soon after Newton's *Principia* appeared, his friend John Locke published *An Essay Concerning Human Understanding*, his most important book on philosophy. In a section discussing language, Locke uses gold to illustrate how words lack any absolute, objective meaning. Compared with a physical lump of stuff, he explains, 'gold' is merely the 'convenience that made men express several parcels of yellow matter coming from Guinea and Peru under the same name'.[26] One problem is that when you hear the term, you associate it with a blend of all the gold items you have encountered in your life, but there is no guarantee that your internal, personal understanding corresponds with the speaker's.

Gold was a subject close to Locke's own pocket: far from being an arcane example to be pondered by linguistic scholars, it mattered for the nation's economy and also his personal benefit. Locke had already invested £600 in the Royal African Company as a founding stakeholder, and in 1695 he became Commissioner of Trade. Every year, the Company generated a fortune in golden guineas, but it also shipped many thousands of the new African currency—people, exchanged for manufactured goods to use as slaves. European greed for gold and silver inspired the plot of Dryden's *Indian Emperour* and fuelled the ever-increasing ship-loads of enslaved peoples transported across the Atlantic during the eighteenth century. For armchair theorists in Britain, it seemed a rational truism that more trade promotes more wealth, but they overlooked the problem of unequal distribution. Locke and his fellow investors in London did indeed benefit financially from global commerce, but at the expense of their African suppliers and their Asian competitors and their English labourers. To profit from that system seems an odd choice for a philosopher who wrote so much about individual rights and liberty.[27]

When Newton was developing his theory of gravity, he assumed that the same laws hold all over the world. By comparison, economic models based on that principle of uniformity may be mathematically effective, but they take no account of cultural differences. Ensconced in the Tower of London, Newton struggled to stabilize the guinea and establish international monetary standards. That entailed imposing rational measurement on attitudes towards Locke's 'yellow matter', a substance that had traditionally acquired various unquantifiable values—as altarpieces in Portugal, as sculpted weights in the Gold Coast, as sacred ornaments in China, as coronation medals in London. African merchants were originally willing to exchange their native gold for objects imbued with great economic and religious worth, such as cowrie shells or copper-lace shawls. Conversely, Europeans invested great time and effort in manufacturing goods not to use themselves, but to exchange for two commodities they desired: a metal that they endowed with financial value, and human beings for the labour force they required to keep accumulating capital.[28]

Thomson's *Rule, Britannia!* still arouses strong sentiments, but few people remember the fifth stanza:

> To thee belongs the rural reign;
> Thy cities shall with commerce shine:
> All thine shall be the subject main,
> And every shore it circles thine.[29]

His triumphant lines celebrate the rights of imperial rule by a tiny trading kingdom, but they represent optimism for the future rather than actuality. Much of the gold and silver mined with such heavy human cost in the Americas and in Africa merely passed through Europe, continuing its journey eastwards to end up in Asia. One writer visualized Europe bleeding to death: 'Europe like a body in a warm bath with its veins opened...and her bullion which is the life-blood of her trade flows to India to enrich the Great Mogul's subjects.'[30]

It was not until the end of the eighteenth century that China and India were ousted from their position as leading players in global commerce. According to one of Francis Bacon's celebrated maxims, three inventions had heralded the modern era: printing, gunpowder, and the magnetic compass. Significantly, all three originated in China, which during Newton's lifetime was prosperous, efficiently run, and dominated world trade through its apparently insatiable demand for precious metals. Whereas wealthy Brits craved luxury Chinese goods—silk, tea, porcelain—East Asian customers showed little interest in acquiring Western manufactured products or scientific knowledge: instead, gold and silver flooded eastward, affecting national economies all over Europe.

Thomson's *Rule Britannia!* and Ramsay's elegy to Newton voiced the smug complacency of a nation that admired itself as a world ruler and glossed over rival claims. While the words of these two British poets have endured, the distinguished Jesuit missionary Jean Crasset is scarcely remembered, perhaps because he told some uncomfortable home truths—that Asian nations were key players in global trade, renowned not only for the luxury goods they exported in exchange for gold and silver, but also for the scholarly books and manuscripts appropriated by British visitors for their libraries back home. 'It is very usual for Civiliz'd and Polite Nations to look upon all others as barbarous,' Crasset remarked; '*Europe* now being the Seat of Learning, and Science, wherein learned Academies are set up for the Discovery of Hidden Secrets in Nature, we take all the Rest of Mankind for meer Barbarians: But Those who have Travel'd into *China* and *Japan*, must confess those People far surpass us in the endowments, both of body and mind.' Similarly, in *Gulliver's Travels*, Swift relied on the high reputation of Japanese civility and wealth to satirize the crass behaviour of Britain's European rivals, the Dutch.[31]

As its population increased, Britain depended more and more heavily on buying in goods from overseas territories to keep its citizens fed and clothed. During the early decades of the eighteenth century, imports were escalating at a far higher rate than exports, a deficit that was made more urgent by the perpetual need to finance expensive wars. To reverse this outward flow of money, the government stepped up earlier protectionist policies. High taxes or even complete bans were slapped on luxury goods arriving from China and India, as well as from European rivals, especially France and Holland. For example, in response to pressure from the Ordnance Office, the Royal African Company stopped buying

Dutch guns and instead traded English firearms—around 66,000 in thirty years—for gold, people, and ivory. Home manufacturers competed by developing less expensive imitations, but they often relied on the skills of immigrant workers and adopted (aka stole) techniques developed overseas. By the end of the eighteenth century, Britain had ruthlessly displaced the previous economic leaders based in Asia.[32]

From his powerful position at the Mint, Newton supported the government's exclusionist policies, and the inventory of his possessions at his death suggests that he followed his own recommendations: his patriotic cellar included cider but no French brandy, and he chose home-woven harrateen rather than Chinese silk for his crimson bed curtains.[33] By stemming the eastward flow of silver, the yawning gap between gold and silver could be narrowed, a pressing problem that Newton never solved. Steering Britain along a mercantilist road of adopting prohibitive policies to boost exports and build up cash reserves, he drew up proposals to bar individuals from melting down coins, or using gold and silver decorations for their clothes and coaches. He sought to embargo exotic luxury imports: 'The like limitations for China earthen ware would save ye Nation much money & so would be a prohibition of importing Cabinets & other lacquered wooden ware from Japan & other parts of ye Indies.'[34]

Buying cheaper and buying British were individual decisions, but collectively they achieved a global impact. Those who were already comfortably off became still more prosperous, mainly at the expense of foreign exporters and the ignored victims of the international slave trade. By the end of the eighteenth century, Britain had become the world's leading industrial nation with the largest global empire, having nudged China, Japan, and the west coast of Africa towards long periods of decline.

Epilogue

Dryden gives the final speech to Cortez, who—despite being a dastardly Spaniard—is determined to retain his honour; in this distorted version of colonial history, it is the anachronistic Pizarro who shoulders the burden of responsibility for cruelty, oppression, and greed. In his last line, Cortez rejoices at being 'doubly blest, with conquest, and with love': this European victor now possesses Montezuma's empire as well as his daughter. For Hogarth's eighteenth-century Whig audience, that must have seemed a satisfactory ending at a time when Britain was struggling to control its territories in the Americas.

Cortez also gives his blessing to an alternative vision, a utopian dream of living in peace and poverty rather than in subjugation to wealth and foreign rule. This honourable route to virtuous happiness is articulated not by a European, but by Guyomar, Montezuma's son, who aspires to establish an independent community living in harmony with nature:

> Northward, beyond the Mountains we will go,
> Where Rocks lie cover'd with Eternal Snow,
> Thin Herbage in the Plains, and Fruitless Fields,
> The Sand no Gold, the Mine no Silver yields:
> There Love and Freedom we'l in Peace enjoy;
> No Spaniards will that Colony destroy.
> We to our selves will all our wishes grant;
> And nothing coveting, can nothing want.[1]

Throughout the play, Guyomar has demonstrated that even supposedly primitive people can hold high moral standards. With Cortez's blessing, he guides his followers towards a very different type of freedom from the Whig liberty that enabled wealthy British people to become still wealthier. If Dryden's play were to be restaged today, many spectators might think that Guyomar's Indians made the better choice.

I recently read a story imagining the emotions of a modern African family emigrating to America, the same geographical journey as the one forcibly undertaken by so many thousands of enslaved people during Newton's lifetime. When the couple's 6-year-old demands a story, her father decides to tell her about the magical 'Door of No Return' in Gorée. Tentatively, terrified of destroying her innocence, he explains that although there were no fresh water supplies on the island, there was a special market for selling human beings. His daughter's reaction is loud and instantaneous: 'Boahema laughed, bless her heart. A laughter so shrill and sudden the people in the row ahead turned back, startled... "Papa," she chortled, "You said this was a *real* story." '[2]

Boahema's exuberant chuckles of disbelief underline that slavery was, indeed, an extraordinary practice, but it lasted for centuries and still survives, even if now concealed. Over the last three centuries, Newtonian rationalists have accumulated vast numbers of facts, but there is little evidence that people have become either more clever or more virtuous. Older and more jaundiced than Boahema, I have no doubts that people really did behave in ways that seem unconscionable to me, but were second nature for them.

I was just finishing a first draft of this book when Cambridge's vice-chancellor unexpectedly announced that he was setting up an enquiry into the university's dependence on profits from the slave trade. Unknowingly, I had anticipated his official initiative by choosing to explore the imperial affiliations of Cambridge's most iconic scientific hero, Isaac Newton. In contrast, I had realized that I was following in the tracks of an eminent Russian physicist called Boris Hessen. In 1931, he shocked his international audience at a large conference held in London by delivering a lecture on 'The social and economic roots of Newton's *Principia*'. A member of a delegation advocating Soviet science policies, Hessen argued that Newton's work stemmed not from any unique genius, but from contemporary ideological conflicts and the technical demands of a rising bourgeoisie.[3]

Despite his Soviet loyalty, Hessen was executed in 1936, so he never knew how famous his speech would become. At the time, many British academics were appalled, decrying it as a Marxist attack on their national figurehead and the principle of scientific freedom. Some chose the easy option of retreating into denial and refusing to engage with Hessen's arguments. But his paper was welcomed by younger left-inclined scientists, and later exerted an enormous influence on how successive historians thought about science's past. Through them, Hessen's speech underpins the argument of this book that Newton participated in a mercantile, imperial community whose values shaped his scientific ideas; conversely, his theories affected the subsequent direction taken by a globalizing society.

Newton is one of Britain's greatest heroes, and contemplating his human flaws can be uncomfortable. His major biographer, Richard Westfall, courageously revealed that he had embarked on psychoanalysis to explore his emotional relationship with his subject. Accusing himself of downplaying Newton's thirty years of financial and political negotiations at the Mint, Westfall confessed that he had sought to preserve unsullied Newton's reputation as an unworldly scholar. Digging deep into his own psyche, Westfall exposed his innermost self-identification as a Presbyterian elder, a staunch Puritan repelled by rampant consumerism and fearful that Newton's activities at the Mint might tarnish his reputation.[4]

Unlike Westfall, I have no qualms about impugning Newton's moral stance and no ambition to emulate him, although my rendition of his last three decades is coloured by my own views and experiences. There are always new ways of interpreting familiar facts, and there are always new facts to be unearthed. That is why being a historian is so fascinating. On the other hand, to embark on a historical research project is to enter a bewildering Borgesian labyrinth. There are dead ends and there are spurious interconnections, but there is no definite goal or advance destination. Rewriting the past entails venturing along paths that nobody else has followed, leaving the security of well-established analyses. The thread guiding Theseus away from the Minotaur has broken, and the birds have eaten the trail of breadcrumbs leading Hansel and Gretel back to the woodcutter's cottage.

Newton has become symbolically so important that—as I know from experience—any attempt to reassess him can arouse bitter antagonism. By presenting novel arguments about such an iconic figurehead, I am exposing not just my knowledge but also my opinions, character, and beliefs to public scrutiny. In case any doubts linger, although I maintain that science is inextricably intertwined with society, I am not a naïve relativist who accepts all truths as equal. Furthermore, I realize that Newton was just one among many wealthy Europeans who were complicit in exploiting other peoples and places for their own financial gain.

During the eighteenth century, when the privileges of freedom included the right to buy and sell human beings, the British economy depended on the slave trade. Newton has left no explicit record of his views, but he presumably shared the majority opinion that what now seems an abhorrent practice was perfectly acceptable. Even without falling into the trap of assessing bygone attitudes with twenty-first-century sensibilities, what right do we have to judge our predecessors when modern behaviour remains so deplorable? When Charles Dickens wrote *Oliver Twist*, child abuse had not yet been defined as a term, let alone a crime—but although it is now firmly on the statute books, perpetrators still exist. People have treated the world and its inhabitants extremely badly. They still do, but the route to improvement lies through exposure and discussion, not concealment. Protesters claim the moral high ground by demolishing statues of imperial oppressors or removing offensive books from reading lists and library shelves. But is denying our unsavoury past an effective way of dealing with its implications?

Moral responsibility is shared by all members of a community. In 1790, the wealthy industrialist Samuel Galton was condemned by his Quaker brethren for transgressing their commitment to pacifism: they wanted to expel him because his family fortune came from manufacturing guns. In his defence, Galton produced several arguments comparing individual responsibility and collective culpability. 'It is alledged that the Manufacturer of Arms, *contributes* to the carrying on War,' he wrote (his italics). 'But do you, not *all* in many ways *contribute* to the War, by supplying Government directly, or indirectly, with *Money*, which is so necessary, that it is called proverbially the *Sinews* of War? Do not such of you as are concerned in *East India Stock*, who *subscribe to the Loan, who purchase Stock, Lottery Tickets, Navy Victualling, or Exchequer Bills, as directly, and as voluntarily furnish the means of War*, as myself?'[5]

Shifting his focus to slavery, Galton blamed anyone who had ever consumed products such as sugar, indigo, rum, tobacco, or cotton. The abolitionist poet William Cowper used mockery to make the same point, laying bare the tensions between compassion and conformity, between good intentions and political action:

> I pity them greatly, but I must be mum,
> For how could we do without sugar and rum?...
> He blam'd and protested, but join'd in the plan;
> He shar'd in the plunder, but pitied the man.[6]

Such conflicts still arise. Unlike many people in the world, I am sufficiently privileged to be guilty of buying Cowper's sugar and rum in their modern manifestations—mass-produced clothes, exploitative delivery services, aeroplane flights that damage the environment. And although I rarely realize it is happening, the concealed technology of consumerism favours someone like me with a pale skin who can wear toning medical plasters and easily obtain soap from automatic dispensers. From my British perspective, it seems that everybody reading this book is enmeshed in a global economic system that promotes inequality, and whose growth has been linked with the rise of the state and the rise of science and the rise of empire since the mid-seventeenth century.

Exploring the past can reveal how we have reached the present, but for me the main point of doing that is to improve the future. Recalling Newton's divinely run universe, the current state of the world was not pre-ordained as if it were a clock wound up in advance. Instead, multiple individual decisions have shaped the direction humanity has collectively taken, and millions of others will affect what lies ahead. Ensuring a better future requires that everybody—you, me—take personal action. In writing this book, I have tried to analyse some of the ways in which our predecessors went wrong, and indicate the mistakes that we must avoid repeating.

Notes

Notes to Prologue

1. Retrieved from entries in the online *Oxford Dictionary of National Biography*, https://www.oxforddnb.com/ (accessed 17 June 2019).
2. Website of Economic History Resources, http://www.eh.net (accessed 17 June 2019).
3. Blair, pp. 153–79.
4. My main sources for the picture are Uglow, pp. 130–70; Paulson, vol. 1, pp. 172–87, and vol. 2, pp. 1–4; Asfour.
5. Dr Samuel Clarke to Mrs Clayton, 22 April 1732, quoted in Saumarez Smith, p. 70. Falk, pp. 260–1: Mrs Clayton, later Lady Sundon, was a friend of Catherine Barton and influential at court.
6. See https://www.researchgate.net/figure/Portrait-of-Newton-in-1689-by-Godfrey-Kneller_fig1_324694115 (accessed 26 June 2019).
7. Pointon, pp. 107–41 (quotation of 1720 at p. 107).
8. Iliffe, *Priest of Nature* and 'Making of a Politician'.
9. Winn, p. 101 (letter from Anne to Mary, May 1687).
10. Blanning, p. 21.
11. Westfall, *Never at Rest*, p. 591 (letter to Peter King, April 1703); Goldie.
12. Challis, 'Neale'.
13. Murphy.
14. Montagu, quoted in Horwitz, p. 153. My main sources for Montagu are Higgitt, Handley, and Falk.
15. Quoted in Handley, p. 9.
16. Quoted from Montagu's letter of 19 March 1696 in Shirras and Craig, p. 220.
17. Quoted in Westfall, *Never at Rest*, p. 586.
18. Westfall, 'Newton and his Biographer'; Traweek, pp. 74–105.
19. For example, Wennerlind, p. 148.
20. Coppola.
21. Paulson, vol. 1, p. 182; Bulman, pp. 277–90.

Notes to Chapter 1

1. McGuire and Rattansi; Craske.
2. Quoted in Saumurez Smith, p. 57.

3. Carswell, pp. 22–30; Quinn.
4. Quoted (1698) in Wennerlind, p. 154.
5. Mint 19/II, 608–11. http://www.newtonproject.ox.ac.uk/view/texts/normalized/MINT00261 (accessed 13 June 2019).
6. *Fable of the Bees*, quoted in Saumaurez Smith, p. 58.
7. White, *Isaac Newton*, p. 359 (quotation from letter to Lord Townshend of 1724).
8. Letter to Catherine Barton of August 1700: Mint 19/II, 30. https://www.historyofparliamentonline.org/volume/1690–1715/member/tily-joseph-1654-1708 (accessed 9 January 2019).
9. Westfall, *Never at Rest*, p. 581.
10. Werrett, *Thrifty Science*, pp. 47–8.
11. Conti.
12. Newman, p. 91.
13. Sheppard, 'Jermyn Street'.
14. Letter from Richard Bentley of 20 October 1709. http://www.newtonproject.ox.ac.uk/view/texts/normalized/OTHE00082 (accessed 26 June 2018); Westfall, *Never at Rest*, pp. 670–1.
15. Dry, pp. 6–9; Villamil, pp. 62–111.
16. Conduitt, p. 97; Westfall, *Never at Rest*, pp. 869–70.
17. Craig, p. 125.
18. Mint 19/II, 409. http://www.newtonproject.ox.ac.uk/view/texts/normalized/MINT00263 (accessed 4 July 2018).
19. Conduitt, p. 102.
20. Quoted in Westfall, *Never at Rest*, p. 609.
21. Mayor, pp. 314–15, 322 (in 1702).
22. Westfall, *Never at Rest*, pp. 580–1; Carswell, p. xvii.
23. Westfall, *Never at Rest*, pp. 579–81; Villamil.
24. See https://shrubsole.com/products/an-exceptionally-rare-george-ii-antique-english-silver-chamber-pot (accessed 19 July 2018).
25. Villamil, pp. 2–3, 49–61; Baker, p. 236: Le Marchand sculpted four ivories of Newton.
26. Saumarez Smith, pp. 33–58 (quoted in Defoe, p. 52).
27. Robins, p. 58 (1711).
28. I am grateful to Andrew Odlyzko for explaining that Newton had shares in one of the companies in 1700, but none after 1709 in the two united companies.
29. Ashworth.
30. Mint 19/II, 131–2. http://www.newtonproject.ox.ac.uk/view/texts/normalized/MINT00333 (accessed 31 May 2019).
31. Quoted in Westfall, *Never at Rest*, p. 621 (draft of a proposed act).

Notes to Chapter 2

1. Craig; Kilburn-Toppin, pp. 197–201.
2. Hahn, pp. 143–63 (Ned Ward quoted at p. 152); Jones and Holmes, p. 263.
3. Westfall, *Never at Rest*, p. 593.
4. Satia, pp. 27–41, 191–218.
5. Craig, pp. 1, 15, 125–6; Charlton; Challis, *Royal Mint*, pp. 358–60; Mint 19/III, 390–9. http://www.newtonproject.ox.ac.uk/view/texts/normalized/MINT00815 and Mint 19/III, 409–10. http://www.newtonproject.ox.ac.uk/view/texts/normalized/MINT00813 (accessed 20 June 2018).
6. Tollet, pp. 25–6 (from 'To my Brother at St John's College in Cambridge').
7. Londry.
8. Nichols, vol. 6, p. 64.
9. Buchwald and Feingold, pp. 239–44.
10. Tollet, pp. 25–6 (from 'To my Brother at St John's College in Cambridge'); Davis.
11. Tollet, p. 96 (from 'Anne Boleyn').
12. Tollet, p. 67 ('Hypatia').
13. Costa (quotation at p. 52).
14. Tollet, p. 129 ('On the Death of Sir Isaac Newton').
15. Tollet, p. 129 ('On the Death of Sir Isaac Newton').
16. Winn, p. 355 (quotation at p. 390).
17. Craig, pp. 63, 76.
18. Dennison, pp. 57–60.
19. Akkerman; Dennison, p. 77.
20. Quoted in Winn, p. 600 (anonymous).
21. Winn (p. 401) reports that Newton was the tutor, but I have based my account on Westfall, *Never at Rest*, p. 576.
22. Winn (Whitwell Elwin quoted at p. xvii). For political aspects of her reign, see Holmes.
23. Ben-Menahem et al., p. 26.
24. This section is closely based on Hone.
25. Newton Mint manuscript quoted in Hone, p. 140 (1704).
26. Mint 19/III, 297. http://www.newtonproject.ox.ac.uk/view/texts/normalized/MINT00747 (accessed 27 June 2018).
27. Anonymous poem of 1707, quoted in Hone, p. 135.
28. Winn, p. 300.
29. Colley, pp. 137–67; Winn, pp. 524–6, 547–50 (Thomas Tickell quoted at p. 606).
30. From *The Spectator*, quoted in González-Treviño, p. 115.
31. Quoted in Winn, p. 550.

32. See http://www.newtonproject.ox.ac.uk/view/texts/normalized/MINT00125 (accessed 21 June 2018).
33. Winn, p. 599.

Notes to Chapter 3

1. Vickery.
2. Tollet, p. 66 ('Hypatia').
3. Higgitt, p. 163.
4. Swift, *Journal*, vol. 2, pp. 380, 383 (11 and 14 October 1711), and *passim*.
5. Villamil, pp. 50–1.
6. Inwood, pp. 149–51, 268–71.
7. See https://en.wikipedia.org/wiki/Avunculate_marriage (accessed 28 June 2018).
8. Goldie, pp. 22–7. See Manuel, pp. 191–212 for a Freudian analysis.
9. Craig, p. 30.
10. Revelation 14:4–5.
11. Iliffe, *Priest of Nature*, pp. 157–88 (quotations from the Yahuda manuscripts, pp. 185, 185–6).
12. Westfall, *Never at Rest*, pp. 496–7, 535; I am grateful to Mark Goldie for this information.
13. Letter of 10 October 1689: Turnbull, vol. 3, p. 45.
14. Iliffe, *Early Biographies*, p. lv.
15. Higgitt is the most judicial consideration. For Montagu, see Falk, pp. 239–62.
16. Westfall, *Never at Rest*, pp. 502–3.
17. Letter of August 1700, Mint 19/II, 30 (accessed 4 July 2019).
18. Westfall, *Never at Rest*, p. 503.
19. Harrison; Falk, p. 247.
20. Swift, *Journal*, vol. 1, p. 230. Stella's real name was Esther Johnson.
21. Swift, *Journal*, vol. 2, pp. 415, 417 (17 and 20 November 1711).
22. Quoted in Lynall, p. 94.
23. Lynall, pp. 89–119, quotations at p. 94.
24. Letter of 1733 reproduced in More, pp. 540–1.
25. My main sources are Higgitt, Handley, and Falk.
26. Quoted in Higgitt, p. 163.
27. Montagu, pp. 195–6; will and codicils in appendix.
28. Quoted in Westfall, *Never at Rest*, p. 601.
29. Quoted in Westfall, *Never at Rest*, p. 600.
30. Lynall, pp. 93–4; Higgitt, p. 163; Westfall, *Never at Rest*, p. 598.
31. Manley, p. 292.
32. Manley, p. 294.
33. Quoted in Westfall, *Never at Rest*, p. 596 (first published 1757).
34. Craig, p. 124. See also http://www.openculture.com/2011/08/voices_from_the_19th_century.html (accessed 29 August 2019).

35. Westfall, *Never at Rest*, pp. 851–68; Stukeley, pp. 290–1, 303.
36. Thomas Mason, quoted in Conduitt, p. 58.
37. Flamsteed to Abraham Sharp, quoted in Manuel p. 313.
38. From *Polite Conversation*, quoted in Lynall, p. 102.
39. Winn, pp. 403–4 (quotation at p. 403).
40. Mandelbrote, pp. 8, 11–14.
41. Reproduced in Westfall, *Never at Rest*, p. 43.
42. Poole, pp. 85–101, 108–11 (anonymous draft quoted at p. 90).

Notes to Chapter 4

1. Carter.
2. Westfall, *Never at Rest*, pp. 846–9.
3. Conduitt, p. 93, 101–2 (drafts to Fontenelle).
4. Letter of 21 October 1706, http://www.newtonproject.ox.ac.uk/catalogue/record/THEM00106 (accessed 26 June 2018).
5. Conduitt, p. 169 (notes on canonization).
6. Werrett, 'Sociomateriality of Waste'.
7. Dry, pp. 5–21 (especially pp. 13–15).
8. Mint 19/III, 44. http://www.newtonproject.ox.ac.uk/view/texts/normalized/MINT00291 (accessed 13 June 2019).
9. Conduitt; see also Rob Iliffe's introduction (pp. xi–lxii) in *Early Biographies*; and Baker, pp. 233–49.
10. Conduitt, p. 104 (revised draft to Fontenelle).
11. Conduitt, p. 103 (revised draft to Fontenelle).
12. Westfall, *Never at Rest*, pp. 154–7.
13. Conduitt, pp. 94, 161, 170–1, 198, 202, 212–13.
14. Robins, p. 2.
15. Iliffe, *Priest of Nature*; Newton's *Observations upon the Prophecies*, quoted in Manuel, p. 349.
16. Buchwald and Feingold, p. 434.
17. Conduitt, p. 81; Stukeley, pp. 256–7; Ben-Menahem et al., pp. 58–78 (quotation at p. 77).
18. Quoted in Buchwald and Feingold, p. 221, my main source for this discussion.
19. Quoted in Buchwald and Feingold, p. 129.
20. Ben-Menahem et al., pp. 45–53.
21. Quoted from Newton's *Observations upon the Prophecies*, in Manuel, pp. 365–6.
22. Revelation 13:18.
23. Lines 1169–72. See https://www.bartleby.com/204/5.html#txt81 (accessed 24 June 2019).
24. Iliffe, *Priest of Nature*, p. 353 (publications of 1725 and 1726).
25. Quoted in Dennison, p. 195.

Notes to ACT II

1. Marschner, pp. 153–4.
2. White, 'Scott, Mary'.

Notes to Chapter 5

1. Baker and Baker, p. 152.
2. The most detailed biography is Carpenter. My other major source for Desaguliers is Stewart, pp. 213–54.
3. Ashworth, pp. 85–92 (quotations at pp. 87, 90).
4. Contrasting accounts of Freemasonry are provided by Jacob, pp. 109–41 (quotation at p. 133), and Carpenter, pp. 81–111.
5. I am grateful to Martin Cherry, the librarian at London's Museum of Freemasonry, for detailed information. The 1723 *Constitutions* is reproduced in Jacob, pp. 279–85.
6. Uglow, pp. 108–9.
7. Quoted in Morton and Wess, p. 11.
8. Parker; quotation in Wennerlind at p. 205.
9. Uglow, pp. 84–91, ballad quoted at p. 86. My other main sources for the Bubble are Odlyzko, 'Newton and Defoe' and 'Newton's Financial Misadventures'; Carswell; Blanning, pp. 61–3; Markley, pp. 210–23; Wennerlind, pp. 197–234.
10. Defoe, quoted in Odlyzko, 'Newton and Defoe', p. 20.
11. Buchan.
12. Quoted in Odlyzko, 'Newton and Defoe', p. 20.
13. Satia, p. 26.
14. Thomas, p. 305.
15. Erskine-Hill, p. 37.
16. Carpenter, pp. 125–9 (quotation at p. 127).
17. Stewart and Weindling.
18. Quoted in Baker and Baker, p. 28; this is the fullest biography.
19. Carpenter, pp. 153–76, Defoe quoted at p. 160.
20. Coppola, pp. 139–44.
21. Carpenter, pp. 142–5 (quotation at p. 142).
22. Quoted in Stewart, p. 242.
23. Richard Bradley, quoted in Carpenter, p. 144.
24. Carpenter, pp. 148–51 (quotation at p. 150).

Notes to Chapter 6

1. Carpenter, p. 227; Handley.

2. Letter of 23 June 1738, quoted at https://andrewbakercomposer.files.wordpress. com/2018/03/long-version-elizabeth-carter-and-thomas-wright.pdf (accessed 2 August 2019).

3. Desaguliers, *A Course*, p. vi.

4. Jacob and Stewart, pp. 61–92 (quotation at p. 74).

5. Westfall, *Never at Rest*, pp. 627–97, Zacharias von Uffenbach quoted at p. 635.

6. Jones and Holmes, pp. 318–19.

7. Letter to Henry Oldenburg of late Jan. 1675, Turnbull, vol. 7, p. 387.

8. Letter to Newton from John Chamberlayne, Mint 19/II, 334–5. http://www. newtonproject.ox.ac.uk/view/texts/diplomatic/MINT00893 (accessed 24 July 2019).

9. Quoted in Westfall, *Never at Rest*, p. 679 (letter of 8 December 1713).

10. Stukeley, pp. 299–300.

11. Metzger.

12. Letter to Halley of 20 June 1686, http://www.newtonproject.ox.ac.uk/view/ texts/normalized/NATP00325 (accessed 23 January 2019).

13. For Montagu, see Higgitt; for Newton as president, see Westfall, *Never at Rest*, pp. 627–97.

14. Quoted in Manuel, p. 317.

15. Iliffe and Willmoth, pp. 244–57 (quotation at p. 255).

16. Arthur Devis, *The John Bacon Family* (1742–3), https://artsandculture.google. com/asset/the-john-bacon-family-arthur-devis/lgGFJht9ViDeXg.

17. Westfall, *Never at Rest*, p. 265.

18. William Whiston, quoted in Manuel, p. 348.

19. See http://www.newtonproject.ox.ac.uk/view/texts/normalized/NATP00045, pp. 1, 21–2 (accessed 30 November 2018) (1718 edition).

20. Schaffer, 'Glass Works'.

21. The final thirty-one are reproduced at http://www.newtonproject.ox.ac.uk/ view/texts/normalized/NATP00051 (accessed 6 December 2018).

22. Quoted in Gascoigne, p. 223 (John Hancock, 1706 Boyle lecture).

23. Cantor and Hodge.

24. Mandelbrote, pp. 123–6; Iliffe, *Priest of Nature*, pp. 157–88, 350–3. https:// newtonprojectca.files.wordpress.com/2013/06/brief-guide-to-the-general- scholium-letter-size.pdf (accessed 7 December 2018).

25. Kuchta, pp. 91–132.

26. Wolf, p. 349 (James Logan, 1727).

Notes to Chapter 7

1. Quoted in Dennison, pp. 41–2.

2. My main sources are Blanning, Dennison, Marschner, and van der Kiste.

3. Mint 19/III, 313–17, 330. http://www.newtonproject.ox.ac.uk/search/results? keyword=george+coronation+medal&all=1 (accessed 20 June 2019).

4. Winn, pp. 545–51, 609, 616.

5. Quoted in Dennison, p. 54.

6. Winn, p. 635.

7. Blanning, p. 7.

8. Quoted in van der Kiste, p. 103.

9. Lynall, pp. 131–2.

10. Letter of June 1716 quoted in Marschner, p. 150.

11. Manuel, p. 285.

12. Conduitt, pp. 93–4, 102.

13. Manuel, pp. 321–45 (quotation at p. 325).

14. Lynall, pp. 129–30.

15. Balderston, quotation at p. 86 from the *London Journal*.

16. Quoted in Colton, p. 918 (*London Journal*).

17. Swift, quoted in Morton and Wess, p. 10.

18. Gascoigne.

19. Conduitt, p. 94.

20. Zedler.

21. Bertoloni Meli.

22. Shapin, 'Of Gods and Kings' (Leibniz quoted at p. 193).

23. Werrett, *Thrifty Science*, pp. 109–28; quotation in Westfall, *Never at Rest*, p. 306.

24. Quoted in Balderston, p. 88.

25. Reproduced in Marschner, p. 117.

26. Carpenter, p. 33.

27. Dennison, p. 124. Quoted from the *Daily Journal*, Carpenter, p. 45.

28. Desaguliers, *Newtonian System*, pp. 22–4.

29. Quoted in Morton and Wess, p. 17.

Notes to ACT III

1. Kinsley and Kinsley; Loftis.

2. My major sources for discussing this play are Brown; González-Treviño; Hutner, pp. 65–88; Kewes; Loftis; and Orr, pp. 135–87.

3. Armintor. I am grateful to James Herriman-Smith for this information.

4. Dryden, p. 30 (I, i).

5. Dryden, p. 48 (II, i).

6. Thompson, pp. 75–97 (Leigh quoted at p. 75); Loftis.

7. Quoted in Winn, p. 21.

8. Dryden, p. 111 (V, ii).

9. Winn, pp. 609–14, quotation at p. 613 (John Johnson); Davis.

10. Queen Anne quoted in Erskine-Hill, p. 34. Tickell quoted in Winn, p. 606 (from *Poem to His Excellency the Lord Privy-Seal*).

Notes to Chapter 8

1. Dryden, p. 31 (I, i).
2. Dryden, p. 31 (I, i).
3. Dryden, p. 30 (I, i).
4. Quoted in Schaffer, 'Golden Means', p. 35 (from *The Wealth of Nations*).
5. Markley, pp. 210–23 (quotation at p. 221).
6. Waddell (quotations at p. 543).
7. My main sources for this chapter are Bernstein, pp. 175–98; Challis, *Royal Mint*, pp. 351–439; Craig; Horwitz, pp. 143–98; Li; Wennerlind, pp. 83–157; and Westfall, *Never at Rest*, pp. 551–626.
8. Mint 19/II, 608–11. http://www.newtonproject.ox.ac.uk/view/texts/normalized/ MINT00261 (accessed 13 June 2019).
9. Quoted in Bernstein, p. 193 (1698).
10. Schaffer, 'Golden Means', pp. 35–6 (Secretary of the Treasury quoted).
11. Li, pp. 217–23, quotation at p. 217.
12. Levenson, p. 112.
13. Quoted in Westfall, *Never at Rest*, p. 561.
14. Bernstein, pp. 114–98.
15. Quoted in Bernstein, p. 195.
16. Stern (quotations at p. 60).
17. My main sources are Westfall, *Never at Rest*, pp. 567–76; and Levenson, pp. 147–237.
18. Mint 15/17, 215. http://www.newtonproject.ox.ac.uk/view/texts/normalized/ MINT01465 (accessed 5 June 2019).
19. Mint 19/I, 475–7. http://www.newtonproject.ox.ac.uk/view/texts/normalized/ MINT00855 (accessed 5 June 2019).
20. Quoted in Westfall, *Never at Rest*, p. 574.
21. Westfall, *Never at Rest*, p. 570 (Samuel Bond quoting Francis Ball).
22. Quoted in Lynall, p. 98 (1724).
23. Kilburn-Toppin, quotations at pp. 223, 207.
24. Quoted in Kilburn-Toppin, p. 217.
25. Schaffer, 'Golden Means'; Turner. http://www.royalmintmuseum.org.uk/ history/people/mint-officials/isaac-newton/index2.html (accessed 30 May 2019).
26. Newman; Mint 19/I, 293. http://www.newtonproject.ox.ac.uk/view/texts/ normalized/MINT00177 (accessed 27 June 2019).
27. Royal Society, MM/5.43. http://www.newtonproject.ox.ac.uk/view/texts/ normalized/MINT01251 (accessed 30 May 2019); quoted in Westfall, *Never at Rest*, p. 564.
28. Craig, pp. 70–5.
29. Mint 19/III, 524. http://www.newtonproject.ox.ac.uk/view/texts/normalized/ MINT00732 (accessed 24 June 2019).
30. Mint 19/I, 458–9. http://www.newtonproject.ox.ac.uk/view/texts/normalized/ MINT00853 (accessed 31 May 2019).

31. Mint 19/III, 456–7. http://www.newtonproject.ox.ac.uk/view/texts/normalized/ MINT00489 (accessed 31 May 2019).

32. Lynall, pp. 94–119 (Sir Michael Creagh quoted at p. 96).

33. Swift, *Gulliver's Travels*, p. 150.

34. Swift, *Gulliver's Travels*, pp. 150, 184–5.

35. Baker, pp. 233–49.

Notes to Chapter 9

1. Asfour; Harris. Almeria and Cortez were played by Sophia and William Fermor; Kitty Conduitt played Alibech.

2. Dryden, p. 80 (4, ii).

3. See https://www.loc.gov/resource/g8200.ct001445/ (accessed 3 June 2019). I am very grateful to Stephen Snobelen for this reference.

4. Dryden, p. 112.

5. Engetsu; Cowan.

6. Clare.

7. Quoted in Sprat, p. xiii (editors' introduction).

8. Moxham.

9. Hunter, pp. 1–58; McCormick, pp. 185–93.

10. Evelyn quoted in Ashworth, p. 28.

11. Sprat, pp. 403–10 (quotation at p. 408).

12. Sprat, pp. 114–15.

13. Sprat, pp. 407–8.

14. Schaffer, 'Golden Means', p. 27.

15. Werrett, *Thrifty Science*, p. 124.

16. Pepys, vol. 1, p. 258 (3 October 1660); Carr, pp. 172–7.

17. My main sources throughout this chapter are Brewer; Davies; Pettigrew; and Zook.

18. Winterbottom.

19. Govier.

20. Carey, 'Compiling Nature's History', Boyle quoted at pp. 272–3.

21. Govier.

22. Hill; Maddison. He does not seem to be related to Thomas Hill in Hogarth's picture.

23. Quoted in Zook, p. 182.

24. Bennett, quotation at p. 83. The clock is at the top left of the frontispiece.

25. Moxham, pp. 254–5.

26. Scott (quotations at pp. 335–6).

27. Ashworth, pp. 15–33.

28. Micklethwait and Wooldridge, pp. 1–36; Robins, pp. 19–40.

29. Pepys, vol. 4, pp. 152–3 (23 May 1663).

30. Green, pp. 1–29, 108–48, 262–95.
31. Both quotations from Swift, *Gulliver's Travels*, p. 275.
32. Fryer, p. 44.
33. Colley, pp. 23–134.
34. Inikori, pp. 215–64 (especially p. 227).
35. John Aikins, quoted in Green, pp. 140–1.
36. St Clair, pp. 1–81; Reed; Woollacott.
37. Defoe, p. 17 (about 2.5 kg), p. 33.
38. Carey, 'Reading Contrapuntally' (quotation at p. 135); Tonks.
39. Carr, p. 180.
40. Royal African Company, p. 1.
41. Thomas, pp. 196–464. For transcripts of correspondence with West African personnel of the RAC from 1681 to 1699, see Law.

Notes to Chapter 10

1. Dryden, p. 31 (I, i).
2. Dryden, p. 98 (V, ii).
3. Dryden, p. 79 (IV, ii); Green, pp. 265–70.
4. Dryden, pp. 87–8 (IV, iv).
5. Dryden, p. 88 (IV, iv); Woollacott.
6. Inikori, pp. 216–27; Pettigrew (quotation at p. 91).
7. Quoted in Markley, p. 4 (Josiah Child, 1681).
8. Robins, pp. 1–60 (anonymous letter of 1708 quoted at p. 55).
9. Odlyzko, 'Newton's Financial Misadventures'.
10. Ben-Menahem et al., p. 59.
11. *Oxford Dictionary of Quotations* (from *On Poetry: A Rhapsody*, 1733). https://www.oxfordreference.com/view/10.1093/acref/9780199668700.001.0001/acref-9780199668700.
12. Bulman, pp. 41–70.
13. Parker.
14. Festa and Carey.
15. Green, pp. 262–95.
16. Delisle de Sales, pp. 18–52.
17. Defoe; Carey, 'Reading Contrapuntally'. I am grateful to Clive Wilmer for this point.
18. My main sources for this section are Schaffer, 'Newton on the Beach' and *Information Order*.
19. Quoted in Schaffer, 'Newton on the Beach', p. 251.
20. Schaffer, *Information Order* (quotation at p. 32).
21. Schaffer, 'Golden Means' (Jean Barbot quoted at p. 34).
22. Quoted in Westfall, *Never at Rest*, p. 845 (referring to copper coins).

23. O'Brien (quotation at p. 291).
24. Quoted in O'Brien, p. 290.
25. Snobelen (quotation at p. 169).
26. Locke, quoted in Schaffer, 'Golden Means', p. 22.
27. Uzgalis.
28. Green, pp. 467–76.
29. Colley. https://en.wikisource.org/wiki/The_Works_of_James_Thomson/Rule,_ Britannia! (accessed 30 April 2019).
30. Robins, p. 59 (anonymous book of 1720).
31. Bulman, pp. 41–70; Markley, pp. 241–68 (Crasset quoted at p. 241); Festa and Carey.
32. Ashworth; Parthasarathi; Satia, pp. 28–9.
33. Villamil, pp. 51, 54.
34. Westfall, *Never at Rest*, pp. 621–2.

Notes to Epilogue

1. Dryden, p. 111 (V, ii).
2. Jackson-Opuku.
3. Bukharin; Schaffer, 'Newton at the Crossroads'.
4. Westfall, 'Newton and his Biographer'.
5. Satia, pp. 1–12, 316–44. Quotation from https://www.revolutionaryplayers. org.uk/letter-from-samuel-galton-jnr-to-the-friends-of-the-monthly-meeting-in-birmingham/ (accessed 16 May 2019).
6. Cowper, pp. 375–6 ('Pity for Poor Africans', lines 5–6, 43–4).

Bibliography

Sources and Referencing

In the course of writing this book, I took advantage of several existing biographies, in particular Richard Westfall's magisterial *Never at Rest*. Because it was published in 1980, I have assumed that much of the information it contains (as opposed to opinions) is essentially common knowledge, and so I have not included specific references for every single aspect of Newton's life. I have provided full footnotes for primary and secondary material not mentioned in the standard accounts, and I have also sourced every quotation.

Akkerman, Nadine. *Invisible Agents: Women and Espionage in Seventeenth-Century Britain* (Oxford: Oxford University Press, 2018).

Armintor, Deborah Needleman. ' "Go, Get Your Husband Put into Commission": Fielding's Tom Thumb Plays and the Labor of Little Men', *The Eighteenth Century* 44 (2003), 69–85.

Asfour, Amal. 'Hogarth's Post-Newtonian Universe', *Journal of the History of Ideas* 60 (1999), 693–716.

Ashworth, William J. *The Industrial Revolution: The State, Knowledge and Global Trade* (London: Bloomsbury, 2017).

Baker, Charles Henry Collins, and Baker, Muriel I. *The Life and Circumstances of James Brydges, First Duke of Chandos, Patron of the Liberal Arts* (Oxford: Clarendon Press, 1949).

Baker, Malcolm. *The Marble Index: Roubiliac and Sculptural Portraiture in Eighteenth-Century Britain* (New Haven and London: Yale University Press, 2014).

Balderston, Gordon. 'Giovanni Battista Guelfi: Five Busts for Queen Caroline's Hermitage in Richmond', *Sculpture Journal* 17 (2008), 83–8.

Batchelor, Robert K. *London: The Selden Map and the Making of a Global City* (Chicago: University of Chicago Press, 2014).

Ben-Menahem, Yemima, Feingold, Mordechai, and Snobelen, Stephen. *Newton's Secrets: Newtonian Manuscripts from the Collections of the National Library* (Jerusalem: Jewish National and University Library, 2007).

Bennett, Jim. 'The Instruments', in Michael Hunter, *The Image of Restoration Science: The Frontispiece to Thomas Sprat's* History of the Royal Society *(1667)* (London and New York: Routledge, 2017), pp. 79–127.

Bernstein, Peter L. *The Power of Gold: The History of an Obsession* (New York and Chichester: Wiley, 2000).

Bertoloni Meli, D. 'Caroline, Leibniz, and Clarke', *Journal of the History of Ideas* 60 (1999), 469–86.

Blair, Ann. *The Theater of Nature: Jean Bodin and Renaissance Science* (Princeton: Princeton University Press, 1997).

Blanning, Tim. *George I: The Lucky King* (London: Allen Lane, 2017).

Brewer, Holly. 'Slavery, Sovereignty, and "Inheritable Blood": Reconsidering John Locke and the Origins of American Slavery', *American Historical Review* 22 (2017), 1038–78.

Brown, Laura. 'Dryden and the Imperial Imagination', in Steven N. Zwicker (ed.), *The Cambridge Companion to John Dryden* (Cambridge: Cambridge University Press, 2004), pp. 59–74.

Buchan, James. 'Mississippi Dreaming: On the Fame of John Law', *New Left Review* 210 (1995), 48–62.

Buchwald, Jed Z., and Feingold, Mordechai. *Newton and the Origin of Civilization* (Princeton and Oxford: Princeton University Press, 2013).

Bukharin, Nikolai Ivanovich. *Science at the Cross Roads: Papers Presented to the International Congress of the History of Science and Technology, held in London from June 29th to July 3rd, 1931* (London: Frank Cass, 1971).

Bulman, William J. *Anglican Enlightenment: Orientalism, Religion and Politics in England and its Empire, 1648–1715* (Cambridge: Cambridge University Press, 2015).

Cantor, Geoffrey, and Hodge, Michael. 'Introduction', in Geoffrey Cantor and Michael Hodge (eds), *Conceptions of Ether: Studies in the History of Ether Theories, 1740–1900* (Cambridge: Cambridge University Press, 1981), pp. 1–60.

Carey, Daniel. 'Compiling Nature's History: Travellers and Travel Narratives in the Early Royal Society', *Annals of Science* 54 (1997), 269–92.

Carey, Daniel. 'Reading Contrapuntally: *Robinson Crusoe*, Slavery, and Postcolonial Theory', in Daniel Carey and Lynn Mary Festa (eds), *Postcolonial Enlightenment: Eighteenth-Century Colonialisms and Postcolonial Theory* (Oxford: Oxford University Press, 2009), pp. 105–36.

Carpenter, Audrey. *John Theophilus Desaguliers: A Natural Philosopher, Engineer and Freemason in Newtonian England* (London: Continuum, 2011).

Carr, Cecil Thomas. *Select Charters of Trading Companies, A.D. 1530–1707* (London: Quaritch, 1913).

Carswell, John. *The South Sea Bubble* (Stroud: Alan Sutton, 1993).

Carter, Philip. 'John Conduitt', *Oxford Dictionary of National Biography*, http://www.oxforddnb.com/view/10.1093/ref:odnb/9780198614128.001.0001/odnb-9780198614128-e-6061?rskey=NRg0Py&result=1 (accessed 5 July 2018).

Challis, Christopher Edgar. *A New History of the Royal Mint* (Cambridge: Cambridge University Press, 1991).

Challis, Christopher Edgar. 'Thomas Neale', *Oxford Dictionary of National Biography*, https://www.oxforddnb.com/view/10.1093/ref:odnb/9780198614128.001.0001/odnb-9780198614128-e-19829?rskey=eC1bBr&result=3 (accessed 5 June 2018).

Charlton, John. *The Tower of London: Its Buildings and Institutions* (London: HMSO, for the Department of the Environment, 1978).

Clare, Janet. 'Introduction', in Janet Clare (ed.), *From Republic to Restoration: Legacies and Departures* (Manchester: Manchester University Press, 2018), pp. 1–22.

Colley, Linda. *Captives: Britain, Empire and the World 1600–1850* (London: Pimlico, 2003).

Colton, Judith. 'Kent's Hermitage for Queen Caroline at Richmond', *Architectura* 4 (1974), 181–91.

Conduitt, John. 'Conduitt Material', in Rob Iliffe (ed.), *Early Biographies of Isaac Newton: 1600–1885, Volume 1* (London: Pickering & Chatto, 2006), pp. 55–107, 127–40, 155–235.

Conti, Antonio. 'Account of 1715 Interview with Newton', in Rob Iliffe (ed.), *Early Biographies of Isaac Newton: 1600–1885 , Volume 1* (London: Pickering & Chatto, 2006), pp. 237–44.

Coppola, Al. *The Theater of Experiment: Staging Natural Philosophy in Eighteenth-Century Britain* (New York: Oxford University Press, 2016).

Costa, Shelley. 'The Ladies' Diary: Gender, Mathematics, and Civil Society in Early-Eighteenth-Century England', *Osiris* 17 (2002), 49–73.

Cowan, Brian. 'The Rise of the Coffeehouse Reconsidered', *The Historical Journal* 47 (2004), 21–46.

Cowper, William. *The Complete Poetical Works* (ed. H. S. Milford) (London: Oxford University Press, 1907).

Craig, John. *Newton at the Mint* (Cambridge: Cambridge University Press, 1946).

Craske, Matthew. 'Conversations and Chimneypieces: The Imagery of the Hearth in Eighteenth-Century English Family Portraiture', *British Art Studies* 2 (2016), http://dx.doi.org/10.17658/issn.2058–5462/issue-02/mcraske (accessed 13 June 2018).

Davies, Kenneth Gordon. *The Royal African Company* (London: Longmans, 1957).

Davis, Paul. 'Dryden and the Invention of Augustan Culture', in Steven N. Zwicker (ed.), *The Cambridge Companion to John Dryden* (Cambridge: Cambridge University Press, 2004), pp. 75–91.

Defoe, Daniel. *Robinson Crusoe* (Oxford: Oxford University Press, 2007).

Delisle de Sales, Jean. *De la philosophie de la nature ou Traité de la morale pour le genre humain, Volume 4* (London, 1789), https://books.google.co.uk/books?id=xqpfpaKCpsQC&printsec=frontcover&source=gbs_ge_summary_r&redir_esc=y#v=onepage&q=%22Drame%20Raisonnable%22&f=false (accessed 28 February 2019).

Dennison, Matthew. *The First Iron Lady: A Life of Caroline of Ansbach* (London: William Collins, 2017).

Desaguliers, John Theophilus. *The Newtonian System of the World, the Best Model of Government: an Allegorical Poem* (London, 1728).

Desaguliers, John Theophilus. *A Course of Experimental Philosophy* (London, 1734).

Dry, Sarah. *The Newton Papers: The Strange and True Odyssey of Isaac Newton's Manuscripts* (Oxford: Oxford University Press, 2014).

Dryden, John. 'The Indian Emperour', in John Loftis (ed.), *The Works of John Dryden, Volume 9* (Berkeley and Los Angeles: University of California Press, 1966), pp. 1–112.

Engetsu, Katsuhiro. 'Dryden and the Modes of Restoration Sociability', in Steven N. Zwicker (ed.), *The Cambridge Companion to John Dryden* (Cambridge: Cambridge University Press, 2004), pp. 181–95.

Erskine-Hill, Howard. 'Pope and Slavery', *Proceedings of the British Academy* 91 (1998), 27–53.

Falk, Bernard. *The Way of the Montagues: A Gallery of Family Portraits* (London and New York: Hutchinson, 1947).

Festa, Lynn, and Carey, Daniel. 'Some Answers to the Question: "What is Postcolonial Enlightenment?"', in Daniel Carey and Lynn Mary Festa (eds), *Postcolonial Enlightenment: Eighteenth-Century Colonialisms and Postcolonial Theory* (Oxford: Oxford University Press, 2009), pp. 1–33.

Fryer, Peter. *Staying Power: The History of Black People in Britain* (London: Pluto Press, 1984).

Gascoigne, John. 'From Bentley to the Victorians: The Rise and Fall of British Newtonian Natural Theology', *Science in Context* 2 (1988), 219–56.

Goldie, Mark. *John Locke and the Mashams at Oates* (Cambridge: Churchill College, 2004).

González-Treviño, Ana Elena. '"Kings and their Crowns": Signs of Monarchy and the Spectacle of New World Otherness in Heroic Drama and Public Pageantry', *Studies in Eighteenth Century Culture* 42 (2013), 103–21.

Govier, Mark. 'The Royal Society, Slavery and the Island of Jamaica, 1660–1700', *Notes and Records of the Royal Society of London* 53/2 (1999), 203–17.

Green, Toby. *A Fistful of Shells: West Africa from the Rise of the Slave Trade to the Age of Revolution* (London: Allen Lane, 2019).

Hahn, Daniel. *The Tower Menagerie: Being the Amazing True Story of the Royal Collection of Wild and Ferocious Beasts* (London: Simon & Schuster, 2003).

Handley, Stuart. 'Montagu, Charles, Earl of Halifax', *Oxford Dictionary of National Biography*, http://www.oxforddnb.com/view/10.1093/ref:odnb/9780198614128. 001.0001/odnb-9780198614128-e-19004?rskey=qD9CNk&result=2 (accessed 6 July 2018).

Harris, Max. 'Aztec Maidens in Satin Gowns: Alterity and Dialogue in Dryden's "The Indian Emperour" and Hogarth's "The Conquest of Mexico"', *Restoration: Studies in English Literary Culture, 1660–1700* 15 (1991), 59–70.

Harrison, Richard D. 'Sir William Norris', *Oxford Dictionary of National Biography*, http://www.oxforddnb.com/view/10.1093/ref:odnb/9780198614128.001.0001/ odnb-9780198614128-e-20290?rskey=uhPiMA&result=1 (accessed 3 July 2018).

Hart, Matthew. *Gold: The Race for the World's Most Seductive Metal* (London: Simon & Schuster, 2013).

Higgitt, Rebekah. 'President, Patron, Friend and Lover: Charles Montagu's Significance to the History of Science', *Notes and Records of the Royal Society* 59 (2005), 155–70.

Hill, Abraham. 'Enquiries on Guiny', *Philosophical Transactions* 2 (1667), 472.

Holmes, Geoffrey S. *British Politics in the Age of Anne* (London: Hambledon, 1987).

Hone, Joseph. 'Isaac Newton and the Medals for Queen Anne', *Huntington Library Quarterly* 79/1 (2016), 119–48.

Horwitz, Henry. *Parliament, Policy, and Politics in the Reign of William III* (Manchester: Manchester University Press, 1977).

Hunter, Michael. *The Image of Restoration Science: The Frontispiece to Thomas Sprat's* History of the Royal Society *(1667)* (London and New York: Routledge, 2017).

Hutner, Heidi. *Colonial Women: Race and Culture in Stuart Drama* (Oxford: Oxford University Press, 2001).

Iliffe, Rob (ed.). *Early Biographies of Isaac Newton: 1600–1885, Volume 1* (London: Pickering & Chatto, 2006).

Iliffe, Rob. *Priest of Nature: The Religious Worlds of Isaac Newton* (Oxford: Oxford University Press, 2017).

Iliffe, Rob. 'Newton: The Making of a Politician', http://www.newtonproject.ox.ac.uk/view/texts/normalized/CNTX00002 (accessed 14 June 2018).

Iliffe, Rob, and Willmoth, Frances. 'Astronomy and the Public Sphere: Margaret Flamsteed and Caroline Herschel as Assistant Astronomers', in Lynettte Hunter and Sarah Hutton (eds), *Women, Science and Medicine 1500–1700* (Stroud: Sutton Publishing, 1997), pp. 235–65.

Inikori, Joseph E. *Africans and the Industrial Revolution in England: A Study in International Trade and Economic Development* (Cambridge: Cambridge University Press, 2002).

Inwood, Stephen. *The Man Who Knew Too Much: The Strange and Inventive Life of Robert Hooke 1635–1703* (London: Macmillan, 2002).

Jackson-Opuku, Sandra. 'Boahema Laughed', in Margaret Busby (ed.), *New Daughters of Africa: An International Anthology of Writing by Women of African Descent* (Jonathan Ball online, 2019), locs. 4539–606.

Jacob, Margaret C. *The Radical Enlightenment: Pantheists, Freemasons and Republicans* (London: George Allen & Unwin, 1981).

Jacob, Margaret C., and Stewart, Larry. *Practical Matter: Newton's Science in the Service of Industry and Empire* (Cambridge, MA: Harvard University Press, 2004).

Jones, Clyve, and Holmes, Geoffrey (eds). *The London Diaries of William Nicolson, Bishop of Carlisle* (Oxford: Clarendon Press, 1985).

Kewes, Paulina. 'Dryden's Theatre and the Passions of Politics', in Steven N. Zwicker (ed.), *The Cambridge Companion to John Dryden* (Cambridge: Cambridge University Press, 2004), pp. 131–55.

Kilburn-Toppin, Jasmine. ' "A place of great trust to be supplied by men of skill and integrity": Assayers and Knowledge Cultures in Late-Sixteenth- and Seventeenth-Century London', *British Journal for the History of Science* 52 (2019), 197–223.

Kinsley, James, and Kinsley, Helen (eds). *John Dryden: The Critical Heritage* (London and New York: Routledge, 1971).

Kuchta. David. *The Three-Piece Suit and Modern Masculinity: England, 1550–1850* (Berkeley and London: University of California Press, 2002).

Law, Robin (ed.). *The English in West Africa, 1681–99* (3 vols) (Oxford: Oxford University Press, 1997–2006).

Levenson, Thomas. *Newton and the Counterfeiter: The Unknown Detective Career of the World's Greatest Scientist* (London: Faber & Faber, 2009).

Li, Ming-Hsun. *The Great Recoinage of 1696 to 1699* (London: Weidenfeld & Nicolson, 1963).

Loftis, John. 'Commentary', in John Loftis (ed.), *The Works of John Dryden, Volume 9* (Berkeley and Los Angeles: University of California Press, 1966), pp. 291–330.

Londry, Michael. 'George Tollet (d.1719)', *Oxford Dictionary of National Biography*, http://www.oxforddnb.com/view/10.1093/ref:odnb/9780198614128.001.0001/

odnb-9780198614128-e-60262?rskey=NFNUGg&result=2 (accessed 20 June 2018).

Lynall, Gregory. *Swift and Science: The Satire, Politics, and Theology of Natural Knowledge, 1690–1730* (London: Palgrave Macmillan, 2012).

McCormick, Ted. 'Projecting the *Experiment*: Science and the Restoration', in Janet Clare (ed.), *From Republic to Restoration: Legacies and Departures* (Manchester: Manchester University Press, 2018), pp. 185–205.

McGuire, J. E., and Rattansi, P. M. 'Newton and the Pipes of Pan', *Notes and Records of the Royal Society* 21 (1966), 108–43.

Maddison, R. E. W. 'Abraham Hill, FRS (1635–1722)', *Notes and Records of the Royal Society of London* 15 (1960), 173–82.

Mandelbrote, Scott. *Footprints of the Lion: Isaac Newton at Work* (Cambridge: Cambridge University Library, 2001).

Manley, Mary de la Rivière. *Memoirs of Europe: Towards the Close of the Eighth Century* (London: for John Morphew, 1710).

Manuel, Frank E. *A Portrait of Isaac Newton* (London: Frederick Muller, 1968).

Markley, Robert. *The Far East and the English Imagination, 1600–1730* (Cambridge: Cambridge University Press, 2006).

Marschner, Joanna. *Queen Caroline: Cultural Politics at the Early Eighteenth-Century Court* (New Haven: Yale University Press, 2014).

Mayor, John Eyton Bickersteth. *Cambridge under Queen Anne: Illustrated by Memoir of Ambrose Bonwicke and Diaries of Francis Burman and Zacharias Conrad von Uffenbach* (Cambridge: Deighton, Bell & Co, 1911).

Metzger, Edward Charles. 'Montagu, John, second Duke of Montagu', *Oxford Dictionary of National Biography*, http://www.oxforddnb.com/view/10.1093/ref:odnb/9780198614128.001.0001/odnb-9780198614128-e-19025?rskey=NlPDJq&result=5 (accessed 23 July 2018).

Micklethwait, John, and Wooldridge, Adrian. *The Company: A Short History of a Revolutionary Idea* (New York: Modern Library, 2003).

Montagu, Charles. *The Works and Life of the Right Honourable Charles: Late Earl of Halifax, Including the History of his Lordship's Times* (London: for E. Curll, 1715).

More, Louis Trenchard. *Isaac Newton: A Biography* (New York and London: Scribner, 1934).

Morton, Alan Q., and Wess, Jane A. *Public and Private Science: The King George III Collection* (Oxford: Oxford University Press and the Science Museum, 1993).

Moxham, Noah. 'Natural Knowledge, Inc.: The Royal Society as a Metropolitan Corporation', *British Journal for the History of Science* 52 (2019), 249–71.

Murphy, Anne L. 'Lotteries in the 1690s: Investment or Gamble?' http://uhra.herts.ac.uk/bitstream/handle/2299/6283/905632.pdf;sequence=1 (accessed 5 June 2018).

Newman, E. G. V. 'The Gold Metallurgy of Isaac Newton', https://core.ac.uk/download/pdf/81546668.pdf (accessed 27 June 2019).

Nichols, John. *A Select Collection of Poems* (8 vols) (London, 1780–2).

O'Brien, Karen. '"These Nations Newton Made his Own": Poetry, Knowledge and British Imperial Globalization', in Daniel Carey and Lynn Mary Festa (eds),

Postcolonial Enlightenment: Eighteenth-Century Colonialisms and Postcolonial Theory (Oxford: Oxford University Press, 2009), pp. 281–303.

Odlyzko, Andrew. 'Isaac Newton, Daniel Defoe and the Dynamics of Financial Bubbles', *Financial History* (Winter 2018), 18–21.

Odlyzko, Andrew. 'Newton's Financial Misadventures in the South Sea Bubble', *Notes and Records of the Royal Society* 73 (2019), 29–39.

Orr, Bridget. *Empire on the English Stage, 1660–1714* (Cambridge: Cambridge University Press, 2001).

Parker, Katherine. 'Pepys Island as a Pacific Stepping Stone: The Struggle to Capture Islands on Early Modern Maps', *British Journal for the History of Science* 51 (2018), 659–77.

Parthasarathi, Prasannan. *Why Europe Grew Rich and Asia Did Not: Global Economic Divergence, 1600–1850* (Cambridge: Cambridge University Press, 2011).

Paulson, Ronald. *Hogarth* (3 vols) (Cambridge: Lutterworth Press, 1992–3).

Pepys, Samuel. *The Diary of Samuel Pepys: A New and Complete Transcription* (ed. Robert Latham and William Matthews) (11 vols) (London: Bell & Hyman, 1983).

Pettigrew, William Andrew. *Freedom's Debt: The Royal African Company and the Politics of the Atlantic Slave Trade, 1672–1752* (Chapel Hill: University of North Carolina Press, 2013).

Pointon, Marcia. *Hanging the Head: Portraiture and Social Formation in Eighteenth-Century England* (New Haven and London: Yale University Press, 1993).

Poole, Robert. *Time's Alteration: Calendar Reform in Early Modern England* (London: UCL Press, 1998).

Principe, Lawrence M. 'Style and Thought of the Early Boyle: Discovery of the 1648 Manuscript of *Seraphic Love*', *Isis* 85 (1994), 247–60.

Quinn, Stephen. 'Goldsmith-Banking: Mutual Acceptance and Interbanker Clearing in Restoration London', *Explorations in Economic History* 344 (1997), 411–32.

Reed, Ann. '*Sank fa* Site: Cape Coast Castle and Its Museum as Markers of Memory', *Museum Anthropology* 27 (2004), 13–23.

Robins, Nick. *The Corporation that Changed the World: How the East India Company Shaped the Modern Multinational* (London: Pluto Press, 2019).

Royal African Company. *An Answer of the Company of Royal Adventurers of England trading into Africa to the Petition and Paper of Certain Heads and Particulars thereunto Relating and Annexed: Exhibited to the Honourable House of Commons by Sir Paul Painter, Ferdinando Gorges, Henry Batson, Benjamin Skutt, and Thomas Knights on the Behalf of Themselves and Others concerned in His Majesties Plantations in America* (1667).

St Clair, William. *The Door of No Return: The History of Cape Coast Castle and the Atlantic Slave Trade* (New York: BlueBridge, 2007).

Satia, Priya. *Empire of Guns: The Violent Making of the Industrial Revolution* (London and New York: Duckworth Overlook, 2018).

Saumarez Smith, Charles. *The Rise of Design: Design and the Domestic Interior in Eighteenth-Century England* (London: Pimlico, 2000).

Schaffer, Simon. 'Newton at the Crossroads', *Radical Philosophy* 37 (1984), 23–8.

Schaffer, Simon. 'Glass Works: Newton's Prisms and the Uses of Experiment', in David Gooding, Trevor Pinch, and Simon Schaffer (eds), *The Uses of Experiment: Studies in the Natural Sciences* (Cambridge: Cambridge University Press, 1989), pp. 67–104.

Schaffer, Simon. 'Golden Means: Assay Instruments and the Geography of Precision in the Guinea Trade', in Marie-Noëlle Bourguet, Christian Licoppe, and H. Otto Sibum (eds), *Instruments, Travel and Science: Itineraries of Precision from the Seventeenth to the Twentieth Century* (London and New York: Routledge, 2002), pp. 20–50.

Schaffer, Simon. *The Information Order of Isaac Newton's* Principia Mathematica (Uppsala: Uppsala University, 2008).

Schaffer, Simon. 'Newton on the Beach: The Information Order of *Principia Mathematica*', *History of Science* 47 (2009), 243–76.

Scott, Jonathan. '"Good Night Amsterdam": Sir George Downing and Anglo-Dutch Statebuilding', *The English Historical Review* 118 (2003), 334–56.

Seidel, Michael. 'Crusoe in Exile', *PMLA* 96 (1981), 363–74.

Shapin, Steven. 'Of Gods and Kings: Natural Philosophy and Politics in the Leibniz–Clarke Disputes', *Isis* 72 (1981), 187–215.

Shaw, William Arthur. *Select Tracts and Documents Illustrative of English Monetary History 1626–1730* (London: G. Harding (G. A. Wheeler), 1935).

Sheppard, F. H. W. (ed.). *Survey of London: Volumes 29 and 30, St James Westminster, Part 1* (London, 1960), pp. 271–84. British History Online http://www.british-history.ac.uk/survey-london/vols29-30/pt1/pp271-284 (accessed 25 June 2018).

Shirras, G. Findlay, and Craig, J. H. 'Sir Isaac Newton and the Currency', *The Economic Journal* 55 (1945), 217–41.

Snobelen, Stephen D. '"God of gods, and Lord of lords": The Theology of Isaac Newton's General Scholium to the *Principia*', *Osiris* 16 (2001), 169–208.

Sprat, Thomas. *History of the Royal Society of London* (facsimile of 1667 edition with introduction by Jackson I. Cope and Harold Whitmore Jones) (London: Routledge & Kegan Paul, 1959).

Stern, Simon. 'R v Jones (1703)', in Phil Handler, Henry Mares, and Ian Williams (eds), *Landmark Cases in Criminal Law* (Oxford: Hart, 2017), pp. 59–79.

Stewart, Larry. *The Rise of Public Science: Rhetoric, Technology, and Natural Philosophy in Newtonian Britain, 1660–1750* (Cambridge: Cambridge University Press, 1992).

Stewart, Larry, and Weindling, Paul. 'Philosophical Threads: Natural Philosophy and Public Experiment among the Weavers of Spitalfields', *British Journal for the History of Science* 28 (1995), 37–62.

Stukeley, William. 'Memoirs', in Rob Iliffe (ed.), *Early Biographies of Isaac Newton: 1600–1885 , Volume 1* (London: Pickering & Chatto, 2006), pp. 243–308.

Swift, Jonathan. *Journal to Stella* (2 vols) (ed. Harold Williams) (Oxford: Blackwell, 1974).

Swift, Jonathan. *Gulliver's Travels* (Oxford: Oxford University Press, 2005).

Thomas, Hugh. *The Slave Trade: The History of the Atlantic Slave Trade 1440–1870* (London: Phoenix, 2006).

Thompson, Ayanna. *Performing Race and Torture on the Early Modern Stage* (London: Routledge, 2008).

Tollet, Elizabeth. *Poems on Several Occasions. With Anne Boleyn to King Henry VIII. An Epistle* (London, c.1760).

Tonks, Patrick. 'Robinson Crusoe's Brazilian Expedition and *The Trans-Atlantic Slave Trade Database*', *Digital Defoe: Studies in Defoe & His Contemporaries* 2 (2010), 85–8.

Traweek, Sharon. *Beamtimes and Lifetimes: The World of High Energy Physicists* (Cambridge, MA: Harvard University Press, 1988).

Turnbull, Herbert Westren. *The Correspondence of Isaac Newton* (7 vols) (Cambridge: Cambridge University Press, 1959–77).

Turner, Robert. 'Of Pennies and the Pyx: An Account of the Origins of the English Coinage and the Control exercised by the Trial of the Pyx' (unpublished manuscript).

Uglow, Jenny. *Hogarth* (London: Faber & Faber, 1997).

Uzgalis, William. 'John Locke, Racism, Slavery and Indian Lands', in Naomi Zack (ed.), *The Oxford Handbook of Philosophy and Race* (Oxford Handbooks online, 2017), https://www.oxfordhandbooks.com/view/10.1093/oxfordhb/9780190236953.001.0001/oxfordhb-9780190236953.

Van der Kiste, John. *King George II and Queen Caroline* (Stroud: Sutton, 1997).

Vickery, Amanda. *The Gentleman's Daughter: Women's Lives in Georgian England* (New Haven and London: Yale University Press, 1998).

Villamil, Richard de. *Newton: The Man* (London: Gordon D. Knox, 1931).

Waddell, Brodie. 'The Politics of Economic Distress in the Aftermath of the Glorious Revolution, 1689–1702', *English Historical Review* 130 (2015), 318–51.

Wennerlind, Carl. *Casualties of Credit: The English Financial Revolution, 1620–1720* (Cambridge, MA, and London: Harvard University Press, 2011).

Werrett, Simon. 'The Sociomateriality of Waste and Scrap Paper in Eighteenth-Century England', in Christine von Oertzen, Carla Bittel, and Elaine Leong (eds), *Working and Knowing with Paper: Towards a Gendered History of Knowledge* (Pittsburgh: University of Pittsburgh Press, 2019), pp. 46–59.

Werrett, Simon. *Thrifty Science: Making the Most of Materials in the History of Experiment* (Chicago: University of Chicago Press, 2019).

Westfall, Richard S. *Never at Rest: A Biography of Isaac Newton* (Cambridge: Cambridge University Press, 1980).

Westfall, Richard S. 'Newton and his Biographer', in Samuel H. Baron and Carl Pletsch (eds), *Introspection in Biography: The Biographer's Quest for Self-Awareness* (Hillsdale, NJ: The Analytic Press, 1985), pp. 175–89.

White, Barbara, 'Scott, Mary, Countess of Deloraine', *Oxford Dictionary of National Biography*, http://www.oxforddnb.com/view/10.1093/ref:odnb/9780198614128.001.0001/odnb-9780198614128-e-68126?rskey=2gLCmV&result=3 (accessed 12 July 2018).

White, Michael. *Isaac Newton: The Last Sorcerer* (London: Fourth Estate, 1997).

Winn, James Anderson. *Queen Anne: Patroness of Arts* (Oxford and New York: Oxford University Press, 2014).

Winterbottom, Anna. 'An Experimental Community: The East India Company in London, 1600–1800', *British Journal for the History of Science* 52 (2019), 323–43.

Wolf, Edwin. *The Library of James Logan of Philadelphia 1674–1751* (Philadelphia: Library Company of Philadelphia, 1974).

Woollacott, Angela. *Gender and Empire* (Basingstoke: Palgrave Macmillan, 2006).

Zedler, Beatrice. 'The Three Princesses', *Hypatia* 4/1 (1989), 28–63.

Zook, George Frederick. *The Company of Royal Adventurers Trading into Africa* (Lancaster, PA: Press of the New Era Printing Co., 1919).

Illustration Credits

0.1 Private collection: collections@paul-mellon-centre.ac.uk; ycba.info@yale.edu

0.2 Granger Historical Picture Archive/Alamy Stock Photo

1.1 Wellcome Collection. CC BY

1.2 ACTIVE MUSEUM/Alamy Stock Photo

2.1 Yale Center for British Art, Paul Mellon Collection

2.2 Royal Collection Trust/© Her Majesty Queen Elizabeth II 2019

3.1 King's College Cambridge. Keynes MS 112/4 (as shown Mandelbrote, p. 8)

4.1 © The Trustees of the British Museum

5.1 Digital Image Library/Alamy Stock Photo

5.2 INTERFOTO/Alamy Stock Photo

5.3 Library of Congress, Geography and Map Division

6.1 Cambridge University Library. Adv..b.39.2.p. 483 (as shown Mandelbrote, p. 125)

6.2 Cambridge University Library. Adv..b.39.2.p. 483 (as shown Mandelbrote, p. 125)

7.1 Granger Historical Picture Archive/Alamy Stock Photo

8.1 Photo 12/Alamy Stock Photo/Alamy: HTMJ1X

8.2 Courtesy of the Royal Mint Museum

9.1 Library of Congress, Geography and Map Division

9.2 Museum of London

9.3 Rept0n1x/Wikimedia Commons

9.4 Rob Fenenga/Alamy Stock Photo

10.1 Cambridge University Library

Index

Note: Figures are indicated by an italic "*f*" following the page number.

Digital users: indexed terms that span two pages (e.g., 52–3) may, on occasion, appear on only one of those pages.